THE
BATTLE
of NEW ORLEANS

THE
BATTLE
of NEW ORLEANS:

"But for a Piece of Wood"

R O N   C H A P M A N

PELICAN PUBLISHING COMPANY
GRETNA 2015

First edition, 2013
First Pelican edition, 2014
Second Pelican edition, 2015

---

*The word "Pelican" and the depiction of a pelican are trademarks
of Pelican Publishing Company, Inc., and are registered in the
U.S. Patent and Trademark Office.*

ISBN: 9781455620272
E-book ISBN: 9781455620289

Printed in the United States of America
Published by Pelican Publishing Company, Inc.
1000 Burmaster Street, Gretna, Louisiana 70053

Table of Contents

Dedicated to

My lovely wife Margaret and my beautiful daughter Becca

Also

To the University of New Orleans History Department (1967-1976).
Their dedication, training, and guidance made this work possible.

"America's glory, which dazzled the world
When the toils of our sires had achieved independence,
Was brightened when Jackson her banners unfurled
To protect the dear boon for their grateful descendants-
When conquerors of Spain
Crossed the boisterous main,
Boldly threatening to rivet our fetters again:
But a happy new year for Columbia begun
When our Jackson secured what our Washington won;

—Samuel Woodworth

Acknowledgments

I am especially indebted to the wonderful and caring staff of the *Williams Research Center of the Historic New Orleans Collection.* Their guidance and support have made this work possible. I wish to highlight the valuable work of Jason Weiss whose travels to Great Britain provided me with access to so very many valuable documents. These firsthand accounts proved enlightening and invaluable. Robert "Bobby" Trichnor was especially helpful in assembling the images need for this book. This list goes on. The entire staff of the Williams Research Center deserves accolades. A researcher could not work with a more professional and helpful group of individuals.

I wish to extend my special thanks to those kind and patient individuals upon whom I imposed the task of reading the drafts of this work while in progress. Were it not for them, this book would undoubtedly lack the cohesion it possesses. I wish to especially thank Christina Vella for her patience and guidance, Lisa Muilenburg for her careful eye on editing, and Dr. Curtis Manning, who both assisted with editing and managed the publication process. My wife Margaret deserves special mention for her personal insights. This book would not be possible without their treasured assistance. There were so many others who given their time during this long process. All have provided invaluable support.

I reserve special thanks to my wife Margaret and daughter Becca, whose patience and support proved invaluable throughout the process.

Again, the goal here is to inform the reader about the background and events surrounding the Battle of New Orleans; the environment in which it was fought; the social circumstances of New Orleans in 1814, how the campaign was won, and, equally important, how the British lost. The story of the Battle of New Orleans has never been given the credit it deserves; this work hopes to rectify that error.

Ron Chapman

Introduction

The United States, like all nations, has been engaged in many wars since its founding. Of these, few military conflicts are so neglected as the War of 1812. In that forgotten war the important Battle of New Orleans has become a mere footnote. The British invasion into the Gulf of Mexico occurred thirty-one years after the close of the American Revolution. Yet, few realize that the successful defense of Louisiana played a critical role in the securing the new nation's territory and independence.

Presidents George Washington, John Adams, and Thomas Jefferson sought desperately to keep America out of the European wars of the French Revolution. They barely succeeded. The continued abuses of both England and France tore at the heart of the nation and raised serious questions about America's ability to protect its interests . . . a vital component of any nation's integrity.

Under the presidency of James Madison, events took on a force of their own. France had made peace with America. In contrast, Great Britain's continued imposition of the Orders in Council, under which they seized American ships and impressed American sailors. This caused persistent calls for a strong response. That occurred June 18, 1812 when War Hawks won control of Congress and forced a Declaration of War.[1]

This work does not furnish a full description of the battles that marked the entire War of 1812. The primary points of focus here are the events that unfolded when the British launched an expedition in the winter of 1814 from Jamaica into the Gulf of Mexico to seize the port of New Orleans.

In a forgotten war, the battles for New Orleans remain neglected struggles. The common interpretation focuses on one battle that took place AFTER the treaty of peace had been signed. Thus, it amounts to nothing more than an unfortunate episode having no impact on succeeding events.

Closer analysis, however, demonstrates that what occurred along the bayous of southeast Louisiana determined American history. Despite notions to the contrary, the fate of America did indeed lay in the hands of a Tennessee General commanding a bizarre assortment of citizen soldiers on a sugar plantation below New Orleans. Furthermore, the main conflict consisted of ten battles occurring over five months.

Few realize the importance this campaign had for the future of the United States and how close America came to losing it on several occasions. The British embarked upon an ambitious expedition. Had the British prevailed, which every reasonable person fully expected, America would be a different nation today. Only because they failed has the event been relegated to the dustbin of history.

For that reason, it is critical that Americans learn what was at stake during the winter of 1814-15 in a place called St. Bernard Parish. Only then can we appreciate the magnitude of Jackson's victory.

Not all historians agree on the importance of this battle. Some argue that the war was ended in the midst of the campaign. This view advances the notion that the Battle of New Orleans was of little consequence. No matter what happened on the battlefield, the outcome had already been determined by a treaty signed December 24th in Ghent, Belgium. The Battle of New Orleans proved to be a very bloody, but unfortunate twist of fate . . . a footnote in history, nothing more.

Accordingly, the war had lost support among the commercial interests in England. These "shopkeepers" wanted the war over because the war was costing British merchants and the British government too much money and promised little gain. In their view, the campaign for New Orleans was a meaningless, bloody exercise in futility. No matter what the outcome, Great Britain would adhere to the treaty, end the war, accept the *status quo ante*, and re-open trade.

The central theme of this study maintains that the Battle of New Orleans was of pivotal importance to the future of America. The Treaty of Ghent had never been formally adopted. King George had not signed it: President Madison had not signed it, and the United States Senate had not ratified it. Thus, had the British won, the *un-ratified* treaty would be of little consequence. New Orleans was too important strategically to be abandoned if taken.

In fact, the British launched this massive invasion while negotiations were underway in Ghent. If they legitimately sought peace, why embark upon a campaign against American interests in the Gulf of Mexico while conducting peace talks? They had reasons!

A conversation between retired President Jackson and the late governor of Ohio, William Allen provides the strongest evidence to support this position. When Allen was a correspondent for the *Missouri Republican* he visited Jackson and reported this account of their conversation. After toasting the admission of Arkansas into the union in 1836, Jackson turned to Allen and stated: "*Allen, if there had been a disaster, instead of victory, at New Orleans, there would never have been a state of Arkansas.*"[2]

Commenting further President Jackson stated: "*If Pakenham had taken New Orleans, the British would have claimed and held the whole of Louisiana Purchase.*" Jackson then discussed the Treaty of Ghent: "*. . . but the minutes of the conference at Ghent, as kept by Mr. Gallatin, represent the British commissioners as declaring in exact words: 'We do not admit Bonaparte's construction of the law of nations; we cannot accept it in relation to any subject-matter before us.*'"[3]

Jackson continued: "*At that moment none of our commissioners knew what the real meaning of those words was. When they were uttered the British commissioners knew that Pakenham's expedition had been decided on . . . I have learned, from diplomatic sources of the most unquestionable authority, that the British Ministry did not intend the Treaty of Ghent to apply to the Louisiana Purchase at all.*"[4]

Jackson finished stating: "*These words were meant to lay the foundation for a claim on the Louisiana Purchase, entirely external to the provisions of the Treaty of Ghent. And in that way, the British government was signing a treaty with one hand in front, whilst the other hand, behind its back, was dispatching Pakenham's army to seize the fairest of our possessions. Now Allen, you have the whole story, and know why Arkansas was saved to the union.*"[5]

The issue of New Orleans and Louisiana tormented the British lion. England steadfastly refused to accept the Louisiana Purchase, even though a British bank (Baring & Baring Co.) had profited from financing the transaction. The Proclamation issued by Colonel Edward Nicholls on August 29, 1814 to the Creole population of Louisiana emphasized that point: "*Natives of Louisiana! On you the first call is made to assist in **liberating** from a faithless, imbecile government **your paternal soil** . . . I call to aid me in this just cause: **American usurpation of this country must be abolished and the lawful owners of this soil put in*** *possession. [Emphasis added]"* Need there be any further proof of British intentions? [6]

The British were further angered that the $15 million the United States paid to Napoleon financed a French war machine that England was forced to fight. Taken all together, Louisiana remained a sticky issue to some very powerful people in Great Britain. What sweet revenge to take this vast territory away from America and give it back to Spain. This openly implies that the intention of the invaders was to replace American rule in Louisiana with that of Spain . . . its "lawful owners."

Article #1 of the Treaty of Ghent further reinforces this view. The Treaty specifically states that lands taken in battle would: "*. . . forthwith [be] restored and delivered to the proper authorities and persons to whom they respectively belong.*" To whom did Louisiana belong? According to Great Britain, Spain retained possession. [7]

Britain believed its ally Spain had been illegally deprived of its Louisiana possession by Napoleon's France. In essence, America had purchased stolen property. Although Napoleon traded King Carlos IV of Spain the province of Etruria (Tuscany) in Italy for Louisiana, the promised exchange of territory never occurred. Besides, Tuscany wasn't Napoleon's to trade. It belonged to Italy. Napoleon never owned Louisiana because he never paid for it and, therefore, could not sell it. It belonged to Spain.

Regarding the *Treaty of Ghent* one must also consider it was signed December 24th . . . fifteen days before the decisive January 8th battle, but well into the campaign to take New Orleans. Had Britain won the Battle of New Orleans, nothing would have prevented her from demanding a renegotiation of the treaty based upon the new set of circumstances on the ground. In fact, the British had a long tradition of stretching out negotiations in order to achieve military advantages that improved their bargaining power. [8]

This is explicitly set down in the body of the treaty itself. *"All hostilities both by sea and land shall cease as soon as this Treaty shall have been RATIFIED (emphasis added) by both parties as hereinafter mentioned."* The second article again affirms the fact that this Treaty goes into effect only AFTER ratification . . . *"Immediate after ratification (emphasis added) of the Treaty by both parties as hereinafter mentioned, orders shall be sent to the armies, Squadrons, Officers, Subjects, and Citizens of the two Powers to cease from all hostilities" (Treaty of Ghent)*[9]. Thus, until ratification occurred, hostilities would persist.

Article XI begins with a further emphasis that the treaty only has bearing when ratified: *"This Treaty when the same shall have been ratified* *on both sides <u>without alteration</u> by either of the contracting parties, and the ratifications mutually exchanged, shall be binding on both parties (emphasis added)".* The insertion of the phrase *"without alteration"* does not prevent "alteration", it merely states that the treaty as written shall be accepted if there are no "alterations" added by either signatory. This opens the door for potential changes should it be to the advantage of one of the parties to so alter. A change in circumstances on the battlefield would give cause for "alteration."

Furthermore, the treaty commands each party to return all territories and items seized, but only *"upon the Exchange of the Ratifications of this Treaty."*[10] But by requiring that lands in dispute should be: *". . . forthwith restored and delivered to the proper authorities and persons to whom they respectively belong"* again raised the issue of the legitimacy of the Louisiana Purchase.

The key point here is the emphasis on "ratification." Why? Is it because Great Britain was expecting a victory in New Orleans? Was such an event anticipated by the references pertaining to "alteration" addressed in the treaty?

The document initialed December 24, 1814, did not become official until ratified by the governments of Great Britain and the United States of America on February 18, 1815, fifty-five days later. [11] Thus, a changed situation on the battlefield could have altered the scope of the treaty, allowed "alterations", and affected the future of the United States. The King of England had to merely refuse to sign or decide to "adjust" the document to nullify the existing treaty and thus keep the gains won by Pakenham. It would NOT require violating the treaty.

It is difficult to believe that had Pakenham: succeeded on the battlefield in Chalmette, occupied New Orleans, opened a second military front in the west, set up a government, secured his position both militarily and civilly, seized the city's riches, occupied fertile cotton lands, eliminated sugar competition, gained control of the Mississippi River, reaped revenge for Great Britain's residual embarrassment over the American Revolution, provided a safe haven for Britain's Native/American allies, and possibly even returned Louisiana to Spain, Great Britain would have surrendered these advantages and quietly folded its tents and departed because of a few un-ratified suggestions scribbled on parchment.

Granted, this is all speculation. Perhaps Great Britain would have honored the Treaty as composed. We will never know because Jackson's overwhelming victory in New Orleans rendered moot any review of the Treaty of Ghent. However, factoring in the circumstances, the implications of a British victory deserves consideration.

British actions clearly demonstrated their intentions. General Pakenham approached New Orleans with a massive army complete with an administrative staff all accompanied by their family members. The British intended to occupy and govern the city while controlling the terminus of America's greatest river system.

Some wonder what the British would have done with Louisiana. Likely, taking it would have satisfied long simmering resentments over the American Revolution and anger about the relationship between America and Napoleon's France. But keeping it might have caused problems they would not welcome. By returning Louisiana to Spain, it would have created a domestic crisis in the United States and may have forced America to once again purchase it . . . this time from its rightful owner, Spain. That alone would have caused incalculable domestic and financial difficulties for the American government. It is doubtful that Great Britain had any intention of keeping it.

However, should they have determined to maintain control of the region, the British had many other reasons for doing so:

First, they could have limited the growth of America. They realized that Napoleon was right when he stated at the time of the Louisiana Purchase: *"I have given to England a maritime rival which will sooner or later humble her pride."*[12] A British occupation of New Orleans and the river that fed it would divide the continent and prove an effective barrier to westward expansion thus limiting the growth of this upstart nation and potential rival.

Second, a victory in New Orleans would allow England to control the Mississippi River and all trade traveling down that waterway. James Monroe, Secretary of War, stated as much: *"Should the enemy take possession of Louisiana, I need not describe to you its pernicious effect, not on the interests of that growing state only, but of all that portion of the United States, lying westward of the Allegheny Mountains. Its whole commerce would be in the hands of an inveterate foe."* Territories west of the Appalachian Mountains needed the Mississippi River system for trade and might have been forced to ally with any power controlling it. Even if England later ceded Louisiana to Spanish control, they could yet influence the region's future. [13]

Third, for years England had demonstrated a strong desire to protect its Native-American allies. Many Indians had sided with Great Britain in the French and Indian War, the American Revolution, and the War of 1812. They were now paying a heavy price for these alliances. Americans were exacting a grave toll on the Indians as their villages were plundered, populations decimated, and lands taken away in revenge. Territory west of the Mississippi could be made available to Native Americans under British protection, but only if Britain controlled the Mississippi River.

Fourth, the cotton economy was important to England. The Industrial Revolution began in Great Britain with the production of woven cloth. Cotton was the new material of choice and highly in demand. Cotton was light, strong, and easy to weave. Without it, England's economy would suffer. Cotton was a critical raw material for England's economic miracle, like oil today. The best cotton came from the American South, but it was not cheap.

Since the invention of the cotton gin, this material became readily available. A steady and cheap supply of raw cotton would augment England's advantage in the cloth industry by generating higher profits. By taking New Orleans and those lands west of the Mississippi River (Arkansas, Texas, Missouri, and most of Louisiana), Britain could sever those territories from the American union. Fertile cotton lands would fall under British control . . . even if returned to a grateful Spain. This would provide necessary competition for the monopoly Southern states were rapidly gaining and mitigate the influence of what, in later years, would become the dominance of "King Cotton".

Fifth, a British occupation would give England the sizable material wealth stored in New Orleans. None other than the Duke of Wellington himself, General Edward Pakenham's brother-in-law, saw avarice at the base of this expedition. In a letter to Lord Longford dated May 22, 1815 he stated: *"I cannot but regret, however, that he [General Pakenham] was ever employed on such a service, or with such a colleague [Admiral Cochrane]. The expedition to New Orleans originated with that colleague; the plunder was its object."* [14]

Sixth, the British could be masters of the rich fur trade that still traveled America's central waterways that flowed down the Mississippi to New Orleans from Britain's own Canadian provinces.

Seventh, the Port of New Orleans was then a much more profitable entity than it is today. Only New York eclipsed it in business and its potential for growth stood proportionate to America's western expansion. New Orleans had become a "boom town" at this time because all trade was by water, and all western water passed by New Orleans. The city and region's location offered great financial advantages. [15]

Finally, the matter of English pride demands discussion. Great Britain had endured an embarrassing defeat as a result of the American Revolution. The precedent of a colony successfully breaking away from a powerful mother country was worrisome. It could prove to be contagious. Soundly defeating America in the War of 1812 would go a long way toward mitigating that humiliation. Americans recognized this and thus described the war as America's "Second War for Independence."

As can be readily seen, the campaign to take New Orleans had dire implications for the future of the United States had Great Britain succeeded. Considering the magnitude of the expedition launched compared to the paucity of defense available to the citizens of New Orleans, nearly everyone expected an overwhelming British victory. Certainly, the officers and men of the invading battle group expected as such, planning to be comfortably settled in New Orleans with their families for Christmas dinner. What happened?

Given the circumstances, an American victory was anything but certain. Any one of a number of events, some extremely small, could have turned the tide for the British and altered the course of American history. Many occasions arose when the British held the advantage, but for whatever reason, failed to seize the opportunity. Consider:

1. Had a sufficient number of barges been procured by Admiral Cochrane to facilitate invasion and maintain supply lines, they would have been able to deploy sooner with more equipment and firepower.

2. Had General Keane followed Colonel Thornton's urgent suggestion to immediately invade New Orleans when first arriving at the Villere Plantation on December 23rd, the British would have totally surprised Jackson and likely taken the city.

3. Had General Pakenham not called back General Gibbs on December 28th when he nearly flanked Jackson's line and breached his defenses, Jackson's defenders may have been routed.

4. Had Pakenham exercised some patience on the morning of January 8th and allowed Colonel Thornton to secure his Westbank position before committing to his major assault, his plan may have succeeded. By waiting one day, the flanking maneuver likely would have worked and victory his.

5. Had the impact of the current of the Mississippi been anticipated and compensated for in the early morning hours of January 8th when Thornton's Westbank assault crossed the river, Pakehham's plan may have succeeded.

6. Most important, had General Lambert exercised determination in recognizing Colonel Thornton's advantage on the Westbank of the Mississippi River and granted his request for reinforcements on the afternoon of January 8th New Orleans may have fallen to a bombardment from the Westbank.

This work demonstrates how close the British came to victory and to imposing their peace on the United States. The Battle of New Orleans deserves much deeper appreciation for its impact on the American experience than it has received over the years. *But for a Piece of Wood* seeks to advance the cause of recognizing the great contribution to our freedoms a motley collection of patriots made from September 1814 through January 1815. It provides proper recognition for the sacrifices made by the humble American participants who confronted overwhelming odds, yet gained a shocking victory in this major military campaign for control of the interior of the American continent during the War of 1812.

It might have turned out otherwise on January 8th . . .

BUT FOR A PIECE OF WOOD

Chapter 1

OVERVIEW: THE BATTLES FOR NEW ORLEANS

Background . . .

The Battle of New Orleans was not an isolated event but part of a far broader plan of imperial conquest.

The War of 1812 marked the United States' baptism into the world community . . . its bloody "right of passage"! This was the first "world war" that America would fight since becoming an independent nation. It began much the same as World War I and World War II. Attempts by America to maintain neutral trade with belligerent European nations at war drew her into an unwanted conflict.

The French Revolutionary Wars and the later Napoleonic Wars dominated the late 18th and early 19th centuries. They raged for 23 years. In 1812, England and France both sought to draw America to its side, while simultaneously attempting to inhibit American trade with the other. This created a confused and dangerous situation for America. The newly created United States could not afford a war, especially one against a major European power.

Once Napoleon Bonaparte became First Consul the war changed character. A military and foreign policy genius now commanded French forces. His aggressive military strategy resulted in victory and thoughts of invading Great Britain itself.

After its naval victory at Trafalgar, Britain enjoyed safety from the threat of invasion and secured uncontested control over the seas. That done, the British navy sought to strangle France by cutting off all trade with the outside world. The Admiralty ordered a naval blockade on continental Europe. A component of this tactic required intercepting neutral shipping destined for the continent.

Britain's Continental Blockade required a large, well-manned navy. Britain could build ships, but it lacked experienced seamen to man those vessels. Prior to the Napoleonic Wars, the British navy employed 10,000 sailors. By 1812 that number had increased to 140,000. The vast majority of this increase came from impressments, forcibly placing men into service. Lord Nelson stated that much of the losses stemmed from 40,000 desertions due in large measure to the brutality of life on British ship.

The King George III issued the first Orders in Council in 1807. Several refinements were later added. This permitted his navy to restrict American commercial shipping. In addition, the Royal Navy began to stop and board American ships at sea and to "impress" American sailors into Royal Service to gain the needed seamen. Many soon resorted to the futile effort of carrying official papers attesting to their American citizenship believing this would protect them from such an outrage. It did not. Americans equated these forced "impressments" to kidnapping American citizens. Tensions between the two nations rose to a fever pitch.

France, for its part, sought to seize American merchant ships in continental harbors thereby preventing them from trading with England. Since Napoleon's Continental System closed all ports to British trade, any ships coming into Europe were suspect and seized for fear they may embark for Britain.

Thus, American interests came into conflict with those of both England and France on the high seas. For most Americans, however, England's actions were more immediate and insulting. The kidnapping of American citizens at sea was viewed as a direct assault on the sovereignty of the United States. America was divided between two contending war parties, but England's actions fostered greater anger in some sectors of the United States than those of France.

Since the founding of the United States, a succession of presidents from George Washington to Thomas Jefferson sought to prevent a war that would destroy the new nation. But anger was growing.

Napoleon eliminated some tensions by ending France's "Quasi War" against the United States. He saw nothing to be gained by it. He won further approval after engineering the Louisiana Purchase in 1803. The south and west leaned toward France. New England merchants, in contrast, supported England.

Thus, America was divided over the issue of war or peace. Indeed, as the situation festered, some wanted war with France (Federalists), while others demanded a show of force against Great Britain (Anti-Federalists). The American/British controversy at sea weighted the controversy in favor of the Anti-Federalists who soon forced these two nations to war.[16]

During the 1810 mid-term elections voters elected a group of anti-British "War Hawks" to Congress. In reaction to the persistent expansion of England's Orders in Council, this new Congress declared war on Great Britain with President James Madison's approval on June 18, 1812. Interesting to note, modern communications might have prevented this war because Great Britain had suspended the offending documents just two days before . . . on June 16, 1812.

American military efforts at first proved worthwhile. When the war began, the United States aggressively moved against English interests in the new world. The Hawks believed that Canada would willingly join with the United States . . . it did not!

Throughout 1813 American victories on land and British victories at sea demonstrated the capacities of these two nations to inflict pain on one another. Soon, the tide would turn against America. Following his ill-advised invasion of Russia, Napoleon suffered a major defeat on October 16-19 of 1813 at the Battle of Leipzig, as well as severe reverses in Spain inflicted by the Duke of Wellington. A militarily humbled Napoleon retreated to France. On March 31, 1814 the allies entered Paris. On April 11th, the emperor admitted defeat. On April 14th he abdicated and sulked into exile on the diminutive island of Elba nestled between Italy and Corsica.

This served Great Britain's cause against America well. It freed Britain's hands. With pressure off of the European theater, England now shuttled more men and material against the United States. By 1814, the British were clearly on the offensive.[17]

Many highly trained and battle-groomed troops who had been pinned down fighting in Europe were suddenly crossing the Atlantic for action in America. By September 1814, 13,000 veteran soldiers were in Canada. By year's end nearly 40,000 seasoned troops had been transported to the new world.[18]

A part of Great Britain's overall plan was the taking of Washington D.C., the seizing of eastern seaports, and the protection of Canada. On a more ambitious note, the British also envisioned a campaign to the

Gulf of Mexico that included taking New Orleans and occupying the mouth of the Mississippi River . . . a powerful strategic move!

The British occupied and burned Washington. They attempted, but failed to take Baltimore. They then launched their invasion plans for New Orleans.

These aggressive and effective military actions aggravated already seething partisan tensions in the United States. These divisions would persist even to the point of nearly severing the union when the Hartford Convention met in Connecticut on December 1814 to January 1815. New England's opposition to the war had reached a fever pitch and secession was openly discussed. Only Jackson's victory in the Battle of New Orleans rendered this convention's deliberations void of meaning and sent the delegates packing home in embarrassment.

The stage was set for Great Britain's massive invasion of the Gulf of Mexico with its ultimate destination being the city of New Orleans. But who would lead this expedition, since the intended commander was gone?

General Sir Edward Pakenham . .

Major-General Sir Edward Pakenham

To achieve the goal of conquering the gulf coast of North America, Great Britain ordered a massive expeditionary force into the Gulf of Mexico. Initially, the British ordered General Robert Ross to command the invasion. However, snipers killed him during the engagement at Baltimore. Seeking a replacement, London ordered Major General Sir Edward Pakenham to take command. Who was this Pakenham?

General Pakenham, brother-in-law of the Duke of Wellington, served with Wellington as a staff officer during the Peninsular Campaign in Spain against Napoleon. Wellington's star would rise higher after he defeated a returned Napoleon at the Battle of Waterloo in (1815). However, while Napoleon lay in exile on the island of Elba, a lull befell military activity on the European continent. During this brief calm, Wellington was offered command of the Gulf expedition. He refused. In his stead, General Sir Edward Pakenham was ordered to Jamaica to command the assembled fleet, train the invasion force, and bring its combined might to bear against New Orleans. In the words of Wellington: *"He is not the greatest genius, but one of the best we have."*[19]

Pakenham was fully versed in Wellington's strategies: importance of supply, good positioning, strong lines of communication, military intelligence, heavy artillery, extended lines of attack, lightening surprise marches, and attacks on the enemy's position.[20] Unfortunately, the circumstances on the fields of Chalmette precluded the application of many of these hard learned tenets of warfare.

Pakenham began his military career in 1794 when he joined the army at age sixteen. On May 28, 1794, he assumed the office of Lieutenant in the 92nd Foot, an Irish Regiment. Three days later he was appointed Captain. On December 6th, he was elevated to Major of the 33rd Ulster Dragoons. This last assignment would give him experience in new world campaigning . . . *"There is no mystery about his rapid promotion. In each case the entry reads 'by purchase'."* Buying one's office was common in the British army, but money was not the whole of it, his family enjoyed good connections.[21]

On February 7, 1801, Pakenham sailed for North America for the first time. By mid-summer he was, *"peacefully installed on the Danish Island of St. Croix and supremely happy."*[22] He spent the next several years living a tranquil tropical life in the islands: Barbados and St. Kitts. All would change due to the collapse of the Peace of Amiens on May 18, 1803 and the resumption of war with France.[23]

On June 20th, Pakenham sailed for the French island of St. Lucia. His British forces reduced the French fort there after a ninety minute siege. The British 64th had endured the brunt of the battle and suffered 138 casualties in this conflict, including Edward Pakenham. He sustained a severe neck wound which gave his head a pronounced tilt once healed. Pakenham was fortunate to be nursed by a French woman who he had chivalrously protected from British abuse in an earlier engagement. Pakenham returned home to mend after three years in the field.[24]

Pakenham sustained a second neck wound on February 1, 1809 while leading an assault on a French camp. *"The shot passed from the right to the left shoulder, quite at the lower part of the neck, what a comical neck"* he wrote home to his mother. He once again returned to London in August of 1809 to heal. Curiously, the first injury that caused his head to have a decided slant due to muscle injury had been corrected by the second wound. Following his recovery, he was sent to Spain to join his brother-in-law, the Duke of Wellington, in the Peninsula Campaign.[25]

The battles in Europe raged until Napoleon's defeat after his misguided invasion of Russia. This resulted in his abdication on April 14, 1814. British attention could now be directed against the United States. The British lion was about to teach this upstart nation a lesson in respect. In the words of now Adjutant-General Pakenham; *"It appears from Madison's speech that we are not to expect peace with America; that fellow and his adherents are sad enemies of ours and are not to be brought to terms but by blows."*[26]

An unfortunate turn of events would alter the course of Pakenham's life. In the American theater of operations, the British were beginning to make effective use of combined naval and land forces. While attempting to take Baltimore, General Robert Ross, a gifted and experienced commander, was cut down by American sniper fire. He was Admiral Sir Alexander Cochrane's first choice for command of land forces in the Gulf of Mexico. His passing created a void. The British needed a new commander. The gauntlet fell to Sir Edward Pakenham. In October 1814, he was ordered once again across the Atlantic, this time to Jamaica to take command to a newly formed expeditionary force.[27] General Sir Edward Pakenham was about to enter the pages of American history.

In a letter to his mother, Edward freely expressed his feelings about this new deployment: *"It was my expectation when I left you to have returned to our little party at the Lodge. Public Events have otherwise determined my private moments. The Affairs in America have gone ill. Staff officers have become necessary, and I have been called on by the Ministers to proceed to the other side of the Atlantic. I confess to you that there is nothing that makes this employment desirable."*[28]

Pakenham's doubts about this expedition were well founded. It was driven by the greed of Admiral Cochrane who had an eye on the vast treasure of cotton, sugar and other goods trapped in New Orleans. Some estimated its value at £3-4 million pounds sterling. On the day before he sailed, Pakenham was quoted as saying that he ". . . *much doubted the policy of the expedition or the correctness of the information upon which the government had decided to make an attempt on that place.*"[29] But orders were orders, and he was not given to question the wisdom of his superiors.

What is particularly sad was Pakenham's premonition when speaking with his friend George Napier just prior to his departure. When advised to take care he responded: "*I promise that I will not unnecessarily expose myself to the fire of the enemy, but you are too old and good a soldier not to be aware that a case might arise in which the Commander-in-Chief may find it absolutely necessary to place himself at the head of his troops in the hottest fire and by his own personal conduct encourage them to victory. If this happens, **I must not flinch, though death be my lot.** [Emphasis added]*"[30] Little did he know how true these words would be as he sailed from Portsmouth November 1, 1814 in the frigate *Statira.*

While on board, Edward Pakenham with his staff officers Gibbs, Burgoyne, Dickson, and Robb carefully studied his collection of maps. The voyage was slow and Pakenham soon realized that the main force under Admiral Cochrane and General Keane was far ahead. When he arrived in Jamaica, Pakenham discovered that an impatient Admiral Cochrane had not waited for him but had already disembarked the main force leaving only General Lambert and the reserves behind. A concerned Pakenham reflected: "*. . . as he is sixteen days ahead of us, I fear we shall not arrive in time to partake of the operation.*" Such was the confidence of Great Britain in victory. [31]

On December 22nd, *Statira* arrived at the mouth of the Mississippi River. The general then learned that Admiral Cochrane had anchored near Ship Island and had begun the process of landing troops. Lieutenant Alexander Dickson noted that: "*Sir Edward Pakenham was much annoyed at the delay.*"[32] Pakenham could not have known that as he sailed to Cochrane's anchorage, shots had already been fired. Furthermore, as a land general he would not have the luxury of picking his field of battle. He would be forced to make due with a theater of operations selected by an Admiral.

On Christmas Day 1814, General Sir Edward Pakenham rushed onto the battlefield . . . to meet his opponent and his destiny.

Major General Andrew Jackson

Andrew Jackson's ancestors originally hailed from Scotland. But for five generations the family had lived in Carrickfergus near Belfast, Ireland. His grandfather was a weaver. In April of 1765, the future general's twenty-seven year old father, Andrew, his wife, Elizabeth, and their two sons (Hugh, two years old, and Robert six months old) left north Ireland. With several other families, they sailed across the Atlantic Ocean for the American colonies.[33]

Andrew and Elizabeth left Ireland because, being tenant farmers, the Jacksons had little hope of ever improving their condition in life or that of their young children. America promised new opportunities.

After two months at sea, the Jackson family arrived in Philadelphia. From there they traveled to North Carolina meeting with Elizabeth's sister, Jane. She was the wife of James Crawford, a local landowner and successful farmer. They settled on neighboring land in the same Waxhaw region.

Having found a suitable location, young Andrew built a house and started homesteading with his family. Tragically, within two years he fell ill. He soon died at the age of twenty-nine leaving a pregnant wife to care for the young family.

A desperate Elizabeth moved in with her sister Jane. On March 15, 1767, she gave birth to a third son whom she named after her now deceased husband Andrew.

Young Andrew Jackson was known for his physical ability, short temper, and toughness. He was eight years old when the American Revolution broke out. He was twelve when his older brother Hugh died of heat exhaustion while serving in the militia during the battle of Stono Ferry in 1779. At thirteen, Andrew himself was drawn into the conflict when British troops with their Loyalists allies entered the Waxhaws under the infamous Colonel Banastre Tarleton.

The two younger Jackson sons participated in the Revolutionary effort. As lads, both Roger and Andrew knew the woods well and kept close watch over goings on by the enemy and reported to the rebels. Near Waxhaw settlement, Tarleton's men surprised the continentals and began to butcher them, even the wounded. A civil war broke out in the district and in an ensuing conflict the rebels were bested. The Jackson boys escaped to the Crawford home, only to be betrayed by loyalist neighbors.

In 1781, British troops surrounded the Crawford house, entered it, destroyed the contents, and captured Andrew and Robert Jackson.

While there, one British officer ordered fourteen year old Andrew to "clean his boots." Andrew refused responding that he was a prisoner of war. The Brit unsheathed his saber and took a swipe at Jackson's head. Young Jackson blocked the stroke, but sliced his hand and suffered a gash on his head as a result. He bore the physical and mental scars the rest of his life.

Both boys were taken prisoner and held in horrid conditions until Elizabeth was able to arrange their release through a prisoner swap. Unfortunately, while in confinement, both boys contracted small pox. Upon release, their condition deteriorated. The ride home was brutal and ater gaining the safety of home, both boys illness grew worse. Robert soon died.

Once Andrew recovered, Elizabeth volunteered as a nurse on a British prison ship to care for rebel prisoners; some were relatives. While there she contracted cholera and she too died.

Thus, the American Revolution rendered a very young Andrew Jackson orphaned. He had lost both brothers and his mother during the conflict and held the British accountable for his sorrows.

Jackson's life after that is interesting. He lived a rowdy life of gambling and fighting. He then became a teacher and later an attorney. In that last capacity he left the Carolina's and in 1788 traveled to what would soon be called Tennessee where he became a businessman, public prosecutor, and later a judge.

While seeking lodgings there he meet the love of his life, Rachel Donelson Robards. The story of their love affair is too involved for discussion here. Suffice it to say that it would become the grist of scandal mongers for years after and become the cause of much pleasure and hardship.

In December of 1796, Jackson became a representative to the U.S. Congress from the new state of Tennessee. In that capacity he steadfastly defended the rights of state militias that often were overlooked and abused by Washington politicians. His victory in gaining them full payment for their services would serve him well later.

In 1797, the Tennessee legislature appointed Andrew to the U.S. Senate. Jackson's personality did not lend itself to a slow moving deliberative body. That, coupled with his loneliness for Rachel and his deteriorating financial situation, caused him to resign after serving only one year of a six year term.

On April 1, 1803, at age thirty-six, Andrew Jackson ran for and won, by one vote, the position of Major General of the Tennessee Militia. He ascended to this elective position despite lacking any military experience.

Andrew Jackson's career continued along a path of both business and local public service until 1810. At that time, relations between America and Great Britain had deteriorated to the point of near open warfare. In fact, many frontiersmen grew convinced that British agents from Canada incited and armed Indians in their campaign of terror along the western frontier.

Westerners became aroused over the brutal attacks of a splinter group within the Creek nation called "Red Sticks." The Indians gained this appellation because they allied with the Shawnee leader Tecumseh and his brother "The Prophet" seeking to annihilate all Whites. They painted their tomahawks red as a sign of commitment. The Red Sticks began a campaign of terror throughout the west killing and scalping men, women, and children.

A particularly brutal attack of murder and kidnapping in a local community enraged Jackson. He knew some of the murdered settlers, and in his capacity as Major General of the Militia he sought revenge. After several attempts to negotiate with local loyal Creek Indians for the return of a captured woman, Jackson went public. In an editorial in the *Democratic Clarion* on July 8, 1812 Jackson made his position known. In a call to his fellow westerners he said: *"It may be but a short time before the question is put to you: Are you ready to follow your general to the heart of the Creek Nation?"*

Not wanting to face Jackson, the loyal Creeks took it upon themselves to find the offending Red Sticks, kill them, and return the kidnapped and emotionally traumatized Mrs. Martha Crawley to what remained of her family.

In the meantime, the war with Great Britain festered. Governor Blount notified Jackson that President Madison had sent him some blank commissions for military officers. The governor signed Andrew Jackson's name on one of them. He now officially became Major General of United States Volunteers. In this capacity, he was ordered to collect troops and travel to New Orleans.

Here politics once again entered the fray. Jackson took his men down the Ohio River to Natchez. Suddenly, he was ordered to surrender the troops under his command to General James Wilkinson in New Orleans. Jackson would have none of it. He had brought 2,000 men some 500 miles from home. He would not abandon them. He refused to turn them over and set out to bring them back to the safety of their hearths and homes.

The return trip was brutal, Jackson gave up his horse for infirm soldiers and paid the costs of the return trip himself. During this return trip his men affixed to him the nickname "Old Hickory" because of his toughness. As a supporter once said about Hickory . . . it is the most difficult wood to work.

After arriving home, Jackson once again found himself involved in a bloody personal conflict. He became party to a dual with the Benton boys. Thomas Hart Benton became angered when Jackson served as a second to Captain William Carroll in a duel with Jessie Benton. Although formerly close friends, Thomas Benton denounced Jackson. Tensions between them erupted into a bloody conflict when both parties met in Nashville. Jackson was shot in the shoulder, suffered a serious wound, almost lost his arm, and was sent to bed for weeks to heal.

During this painful recovery, Jackson learned of a renewed Indian crisis . . . an Indian massacre. He jumped from bed, placed his arm in a sling and took to action: *"The health of your general is restored. He will command in person."*[34]

Jackson responded to the news that a massacre of hundreds white settlers (men, women, and children), Negro slaves, soldiers, and friendly Indians had taken place at Fort Mims, Alabama. The Red Sticks had taken to the war path again, and Jackson prepared to exact vengeance.

These two adversaries, Sir Edward Pakenham and Andrew Jackson, came from totally different backgrounds. One was the son of devoted family and catered privilege; the other orphaned early and born to toil and self-determination. Yet both displayed unbounded honor and courage. Despite their many differences, they soon would meet on a sugar plantation in Chalmette, Louisiana. Everything they had done all of their lives prepared them for this singular event.

Chapter 2

THE SOUTHERN CAMPAIGN OPENS

The Battle of New Orleans concluded a far broader British campaign encompassing the entire southeastern territory of the United States. In addition to taking New Orleans and all that came with that enterprise, the British hoped to retake Creek Indian territory, build a base in Florida, and occupy Louisiana.

It seems everyone had designs on the southeastern corner of North America. Although Spain controlled Florida, Britain still had connections there. Great Britain had occupied the area from 1763 until 1783, gaining it by treaty at the close of the French and Indian War. For twenty years Florida remained loyal to England and should be considered the fourteenth American colony. This colony did not rebel in the American Revolution because it was populated with loyalists fleeing from the troubled east. Britain may have returned it to Spain at the conclusion of the American Revolution in accordance with the Treaty of Paris of 1783, but they did still have roots there.

The United States, for its part, had only recently gained control over portions of West Florida (that area from Perdido River to the Mississippi River above the lakes). The people of West Florida rebelled against Spain and set up their own republic in 1810 for seventy-four days. America soon annexed West Florida up to the Pearl River that same year. The United States made it part of the state of Louisiana in April of 1812. Congress, by a second act, secured the territory further eastward to the Perdido River and attached that to the Mississippi Territory. Although this did not include the post of Mobile, it did include nearly all else.[35]

As war threatened between the United States and Great Britain, the importance of Mobile became apparent to both sides. Seeking to seize an advantage, General Wilkinson, commander of American troops in the old southwest, was ordered by his superiors to take possession of Mobile itself. Colonel John Bowyer marched south and approached Fort Charlotte (old Fort Conde') from the north. On April 12, 1812, Wilkinson joined him and landed close to Fort Charlotte. He sounded a bugle and advanced the combined American forces. With little resistance, the fort's Spanish Commander, Captain Cayetano Perez, evacuated the fort on April 15th and retreated to Pensacola, thus turning Mobile over to the United States. This would soon prove of the greatest importance.[36]

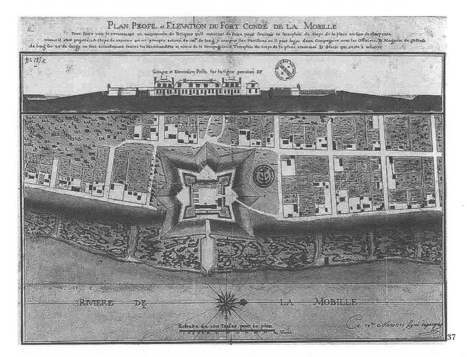

Fort Conde located at Mobile, Alabama.

General Wilkinson reinforced Fort Conde and then sent nine pieces of artillery to Mobile Point establishing a battery there as well. Wilkinson sent Colonel Bowyer to build a third fort at Perdido farther to the east. However, Bowyer's effort was abandoned because he needed to concentrate energies near Mobile. He aided Captain Reuben Chamberlain's construction of the fort at Mobile Point which was to be called "Fort Bowyer." This fortress on a point of land projecting into the Gulf of Mexico, commanded the entrance to Mobile Bay (Today's Fort Morgan). [38]

When war was finally declared on June 18, 1812, the United States now possessed this strategic position. Americans began completing a formidable bastion on Mobile Point that protected the seaward approaches to the town.

With the Americans distracted defending Mobile, Lieutenant James Stirling of the *HMS Brazen* landed at Pensacola in September 1812. Once there, he recognized the importance of this site and reported the same to the British Admiralty. He saw this location as a staging area for support of Britain's Indian allies, especially the Creeks, whom he reported: "*. . . still have the highest attachment to the English, and the greatest hatred to the American name . . .*"[39] The British planned to enlist Indians as allies in the war against America.

In December 1813, the British engineered closer contacts with local tribes when Lieutenant Edward Hanfield arrived in Pensacola and met local Indian leaders searching for arms. The Indians communicated to him their desires (in their words): "*. . . we hope you will eade and assist us as your allies and friends . . . now the Americans has maid war against our nations and we aply for armes and amenisun to defend our silves from so Greid a Enemy . . . and we hope you will send sum of our old friends, the British troops to eade and assist us against our enemeys.*"[40]

Contacts grew between British naval officers, Spanish officials, and local Indians. Pensacola fast became an important piece in Britain's game plan for their gulf campaign and a growing cause for alarm among Americans.

January 25, 1814, marked an important day for Sir Alexander Cochrane. On that date, the Admiralty awarded him total command of the British fleet in the southern theater and promoted him to Vice-Admiral of the Red and Commander in Chief of His Majesty's Ships and Vessels upon the North American Station. This promotion gave him a free hand. He immediately undertook coordinating operations with local Indians to advance his plans for a southern invasion.[41]

That same month, Admiral Cochrane requested that the Lords Commissioners of the Admiralty promote Edwards Nicholls to the rank of Brevet Major and have him serve as commander of the marines aboard of the *HMS Tonnant* (Cochrane's flag ship). Nicholls would play a significant role in the future offensive operation working with the Indians.

The British advanced their design against the southern United States during the spring of 1814. Having early recognized the need of enlisting the local tribes against their American foes, they now aggressively sought to achieve that goal. They planned to capitalize upon the long simmering tensions between local Indians and white settlers.

Indian problems began many years before. The Shawnee warrior Tecumseh and his brother "The Prophet" sought to unite western and southern Indians in a conspiracy to kill off the white man and take back their land well before America's war with Great Britain began. In 1811, they made a pilgrimage to the Creek tribes located in Eastern Alabama and Southern Georgia. Although Tecumseh failed to gain complete support, a faction, calling themselves "Red Sticks", joined him. They resented white settlers moving into their territory bordering the Tombigbee and Mobile Rivers and were ready to fight to secure their ancestral lands.[42]

Tecumseh returned in the autumn of 1812 seeking support again for his crusade against whites. On this occasion, he confronted stronger opposition. Many feared taking the warpath against Americans. Tecumseh warned his opponents that they would soon see the *"arm of Tecumseh like a pale fire, stretch on the vault of heaven."* His British allies had informed him about the coming of a comet, which information he skillfully employed to enhance his cause.[43]

At this same meeting, he met his strongest opponent, a man named Big Warrior, one of the Creek chiefs. After a heated meeting he and his brother, The Prophet, stated that: *"You do not believe the Great Spirit has sent me. You shall believe it! I will go directly and go straight to Detroit. When I get there I will stamp my foot upon the ground, and shake down every house in Toockabatcha!"*

When he had left, the southern Indians noticed the comet in the sky which convinced many that Tecumseh was indeed a messenger sent from the Great Spirit. British astronomical intelligence served him well. However, the Indian traditions tell that they also felt a great shaking of the earth which alarmed them extremely. Many were convinced that this was Tecumseh stamping his foot as he foretold. (Some have argued that this was the great New Madrid earthquake, although that event actually occurred eight months before, however, aftershocks may have continued.)

With the outbreak of war between the United States and Great Britain in 1812, prospects for help arose. By 1813, Tecumseh learned that British agents would establish a base in the Spanish capital of Pensacola, Florida. From this location they would supply Indians with arms, ammunition, and other essentials. With British assistance, the War of 1812 would set the frontier aflame.

Now, in the Spring of 1814, the time had come for a concerted effort on the part of the British to help those Indians on the warpath and encourage others to join them. The new arrangements between Spain and Great Britain would serve that purpose well.

Not all Indians were in agreement. Tensions festered among the Creek Indians themselves, as some supported white settlement and even had become "westernized" farmers themselves. Soon, the arguments between these factions degenerated into a civil war as each took arms against the other. Seeking help, the Red Sticks redoubled efforts to secure military aid from the British now operating out of Pensacola.

Hearing that the Red Sticks were in Florida getting arms from the Spanish (actually the British), American officers Major Daniel Beasley and Captain Dixon Bailey gathered their forces and lay in wait. They made a surprise attack on the Indian supply train on its return. The Americans initially succeeded, but let their guard down and were driven off while looting the supplies. This action set the stage for a far greater venture on the part of the angry Creeks who pledged revenge.

On August 13, 1813, residents along the Alabama River felt threatened. The Red Sticks had promised retaliation. Creek Indians from the Lower Towns who remained loyal to America, along with white men, women, and children, accompanied some military personnel and sought protection within the walls of Fort Mims. A total of 517 retreated to this protective enclosure. Red Eagle (a mixed race Indian whose American name was Weatherford), attacked the fort with over 1,000 braves and within a short time overran the defenses and massacred the inhabitants, killing and scalping nearly all of Fort Mims' occupants and even dashing out the brains of young children against the fort's walls. They took the surviving Black slaves as their own.

44

Creek "Red Stick" attack on Fort Mims

This brutal slaughter caused panic throughout the region and resulted in Andrew Jackson being given command of offensive actions against the Creeks. Although suffering from a severe shoulder wound inflicted in his dual with the Benton boys, he took to horse, deployed his troops, and conducted several successful campaigns against the Creeks.

Jackson's going was not easy. Persistent lack of supplies plagued his men and caused dissention. He began to encounter problems among his own troops concerning the lack of supplies and terms of service, Jackson prevailed upon them through the force of his personality, threats, and executions to stay with him. After putting down some internal resistance, he commanded two bloody offensives against the Indians.[45]

The first action took place at the Indian village of Tallushatchee. He surprised the Indians in their camp and mercilessly slaughtered them. The soon to be famous Davy Crockett, who traveled with Jackson, described the action: "*We shot them like dogs!*"

The second attack took place March 27, 1814, when Jackson's men surprised and the remaining Red Sticks at Horseshoe Bend. After a bloody conflict that lasted two days, Jackson's militia accounted for over 557 enemy dead within the Indian compound and an estimated 300 more who drowned in the river. Only twenty escaped his wrath. He earned the nickname "Sharp Knife" among the Indians for his ruthless attacks. Because of these aggressive actions, his western neighbors considered Jackson a hero.

It was during this battle that Jackson discovered a young infant Indian boy near his mother's body. When none of the Indian women would take the child, he sent young Lyncoya to Rachel at the Hermitage in Nashville where he raised him as his own child. This provides an interesting insight into Jackson's personality. (The young man died of tuberculosis in 1828)

Soon after Horseshoe Bend, Jackson received a promotion. On May 13, 1814, Major General William Henry Harrison, hero of the Battle of Tippecanoe, resigned from the army. President Madison appointed Andrew Jackson to take his place as Major General in the Army of the United States with command over the 7th Military District. He was forty-seven years old and now a general in the United States Army, no longer a state militia commander. [46]

In his new position, Jackson imposed a peace treaty on the Creek Indians. He was anything but magnanimous. He traveled to Fort Jackson in the Mississippi Territory, called the Creek chiefs together, and dictated HIS terms: the Creeks were ordered to surrender 22 million acres, nearly one half of the nation's lands. Even friendly Creeks who had fought with him endured his wrath. His response to them was that they should have captured Tecumseh when he first arrived and sent him to: "*. . . their Great Father the President, or have cut his throat!*"

From Jackson's perspective, their negligence cost American lives, so they too must pay. Furthermore, he ordered that the Creeks break all relations with the British and the Spanish, who controlled Florida. On August 9, 1814, thirty-five Creek chiefs affixed their mark to the Treaty of Fort Jackson.[47]

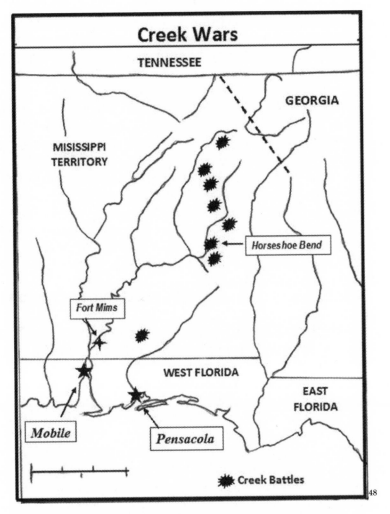

Map shows General Jackson's Campaigns against the
Creek Indians in the South East region.

Having suppressed the Indian uprising, Jackson now focused on a
more pressing problem . . . the persistent British and Spanish menace
in Florida. The British involvement was long and involved, and their
desire to enlist Indian support continued despite Jackson's treaty.
Those surviving "Red Stick" Creeks fled to Florida and remained on
the warpath.

Great Britain obviously had designs on New Orleans and the
Gulf Coast for a long time. To achieve their goal, Admiral Cochrane
indicated on March 22, 1814 his plans for the gulf region by letter to
the British Admiralty . . . *"I beg, have to request, that I may be furnished*

with a copy of the distribution of the squadron in order that I may judge of what additional force may be required to watch the points of attack so as to completely blockade those parts of the coast and if possible obtain pilots and information of the enemy's force and movements do as to enable the expedition on leaving this to proceed directly without delay to its ultimate object.[49]

Then on April 25th, he issued his own proclamation from his headquarters in Bermuda that expanded Admiral Sir John Warren's original proclamation for the blockade of the American coast to *". . . all remaining ports, harbors, bays, creeks, rivers, inlets, outlets, islands, and seacoasts of the said United States of America."* This was in preparation for his next move. Cochrane was tightening the noose. [50]

Despite Jackson's victories during the Creek Indian War, the British hoped to re-enlist those Indians who had escaped to Spanish territory with a mind toward re-opening hostilities. The connivance of the Spanish governor in these discussions proves Jackson's view that the Spanish had negated their neutrality.

In the same letter, Cochrane advises that the British must promote Major Nicholls to Colonel in order that he might have greater authority with the local Indian Chiefs. Cochrane instructed Nicholls to take a company good corporals and sergeants of marines up the Apalachicola River to drill and train the Indians in the: *". . . species of warfare that is by far the most destructive that can be adopted against such a perfidious enemy."* Thinking ahead to the invasion of New Orleans, he also sought: *". . . boats of light draught to bring heavy arms to Lake Pontchartrain [that can also] carry about 100 men."*[51]

He then turned an eye toward Mobile. The British sought a coordinated attack involving a variety of assets; *". . . landing 3,000 British troops at Mobile to be joined by the Indians and disaffected free men of color [who] would drive the Americans entirely out of Louisiana and the Floridas."*[52]

The British began to draft a plan to invade and occupy the region. They decided to set sail with their families, a major military force numbering in excess of 14,000 men and over 60 ships. The armada contained"*. . . all the officers necessary for civil administration, which shows what we must think of their assertions that they came to restore to their allies, the Spaniards, a province they had lost."*[53] This is yet another reference to the Louisiana Purchase.

Captain Hugh Pigot serving in His Majesty's Service reinforced Cochrane's plan when he sent a determined letter to the Admiral. He laid out a plan for arming and training those Creeks who had fled to Florida to escape Jackson's wrath. He desired them to join with the equally angry Seminoles. Pigot believed these disgruntled refugees could be employed to attack American interests. He states that: *"The present number of the warriors of the Creek nation friendly to the English and now ready to take up arms is about 2,800 soldiers . . . near Pensacola.*[54]

Captain Pigot's letter provides details of the anticipated support of local tribes and the status of American defenses: *"The Creeks are armed will come over to them (Seminoles) in great numbers, many have already taken refuge with these tribes."* He suggests that a combined attack against the fort at Mobile could be arranged because it would be *"easy"* it being *". . . the only garrison the United States has until you come to New Orleans. The town is defended by a fort with 200 troops and several pieces of heavy artillery."* He further stated that: *". . . the Creeks would assist in any orders to dispossess the enemy of that country that separates one part of the Creek nation from another and they from their friends the Choctaws."*[55]

Pigot expresses the belief that these Creek Indians would *". . . act in concord with any British force that might be landed for the annoyance of the southern states. They are a native race of men generally (?) handling the use of muskets and extremely anxious to make an entry into Georgia, which I have endeavored to persuade them from until having received support."*

The Captain goes on to explain that the Indians need arms and ammunition, as well as flour and bread, but that they possessed sufficient supplies of horses and "bullocks" of their own. He also insinuates that *". . . the Negros of Georgia"* might be willing to participate in any effort if the offer is made. The British are widening the conspiracy against America to include a slave revolt.

Anticipating the need for a senior officer to work with the local Indians, Admiral Cochrane decided on his own to promote Major Edward Nicholls to the rank of Lieutenant Colonel and placed him in command of the Colonial Corps of Marines. The Admiral gave him the duty to act as liaison training officer with local tribes.

Captain Pigot of the *HMS Orpheus* notified Nicholls that he would be responsible for bringing supplies to the local Indians: pistols, 1000 stand of arms, flints, balls and cartridges, gunpowder, a launch, oars, sails, and tobacco.[56]

The captain notified the admiral that he has ordered George Woodbine to work with the Indians at their request. He had temporarily appointed Woodbine, a member of his ship's company, to the rank of lieutenant of the marines and upon landing to be awarded the brevet rank of captain. *"The Indian chiefs having expressed great desire to have a British force with them that they might be drilled and trained in the use of the bayonet."*[57]

The good captain then developed his overall idea. These Indian troops with *"a handful of British troops accompanied by a few gunboats would (take) possession of Baton Rouge from which New Orleans and all the*

Mississippi would become an easy conquest. I am informed the disaffected in Barataria consists principally of French Creoles and Indians that would cheerfully assist in any altercations against the Americans if afterwards protected by Great Britain." He expected help from Lafitte's 800 men.

The overall plan to coordinate armed Indian forces working in conjunction with freed slaves and Lafitte's Baratarians in an attack on New Orleans began in the summer of 1814 with this letter from Captain Pigot of the *HMS Orpheus.* (More on the Baratarians later)

Five Creek Indian chiefs sent a letter to Admiral Cochrane in June in which they thanked him for his support and responded to his letter dated April. One cannot escape the feeling of warmth between the Indians and the British officers. The chiefs: *". . . acknowledge the receipt of your letter which breathes nothing but kindness and convince us that your and our father, the great and good King George, all of his officers will never forget his dutiful children and the part of the world for the present of arms and ammunition . . . which your captain whom we have visited on board his frigate has delivered to us."*[58]

The chiefs further urged the Admiral to: *"Accept the warmest thanks of all of us and our people be assured our ever beloved Father and King will honestly hear of our chastising there (sic) wicked and rebellious Americans."*[59]

Within this communication the Chiefs describe their mission as to *". . . forcibly land and attack and take the town of Mobile which by that means we could immediately have all the Choctaw Indians and the rest of the tribes on our side".*

Admiral Cochrane sent these letters to the Lord Commissioners of the Admiralty in Great Britain. Attached to his letter, Cochrane appended a list of the seventeen (17) tribes willing to send warriors including the number from each tribe. The total figure amounted to 3,255 men, the largest detachment coming from the Pensacola at 800 braves.[60]

Everything appeared to be flowing in the Admiral's favor. This impressive number of allies likely affirmed his convictions about success. It appeared that a combined force of Indians, freed slaves, and British forces would soon take Mobile, then move to control New Orleans and the entire gulf region.

After having communicated his support through newly promoted Lieutenant Colonel Nicholls to the Creeks, Admiral Cochrane received another letter from the Indians again confirming their warm attachment. The Indian chiefs addressed this communication to the *"Great and Illustrious Warrior."* In it these chiefs state: *". . . our hearts are filled with the glorious love of liberty and protected by our great and good father we will live or die free of which we have given hard proof by choosing to abandon our Country rather than live in it as slaves. We thank you for the supplies you have sent and promise to send. We receive them with unbounded gratitude.*[61]

The native leaders go on to state that: *"the chief you have sent to us [Colonel Edward Nicholls] we receive as we ought we will obey him in all things, we have made him our head warrior and commander in chief. We will get all the Black men we can to join your warriors."*[62]

Admiral Cochrane responded *"To the Great and Illustrious Chiefs of the Indian Nations."* In this dispatch he provides his Native/American friends with assurances of support from King George: *". . . that you are zealous in your wish to free yourself from the chains that the wicked Americans have prepared for you and your children. Yes, Great Warriors, your Father King George will not suffer his Indian Children to be made slaves by his rebellious Subjects."*[63]

Cochrane's efforts to forge close relations with the Southeast Indians were proving successful. He explains to the Indians that Major Nicholls is an experienced soldier under whose tutelage they can expect *"victory over their foes."* He advised them that they must maintain *"strict discipline must be subject to, and an implicit obedience to orders . . ."* In return, the admiral has given his Indian allies two field pieces, 1,000 stand of arms, and 1,000 swords. He adds that *". . . whatever number of warriors you can bring onto the field I will engage to arm them, which arms shall remain as their property after you have driven the Americans from your territories."*[64]

In this letter Cochrane takes the opportunity to urge his Indian friends to increase their numbers by making peace with those tribes at war with the Creeks and gaining their support in this all important effort as allies. *"Send to your deluded brothers now fighting against you and tell them that by adhering to the cause of the Americans, they are forging chains for themselves and their children."* In addition, he urges them to *"Encourage also by every means the emigration of Negroes from Georgia and the Carolinas. I have ordered the Chief I now send to you to organize, clothe, and arm as many as can be got to engage in the common cause."*[65]

Cochrane ends this letter informing them that *". . . great fleets and armies are now coming over the great water, when he (Madison) will be forced to beg a peace, Your rights will not be forgotten if you are true to yourselves."*

From these communications it is evident that the admiral sought to tie together all the alienated domestic elements in America and forge them into an effective fighting force to assist his invasion.

On July 23rd 1814, Cochrane composed a letter to the Lords Commissioners of the Admiralty accompanied with all these communications he had conducted with the Indians. He informed them that pursuant to his letter of 20th June, he had placed under the command of Nicholls: the Royal Marines, the officers, and men needed to assist the local Indians along with "*. . . two howitzers, a field piece, and 300 suits of clothing [and] have embarked him and his detachment with 1,000 stand of arms on board the Hermes and Carron*" and then to proceed to the completion of his mission. Cochrane also furnished Nicholls with $1,000 for "*extraordinary expenses.*" Attached to his letter Cochrane listed the men detached to Captain Percy of the *HMS Hermes* whose ship would land these troops.[66]

The admiral enclosed a copy of the orders he gave to Edward Nicholls of the 156th Company of the Royal Marines on the 4th of July 1814. Accordingly, Nicholls was ordered to land in Florida and to raise 500 men "*. . . amongst the Creek and other Indians . . . and such Negroes and others as may be induced to desert from the territory of the United States.*"

The British devoted considerable effort to employing Black slaves in their invasion plans. Cochrane advised Nicholls to print a "*. . . proclamation which you will distribute among the Black population and further assure them that those who emigrate from America shall have lands given to them in some of the British colonies on which to settle and that at any future period when there may be peace with America they shall not be returned to their former masters.*" This is a curious document considering that great efforts were expended by slave owners to prevent their slaves from learning to read or write. One wonders what value a proclamation would have made other than to put slave owners on watch and any slave caught in possession of such a document in great jeopardy.

Admiral Cochrane also harbors concerns about his native friends tendencies toward committing outrages. He recognizes the repugnance the Fort Mims massacre fostered among most civilized people and did not want a repeat of such atrocities, especially with British troops involved. He warned Nicholls how imperative it was that he "*. . . induce the Indians to desist from the practice of scalping and other species of cruelties which have been in the habit of practicing towards their prisoners.*" Cochrane is painfully aware of the outpouring of public outrage should his Indian allies perform such horrific cruelties again.

Having expended considerable energies aligning Indian and Black allies to his cause, Cochrane then affirms with Nicholls the main object of the campaign. The: "*. . . wresting of New Orleans from the United States being the object of much to be desired, you will use your best endeavors to obtain information of the nature of the country between the Rivers Apalachicola and the Mobile Territory, particularly whether the Indian tribes situated near the Mississippi would unite with our force or any others that might be sent to you in the reduction of New Orleans.*"

Unfortunately for the admiral, his attention also had to encompass issues of foreign policy. Cochrane recognized the delicate nature of Britain's relations with Spain. He knew that he must operate from Spanish Florida, but he also understood that the Spanish were fickle. One could not depend upon them. His concerns proved well founded. He warned Nicholls that he *". . . must be cautious responding in self-defense, not to commit any act of hostility against the United States while in the Spanish boundary or in any other way to infringe on the neutrality of the Spanish territory."*

On the other hand, should a war erupt between Spain and the United States the advantage must be taken. Cochrane ordered Nicholls to *". . . in that case afford every possible assistance to the Spaniards cooperating with them should it be necessary, against the common enemy."* He suggests under those circumstances that he should *". . . move to the westward and the scene of action will be between Mobile and the New Orleans territory."*[67]

In addition to these orders, he instructed Nicholls to coordinate with Captain Woodbine, who had been appointed and deployed earlier by Captain Pigot of the *HMS Orpheus* to instruct the Indians in use of fire arms. Theirs was now to be a joint operation with Nicholls as superior officer.

While juggling the disposition of the Indians, Black slaves, and their British allies, Cochrane also addressed a matter of the greatest concern. Where to open the attack?

Admiral Cochrane proposes to the Lords Commissioners his plan of operations. He suggests that he: *". . . has no doubt in his mind that three thousand British troops landed at Mobile where they would be joined by all the Indians, with the disaffected Freedmen and Spaniards, would drive the Americans entirely out of Louisiana and the Floridas."* The Admiral anticipated opening this offensive operation either in October or the beginning of November 1814. The importance Cochrane places on Mobile should be of note. [68]

To achieve this goal he directs that the Indians be given a 1,000 stand of arms in addition to that which has already been supplied along with two additional field pieces, a howitzer and a nine pounder *". . . with a large cache of ammunition."* He also suggests giving 1,000 *". . . sets of Dragons accoutrements . . . and a number of carbines for the young Indians."* He suggests that since Napoleon has been captured, there should be no problem finding the weapons he needs from the demobilized troops in England.

At this time, Admiral Cochrane awards Major Nicholls with the full rank of Lieutenant Colonel *". . . to give him a consequence with the Chiefs."* He then requests of the Lord Commissioners that they provide him with *". . . vessels of light draught of water to carry heavy guns into the lake 'la Pontchartrain'."* These boats must be designed to operate between Mobile and the Lakes adjoining New Orleans and large enough to carry about 100 men. He is preparing for the invasion of New Orleans. Such barges would play a major role in the coming assault.[69]

Suddenly, his carefully laid plans went awry. Pensacola, although belonging to Spain, was intended to be a land base for the British expedition. After all, with Napoleon safely ensconced on the island of Elba, Spain should now be an ally. Furthermore, since British troops under Lord Wellington had liberated Spain from Napoleon's control, they owed a debt of gratitude.

The Spanish governor, Mateo Gonzales Manrique, grew concerned. Andrew Jackson had taken notice of the British and Indian operations in Florida and had every intention of disrupting their collaboration. Accordingly, General Jackson informed his superiors in Washington of his plan to neutralize this nest of hornets. What were Jackson's intentions regarding Spanish Florida? He was a man of action with a reputation for taking matters into his own hands. If he saw a threat, he would not hesitate to eliminate it. The Spanish governor began to waver.

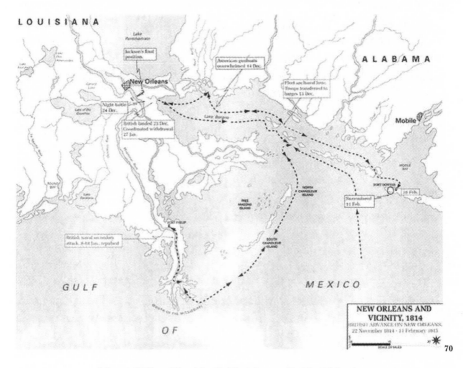

Map of West Florida & Northern Gulf of Mexico

Admiral Cochrane's letters indicate that the British overall plan was to take Mobile first then move inland. The importance of its being a former British colony cannot be forgotten. From Mobile they planned to march toward the Mississippi. Since this was once a British Colony (1767-1783) they may have found support. If not, they at least could deploy their entire army in one piece, forage as they traveled overland to Manchac or Baton Rouge, then cut off access to New Orleans from the Mississippi River. It must be recalled that Jackson received continued support from upriver until days before the January 8th battle.

This opened two opportunities: either secure a position north of the city then descend down river to attack New Orleans or invade the city by means of Lake Pontchartrain. This is exactly what General Jackson feared they might do.

Jackson recognized the critical importance of successfully defending America's key position at Fort Bowyer on Mobile Point. Therefore, he immediately advanced on Mobile to reinforce the American position there. Only then did he discover that Fort Bowyer on Mobile Point had been abandoned. A dismayed Jackson ordered Major William Lawrence and 160 men to secure the fort immediately and prepare it for an impending attack. Events were speedily coming to a head. [71]

On September 9, 1814, Captain William Percy of the *HMS Hermes* composed a very interesting and comprehensive letter to Admiral Cochrane from Pensacola. He reports leaving Havana on August 5th and arriving at the mouth of the Apalachicola River on the 10th where he landed the marines under the command of Lieutenant Colonel Nicholls on Vincent's Island to work with he Indians. He then proceeded to Prospect Bluff to meet with Captain Woodbine only to discover that Woodbine had gone on to Pensacola in the *HMS Sophie* seeking those Indians Jackson had driven into Spanish territory.

When Percy returned from Prospect Bluff, he found a vessel hired by Woodbine removing the arms and ammunition for transport to Pensacola. The Spanish governor had apparently indicated a willingness to assist Great Britain and allowed Pensacola to become the British staging base. [72]

Colonel Nicholls requested Captain Percy to re-embark his detachment and land them at Pensacola to join with Woodbine, now that they had Spanish permission. Percy, however, appears to have doubted Spanish faithfulness, since he had no formal request for British assistance from Florida's governor, only Woodbine's comment. Percy made it clear to Nicholls that he would help him, but he also informed Nicholls of his concerns about Spanish constancy: "... *my determination in the event of not receiving a request from the [Spanish] governor . . . to return to the anchorage off of the Apalachicola as I had promised the Captain General at the Havana, not to land on Spanish territory without being requested to do so.* [73]

Upon arriving at Pensacola on August 23rd, Captain Percy discovered a letter awaiting him from the Spanish governor urging him to disembark the marines immediately: *". . . as they were threatened to be attacked by the Americans."* Spanish cooperation now seemed unquestioned. Percy landed Nicholls and his men.

The British occupied Fort San Miguel and hoisted their colors below those of Spain in accordance with the Spanish governor's dictates. The British firmly planted themselves in Pensacola and began to develop it as a base of operations for their Gulf expedition.

Percy then turned attention to potential allies thriving at the mouth of the Mississippi River. He focused on Jean Lafitte and his Baratarians. On August 29th he *". . . directed Captain Lockyer of HMS Sophie to proceed to Barrataria (sp) taking with him . . . letters from Lieutenant Colonel Nicholls . . . (if) finding them disposed to co-operate with His Majesty's forces against the enemy to hold out to them that should they be considered British subjects."* Lafitte knew the approaches to the city well and could be of invaluable assistance to an invading force approaching by water.

With everything moving according to plan, Percy next unfurled his charts and sketched a design for attacking their initial target . . . Fort Bowyer at Mobile. He collected flour to feed the squadron then assembled arms and ammunition for the local Indians because he intended to attack the fort with *". . . the very numerous tribe of the Choctaw who are supposed to be friendly towards us."* This was an opportunity to test the alliance's effectiveness.

Percy laid out his plan of attack to Admiral Cochrane. He has learned from informers about the defenses of Fort Bowyer: *". . . every information I have been able to obtain that it is a long wood battery of very little strength mounting at the most fourteen guns of small caliber. The men are exposed as high as the knee and there is depth of water sufficient for the squadron to anchor within pistol shot of their guns. The capture or destruction of it will enable us to effectually stop the trade of Louisiana and to starve Mobile."* [74]

Percy heard that General Jackson had re-fortified the fort after first learning that the guns had been removed, but appears to show little concern about this development. He requested that Colonel Nicholls employ 100 Indians to assist in the attack on landward side of the fortification to divert attention while he mounted an attack by sea.

Nicholls responded that he would achieve the task with 130 Indians, 40 marines, and a howitzer.

Percy then notified Admiral Cochrane that he intended to set sail the next day for Mobile. He anticipated a brief skirmish followed by a splendid victory. The invasion was on!

Among Americans, concern grew about Britain's continued operations in the region. A letter from former Postmaster General, Gideon Granger, expressed most people's forebodings and fears for the future of the union: *"I tremble every day for the fate of New Orleans and Mobile. Have we a well appointed army there? Can the President answer for it to the nation if not? Much indeed do I fear that New Orleans is lost forever and that the west will be forced to secede."*[75]

On September 14, 1814, the British launched the planned combined land and naval operation against Fort Bowyer at Mobile Point. They anticipated a quick victory. It turned out quite the opposite. The British sustained the first of what would become several unexpected reversals.

Within forty-eight hours, on September 16th, a much chastened Captain Percy had to report to his commanding officer the results of his misadventure against Fort Bowyer. One can only imagine his embarrassment at having to repair to the cabin of the *HMS Seahorse*, the vessel to which he escaped, to inform Admiral Cochrane that he had not only failed in his mission, but has lost good men and his ship, the *HMS Hermes*.

Percy opens his report accordingly: *"You will have received a copy of my letter of the 9th instant acquainting you with my intention to attack Fort Bowyer on Mobile Point. It is with the greatest regret that I have to inform you of our miscarriage in that affair."*—Captain William Percy.

Percy detailed the events of the action as they unfolded. After welcoming Colonel Nicholls on his return from Barataria, he sailed to Mobile and landed the colonel's forces under command of Captain Woodbine about nine miles east of Fort Bowyer. His flotilla then proceeded westward approaching the fort by sea. At 3:10 P.M. on the 13th, the *Hermes, Sophie, Carron,* and *Childers* passed the bar. At 4:16 P.M. the fort opened fire. At 4:30 P.M. the *Hermes* dropped anchors fore and aft then delivered a broadside soon followed by second barrage delivered by the similarly secured *Sophie*. Unfortunately, the wind died away and an ebb tide commenced pulling water out of the bay. The two supporting ships of the squadron drifted from their "appointed station" leaving the anchored *Hermes* and *Sophie* alone within range of the fort's guns.

While this action was underway, Captain Woodbine's detachment of Indians and marines opened fire from the land side to the east of the fort and commenced their attack. They were driven back by a raking fire of grape shot and ball. The land attack failed almost as soon as it began.

It is most interesting to read the account of the action from the pen of Captain Percy himself drafted in the wardroom of the *HMS Seahorse*. Percy continues:

"At 5:30pm the bow spring being shot away the Hermes swung with her head to the fort, and grounded, where she lay exposed to a severe raking fire, unable to return it except with one carronade and the small arms from the tops. At 5:40 following the ship floated forward, I ordered the small bower cable to be cut, and the spanker to be set there being a light wind with the intention to bring the larboard broadside to bear and having succeeded in that, I let go the bestbower anchor to steady the ship forward and commenced action. At 6:10 finding we made no impression on the fort, and having a considerable number of our men [wounded]and being able only occasionally to fire a few guns on the larboard side in consequence of the light wind had on the ship, I cut the cable and spring and attempted to drop clear of the fort with the tide then running, every sail having been rendered perfectly unserviceable and all the rigging being shot away in doing which, unfortunately, His Majesty's Ship again grounded with the stern to the fort."

The Americans seized the advantage and fired grapeshot and round ball into the stranded vessel. Percy reported that he then met with Nicholls and Lockyer on board the damaged *Hermes* to discuss the landing party assembling on the *Sophie* to assist Woodbine's men on the beach. Both *". . . agreed that it was impractical under existing circumstances at the time"* to affect a reinforcement. They advised that the land forces be withdrawn.

Captain Percy reluctantly decided, with concurrence with Captain Lockyer and Captain Spencer, that the *Hermes* *"could not by any means be got off"*. She was hard aground. Percy ordered the squadron's boats to approach and remove the crew and wounded from the *Hermes*. He then destroyed her: *". . . I had the melancholy satisfaction of seeing His Majesty's ship blown up."* The remaining British ships set sail, abandoning Fort Bowyer.

Andrew Jackson reportedly heard the *Hermes* explosion in Mobile.

Among the British wounded was Lieutenant Colonel Edward Nicholls who sustained a severe wound to the head . . . a piece of wood splinter entered his right eye causing blindness. Percy ended his report by attaching the "Butcher's Bill" from the action listing dead and wounded by name, rank, position, and type of injury.

Captain Percy's attitude had altered significantly. He had replaced his bold promise of quick victory in his letter of a few days before, with an embarrassing and humiliating report to his commanding officer admitting a total defeat. Furthermore, the impact this had on Britain's Indian allies cannot be measured. Already living in fear of "Sharp Knife's" [Jackson's] wrath, after participating in this sorry affair, many Indians soon melted away back into the woods.[76]

The British assault failed on land and sea. A chastened squadron withdrew at 7:20 P.M. that same night and returned to the fleet, a mere four hours after first engaging. Victory belonged to Major Lawrence and his American defenders. Few realize the importance of the Battle of Fort Bowyer. An American defeat here might have sealed the fate of New Orleans.

Following the action, Jackson secured his base at Mobile, Alabama. The general then requested additional troops from Tennessee to confront the British who had landed a significant force at Pensacola and were fortifying a base there. Additionally, he possessed intelligence about how the British were again arming those Creek Indians who had escaped his net and that this combined force had designs on New Orleans.

Jackson smelled blood. He had never forgotten the horrors visited upon him and his family at the hands of British soldiers back in the American Revolution and welcomed revenge. In a letter to his wife Rachel he stated: *"I owe to Britain a debt of retaliatory vengeance. Should our forces meet I trust I shall pay the debt."*[77]

On October 25, 1814, Jackson left his base at Mobile, moved east, and opened an expedition against the British and Spanish in Florida. The general took a dangerous step with this move because there was peace between the United States and Spain. An invasion of Florida would cause an international incident at the least and war at the worst. Jackson, however, had no concerns for such international niceties. In his mind, the Spanish had betrayed the United States and their own neutrality by allowing the British an open door in Pensacola. The threat to the United States was real, and it was his duty to confront it forcibly.

Before crossing Florida's border, he composed a letter to Secretary of War Monroe apprising him of the situation. Like Caesar at the Rubicon, Jackson's action here would once again define his personality: *"I feel I stand justified to my government . . . should I not . . . the consolation of having done the only thing in my own opinion which could give security to the country . . . will be ample reward for the loss of my commission."*

He frankly did not care what politicians in Washington thought, he was going in! [78]

Jackson's reinforcements arrived on November 1, 1814. He hastily assembled his troops at Fort Montgomery, north of Pensacola. Then he and his 4,000 men marched south toward the Spanish/British stronghold in Pensacola on November 3rd.[79]

On that same date, Captain William Percy writing from *HMS Seahorse* at Fort Barrancas in Pensacola composed a letter to the Spanish Governor and Captain General in Havana. He informed him that the Spanish governor in Pensacola appeared less than determined to defend his command.

He reported that when he had arrived off of Apalachicola River he had received a letter from Don Mateo Gonzales Manrique, Governor of Pensacola, requesting British assistance *". . . to repel a threatened attack by the American Army then in that neighborhood."* However, he goes on to report that when his squadron and Colonel Nicholls's forces actually arrived in Pensacola *". . . they found the fortifications in a ruinous state and no appearance of any intention on the part of the government to repair them."*[80]

Percy further reported that he and Nicholls offered British assistance to repair and defend the facilities, but that he is: *". . . sorry to have to add that the assistance has been rendered negatory by the total want of all cooperation on the part of the principle (Spanish) officers who have on all occasions shown jealousy of us."*

Relations would deteriorate further. The tensions between Spanish and British officials became palpable. Neither trusted the other, and both faced considerable problems. The British desperately needed a land base from which to launch their expedition against New Orleans either by a march inland or as a supply port for a naval invasion. Fresh food was critical. The Spanish, on the other hand, had to face the prospects of a determined General Andrew Jackson and his army camped just outside of the city.

The British turned up the heat. Their frustration with the plodding Spanish had reached the breaking point. The day before Percy's letter to Havana, Captain James Gordon of the *HMS Seahorse* notified the Spanish governor of Pensacola that: *". . . we have come to a determination to move off all the Indians and Troops under the Lieutenant Colonel's [Nicholls] orders for the protection of Pensacola (which protection was claimed by you) unless you put the fort here and also that at the entrance of the harbor into the immediate possession of the English in conjunction with Spanish forces under your orders—**we expect and answer in one hour** [emphasis added]."*[81]

On November 2, 1814, Major General Andrew Jackson marched toward Pensacola with four thousand men. Four days later, Jackson and his army bivouacked within two miles of the city. Jackson then sent Major Pierre under a flag of truce to inform the Spanish governor that he had no intention to attack a neutral power but had every intention of denying an enemy of the United States any succor. The British opened fire from Fort Michael on this approaching delegation.

A furious Jackson dashed off a letter to the Spanish governor demanding an explanation for this violation of a flag of truce. Dated November 6, 1814, from the Head Quarters of the 7th Military District near Pensacola, Jackson released a captured Spanish soldier to deliver his angry response. It read in part: *"I am at a loss, Sir, to know what motive has influenced your conduct on this occasion, and being willing to spare unnecessary effusion of blood, I send you this by one of your corporals I made a prisoner at Bayles and shall expect an answer in the course of two hours . . . whether this unheard of conduct is contrary to the usages of war . . . has been the result of an accident or premeditated design."*[82]

That same day, a frightened Governor Manrique wrote two hasty notes to his British counterparts in Pensacola in which he enclosed a copy of Jackson's letter. In a difficult to translate and confused communication the governor wrote to *"The Commander of Land and Sea of His British Majesty anchored in this bay"*

The governor signed the first letter, accompanied with Jackson's angry dispatch, simply "Gonzales." It suggests that the Americans don't appear to have hostile intentions and requests intelligence from "VSS" about the size of Jackson's army, mentioning that the Spanish corporal released by Jackson gauged the American forces at about 3,000 strong with twelve cannons. Gonzales suggests that *". . . these forces we can repel if VSS combines what he can to the one (forces) under my command."* The identity of VSS is not disclosed, but undoubtedly British.

The second letter, which is formally signed by Governor Mateo Gonzales Manrique, the governor declares that he is presently under attack *". . . which circumstance is known by the commander of Land forces* [Nicholls?]. It urges assistance from "GS" and he appears to be suggesting that if help is not forthcoming, he wants it verified that he sought help. Again the identity of "GS" is not disclosed.

The Spanish governor may have been trying to cover his tracks with Havana by urging support against the Americans when he knew it was impossible to gain. His early hesitation prevented any efforts for formulating a defense. That might explain his closing comments where he appears to be attempting to establish a record that he sought help: *"I put it on your notice so you can find out a protest against GS when there is a chance to verify the virtue of my requisition for this [help?]."*

Whatever the circumstances surrounding these cryptic notes, the fact remains that General Jackson, tiring of fruitless negotiations, marched into Pensacola on November 6th. Jackson's men boldly attacked the city from along the beach, and then overran the protective batteries under a hail of cannonballs, grape-shot, and musketry. Within a short time, Governor Manrique appeared with a white flag of truce and offered to surrender the town rather than see it destroyed.

Jackson demanded all forts to be surrendered immediately, which was done after a short delay. However, Fort Barrancas, at the mouth of the harbor remained in the hands of the British. Jackson planned to take the fort by surprise the following morning, with the intention of turning the fort's guns against His Majesty's fleet riding at anchor just off-shore. However, the British occupants beat him to the draw. They abandoned the fort and blew it up as the British fleet exited the harbor. Captain Lockyer who was in command of this operation destroyed the fort with over ". . . *three hundred double barrels of gunpowder, a large magazine of every sort of ordinance stores and provisions for five hundred men for one month, spiked the guns, destroyed the carriages, [and] blew up the blockhouse.*" [83]

Retreating from Pensacola deprived the British of a land base for operations and a source of supplies for their intended expedition against New Orleans. It also deprived them of many of their Indian allies who became disenchanted with the ineffectiveness of British arms and were frightened of being attacked by Andrew "Sharp Knife" Jackson.

On November 9, 1814, Captain James Gordon of the HMS Seahorse sent a dispatch to His Excellency Juan Ruiz Apadaca (?) Captain General in Havana in which he politely stated: *"I think it necessary to inform you by the very first opportunity that the American Troops about three thousand strong under the command of General Jackson entered and took possession of Pensacola on the 7th of this month.*"[84]

He goes on to criticize the local Spanish governor, writing that: *". . . if the governor had allowed the detachments and Indians under Lieutenant Colonel Nicholls command with the seaman and marines I could have landed from the squadron to have strengthened the Barancas in conjunction with the Spanish Troops; I am confident that General Jackson would soon have been obliged to have evacuated Pensacola for want of provisions.*"[85]

Gordon explains how he destroyed the fort and that he had taken with him over 200 Spanish soldiers who he intended to deliver safely at the nearest Spanish port.

Captain Gordon next sent a detailed letter to Admiral Cochrane on November 18th from Apalachicola, where he had anchored his squadron. In this communiqué he further adds to the denunciation of and frustration with Governor Manrique for his failure to defend his city: *"I am sorry to say that the Governor and his Officers determined we should not strengthen Fort Barrancas at the entrance of the harbor; nor would they do so although the ships company of the Hermes had some time before made ready fascines for that purpose."*[86]

He went on to state that the Spanish governor refused to give permission for Colonel Nicholls to advance against the Americans because that *". . . should be considered a breach of neutrality . . . and that it is not in the power of the Governor to declare war."* The Governor also: *". . . wished that the English Colours should not be hoisted on the Fort again with the Spanish [flag]."* Up to that time the English ensign has flown below that of Spain on the forts.

Captain Gordon's frustration must have been extreme because he angrily announced: *". . . under such terms we declined having any more to do with him, that I should leave the place whenever I got everything embarked which we hoped to be in three days."*[87]

An angry Gordon explains that the governor *". . . would not do anything to check the enemy's advances."* Then, Gordon states, that after Jackson's advanced guard approached and were fired upon, the governor had the audacity to contact Gordon and Nicholls: *". . . to demand our assistance wanting the ships companies to be landed and Indians brought back; I told him I could have nothing more to do with him . . . that from his conduct I was certain he had betrayed his trust."*[88]

Gordon refused any further contact with the local Spanish authorities. He spitefully destroyed the other fort on Santa Rosa Island on his way out of port. At this point he mentions a letter from the governor where it appears the governor is attempting to stuff the record with his request for aid, which is likely the note referenced earlier. Gordon sailed for Apalachicola where he disembarked the 200 Spanish soldiers who had left Pensacola with him.

Gordon goes on to report that he has taken with him forty-seven men from the *HMS Hermes* *". . . to use in case of my being able to get hold of small vessels for the purpose mentioned in your secret Instructions."* This refers to the barges needed for use in the invasion of New Orleans.[89]

The duty now fell to Admiral Cochrane to compose a detailed report to the Lords Commissioners of the Admiralty in which he was obligated to discuss the failure of the attack on Fort Bowyer, the loss of Pensacola, and the abandonment of their Indian allies. No officer would envy him the job of having to report such failures to his superiors in London. He penned his report from the cabin of his flagship the *HMS Tonnant* on December 7, 1814.[90]

Obviously, tensions between the Spanish and the English had reached a critical point. Cochrane wrote: *". . . the imbecility of the Spanish Government in West Florida and their natural jealousy, leave the Americans every opportunity of encroaching upon the Indians as it appears to be the object of the American government to cut off all communication between the Indians and Great Britain by driving the Creeks out of their country.*"[91]

The significance of these failures is not difficult to calculate in terms of the Battle of New Orleans. The failed attempt at Mobile removed any hope of a land based invasion toward New Orleans. By abandoning Pensacola, the British lost an important staging area and critical depot. The Indians fled once they saw Jackson appear, the Spanish surrender, and the British flee. Their disappearance removed any hope of assistance from that sector. There never was any indication of assistance from the slave population. As for the Baratarians, no word had come from that quarter either.

Cochrane's planned invasion of New Orleans had come under a cloud. He could no longer depend upon a coordinated event incorporating the efforts of an assortment of allies. All of Cochrane's plans had unraveled, leaving him alone with his fleet, army, and the sole remaining alternative of taking New Orleans by a precarious naval invasion.

Having secured the Gulf Coast, neutralized Spain, and removed the Indian threat, Andrew Jackson turned to challenge his major opponent . . . Great Britain. Jackson had been ruminating on this confrontation for thirty-three years. He now fixed this foe clearly in his sights. Jackson brought more than just the imperative for national defense to the battlefield. There is an old saying . . . *"Vengeance is best served cold!"*

It did not take long for Jackson to react to the magnitude of the force he confronted. Intelligence provided sufficient evidence of his opponent's strength. *"Recent information from the most correct sources has been received of an expedition of 12,000 to 15,000 men, sailing from Ireland early in September last intending to attempt the conquest of Louisiana. You will therefore, see the necessity of preparing for service, at an hour's notice.*"[92]

So much was at risk. A point deserving serious consideration concerned the treaty that had ended Napoleon's rule. One of the conditions of the peace with France that resulted in Napoleon's abdication was a demand for the transfer of Louisiana from the United States to Spain. The territory: *"England claimed, was fraudulently conveyed by Bonaparte to this country, and which England, should its ally, Spain, not prove strong enough to retake, would take for her."* This provides further evidence of Britain's intent. If Britain were to abrogate the Louisiana

Purchase and return Louisiana to Spain, this rich territory would deprive America of its ability to expand. [93]

Driven by imperial determination and personal greed, the British fleet and army sailed confidently westward along the Mississippi Gulf Coast seeking an access point for invasion. Despite recent reversals, the prize was still theirs' for the taking and they had every confidence of success.

So assured were the British of victory that Sir Fredrick Stovin, a Colonel in the British army, wrote to his mother in England from his ship on December 5, 1814: "*We are laying off Pensacola making our arrangements for the attack of New Orleans which I conclude we should commence in about 5 days. I have no doubt of our success . . .*" As for the promise of wealth Sir Fredrick goes on to state: "*. . . [we] expect a good deal of prize money for the large quantity of cotton which is there at N.O.*" British expectations of victory and wealth soared. [94]

Their plans of having Indians and freed slaves as allies, the Baratarians providing intelligence on access routes to the city, Mobile as a point of entry, and Pensacola secure as a nearby supply depot had all collapsed. Despite these reversals the British, nevertheless, held to their conviction that all would end well.

In the midst of all this activity in the gulf, on August 8, 1814, three Englishmen and five American delegates arrived in the Belgian city of Ghent to open peace discussions. Peace talks began as the British were actively planning the invasion of Louisiana. The British were represented by Lord Gambier, a naval admiral, Henry Goulbourn, a Member of Parliament, and William Adams, a doctor of civil laws. President Madison sent the following delegates to represent the United States: John Quincy Adams, James A. Bayard, Henry Clay, Jonathan Russell, and Albert Gallatin.[95]

On October 24, 1814, while participating in the negotiations for the Treaty of Peace, Lord Bathurst presented Major-General Pakenham his new commission along with orders to embark to Louisiana to: "*. . . assume command of the forces operating for the reduction of that province.*"[96]

So convinced were they of victory, the British had even determined a name for their newly conquered territory: "***The Crown Colony of Louisiana***"[97]

Chapter 3

THE SITUATION IN LOUISIANA . . .

What made the English so assured of victory? Why did they believe they would so easily prevail against Louisiana's defenses?

As we have seen, the war had already hopelessly divided the United States into angry camps. Divisions in New Orleans were even more distinct. Louisiana displayed a unique situation. It had only recently become a state through a hotly contested process. Culturally, it did not blend well with the rest of the nation. The city's French and Spanish population persistently conflicted with the ever intruding American immigrants. This helped augment tensions. Louisiana was not a secure fit for the United States.

The announcement of the Louisiana Purchase in 1803 came as a surprise, and the territory's being divided and becoming an American state in 1812 was not welcomed by many of the traditional French and Spanish Creole residents of New Orleans nor the surrounding parishes. In general, many Creoles disliked Americans, and, in particular, some even resented being considered American citizens.[98]

Many Creoles felt dispossessed in their own land. The new immigrants threatened their traditions, laws, language, and cuisine. Their general approach to life was different from those of the ever increasing numbers of Americans settling in the city. A brutish wave of "Kaintucks" who washed down the Mississippi River with every spring flood over-ran Creole customs. The business types from the North expressing their "Protestant Ethics" further aggravated an already sour relationship with local Catholics. New Orleans was rapidly becoming a divided city. French and Spanish occupied the one side, Americans the other. Although there obviously was considerable crossover, the median on Canal Street still retained its traditional status as the "Neutral Ground" between these contending social elements.

By 1812, the Creole population had been significantly augmented by thousands of French speaking refugees from Santo Domingo "who *attained their greatest numerical strength as compared to the American population"* just as the war started. These recent arrivals would account for a significant portion of the population. They *". . . were newcomers, unfamiliar and possibly unsympathetic with American ideas."* They were keenly attached to their new found French friends and shared their fears. According to New Orleans Historian John Kendall, this Haitian addition to New Orleans also *". . . challenged the rival civilization (American)."*[99]

In 1805, the total population of New Orleans was 8,475. Within four years the number had increased as a result of immigration from Santo Domingo (Haiti) to a total of 9,059. Of that number 2,731 were white, 3,102 were free people of color, and 3,226 were slaves. Additional numbers arrived in succeeding years. The influx of French culture aggravated the growing tensions between Creoles and Americans.[100]

One local Creole earnestly set forth his dissatisfaction in a pamphlet published in 1804 which he signed by the simple appellation: "Native". In it he stated that: *"Governor Claiborne fell, as it were from the clouds, without the least knowledge of the country, its inhabitants, their manners, their customs, the very language, or their laws, which he was enjoined to follow."*[101] The introduction of English as an official language caused the greatest concern. In the Creole view they were rapidly becoming *"strangers in their native soil."*

The Vieux Carre' (Old Square) established by the French was surrounded by three plantations: Marigny Plantation was located just down river from the city, Treme Plantation belonging to Thomy Lafon, a free man of color, thrived immediately behind the city toward Lake Pontchatrain, and St. Marie Plantation ran upriver from the city above Canal Street.

As the population grew the need for expansion became evident. Fauburgs (Suburbs) grew up. Fauburg Marigny became the home for most of the traditional Creoles. Fauburg Treme soon evolved into a mixed race community composed of many *"gens de couleur libre"* (Free People of Color) as well as white Creoles. The ever increasing

American population moved upriver to the new Fauburg St. Marie, which soon became the commercial center of New Orleans . . . what are today the Central Business District and the Garden District.

The tensions between the Americans and Creoles were strong. Even less discussed were the animosities that grew between Free Blacks and the more racially conscious Americans who could not accept a large population of African-Americans with rights, substantial money, successful businesses, and social standing. Many were recent arrivals from Haiti. The existence of Free Black Militias proved to be particularly disturbing to some.

The French and Spanish cultures expressed a decidedly different attitude towards slaves, manumission, and a Free Black population than Americans. The Black Codes under the French and Spanish were less severe and the Catholic Church required all souls to be saved through Baptism. A more relaxed attitude prevailed. The Free Black population soon after statehood began to feel the animosity and discrimination that had never so fully infected Louisiana before. These strong racial attitudes would become more pronounced as time wore on.

Robert Breckinridge McAfee, a veteran of the War of 1812 and author of a book about the conflict best described the attitude of most Americans toward the residents of Louisiana: *". . . the population in general was composed of Frenchmen and Spaniards, who had, whether foreigners or natives, been bred under the most despotic forms of government, and had not yet become familiar with our institutions."*

Robert best described the situation with his own words. He presented this analysis about why Louisiana was wholly unprepared for war: *"Local jealousies, national prejudices, and political factions, dividing and distracting the people, prevented that union and zeal in the common cause, which the safety of the country demanded. Hence there was a general despondency and want of preparation for the approaching crisis."*[102]

Here the British saw advantage. These social divisions would lead the British to a mistaken conclusion about the depth of New Orleans' social problems. They saw an opportunity to divide and conquer. Some faction would likely come to their support. Colonel Dickson reports as much in his diary: *"The British government had given away to feelings of optimism concerning the helpful nature of the inhabitants of the invaded territory in the past, and they were now doing the same thing again. In fact, when the Spanish colonists seem to have been friendly toward the British when they encountered them, the same could not be said of the French."*[103]

The basis of the Proclamation composed by the British and distributed among the population focused on this underlying tension and sought to find advantage in it. This Proclamation also betrayed their desire to return Louisiana to Spain: *"Natives of Louisiana! On you the first call is made to assist in liberating from a faithless, imbecile government, your paternal soil: Spaniards, Frenchmen, Italians, and British, whether settled or residing for a time, in Louisiana, on you also, I call to aid me in this just cause: The American **usurpation in this country must be abolished, and the lawful owners of the soil put in possession** . . . [Emphasis added]."*[104]

Louisiana had become a state only several weeks before the declaration of War with England. That process too was highly controversial. Local tensions were repeated on a national scale. Many Congressmen opposed statehood. Josiah Quincy, a Congressman from Massachusetts, even threatened secession from the union if Louisiana were admitted as a state. He believed Louisiana statehood would nullify the contract between states that bound them to the Constitution.

Concerns arose over the fact that Louisiana was the first state to be admitted west of the Mississippi River and a part of the very large Louisiana Purchase. Would more states enter from this new territory? If so, how many? What would be the impact on the power of the original states?

In addition, many could not countenance the prospects of a state with such an unusual background entering the union on equal footing. Louisiana was Catholic and had been under the rule of kings and emperors and thus had no democratic traditions. Its legal system was foreign, and all transactions were in French or Spanish. Furthermore, the overall culture was foreign.

As for the local population, many supported statehood but resented the temper of the debate. Of special concern was the fact that the U.S. government denied the right to vote based upon race. Louisiana's Free Black population could not vote on the issue of statehood. This is likely the very first instance that the federal government officially linked race to voting. Not that Free Blacks were actively voting before, but for the federal government to deny that right was considered an intrusion into state's rights. [105]

Despite these highly charged emotions, Louisiana did become a state April 30, 1812 as the eighteenth state of the union. Although the process was far longer than any preceding state's admission to the union, it was attained. But this highly charged event transpired a mere eleven weeks before the Declaration of War with Great Britain. Emotions remained raw on all sides.

Almost immediately, the people of New Orleans felt the impact as British ships blockaded the Mississippi River. By April of 1813, local banks were charging interest rates of from 3% to 4% per month. The war devastated the local economy. On top of that, the Creek Indian wars caused deep concern especially because ". . . *bands of drunken Choctaw Indians perambulated the city streets. The authorities were loath to restrain them for fear of provoking a rising. . ."*[106]

Taking all of this together, it appears logical for the British to believe that many Creoles and Free People of Color would turn to their side. They were not welcome by Americans. At a minimum, the British believed they could neutralize them as a fighting force when hostilities began. Many assumed these ethnic tensions would hamper any attempt at an effective, coordinated defense of the city by the Americans.

Governor Claiborne expressed his feelings about this matter in a strident letter to Jackson dated November 10th. The fact that British agents distributed subversive leaflets throughout the city concerned him greatly:

"An English commander has dared to make his first call on the Louisianians, and to invite them to outrage the very ashes of their fathers, and welcome an English army on their paternal soil! He added insult to injury by first inviting us to the separation of our country, and they by supposing us capable of cowardly displaying at our dwellings a foreign flag as passport to his protection"[107]

Governor Claiborne had justification to register his outrage about attempts to foment treason. Rumors persisted that some city dwellers feared a conflict with Great Britain. The thought of their precious city destroyed in war was beyond their comprehension. According to their thinking an immediate surrender proved the prudent alternative to destruction and defeat.

How deep did these resentments run? That is what the British sought to probe.

The British were further reinforced that they may be right about discord within the Louisiana ranks because of events half a continent away. Divisions appeared among the general American population as well. Discontent with *"Mr. Madison's War"*, as the War of 1812 had been termed by his New England opponents, raged. In October of 1814, as the New Orleans campaign exploded, New England dissidents called a meeting for December 15, 1814.

Twenty-eight delegates representing anti-war elements met at the Hartford Convention in Connecticut. Members considered secession from the Union based upon their anti-war sentiments and long held pro-British feelings. *"Blue Light Federalists"* in Connecticut had even openly supported British military operations by lighting channels with blue lights to warn the British ships of American blockade runners. This Hartford Convention met during the Battle of New Orleans and only disbanded after the announcement of the Jackson's victory.[108]

Much of the fear among some Creoles stemmed from the reputation of Andrew Jackson himself. Lest we forget, the Russian Czar burned Moscow rather than allow it to fall into Napoleon's hands. Some Creoles believed that Andrew Jackson was more than capable of the same horrendous action to keep New Orleans from falling into enemy hands. They feared for their city. They believed that an immediate surrender might be the safest course of action.

Indeed, that very concern caused a rift between Jackson and some French members of the legislature. On the eve of the main battle, it was reported to Jackson that some members of the legislature were considering surrendering the city should his attempted defense fail. Jackson's response was . . . *"Then blow them up!"* This comment, when transmitted to the legislature, caused an immediate stir.

The City of New Orleans could not be considered a stalwart ally under the stress of invasion. Taking all of this into consideration, British efforts to undermine support and perhaps even gain advantage proved a worthy effort.

As another component of their program to divide and conquer New Orleans, the British sought out the Baratarians. Although avowed enemies of British and Spanish merchantmen, they nevertheless occupied a strategic location on the coast of Louisiana and exhibited an uncanny knowledge of its inland waterways. Furthermore, their legal problems with American authorities were well documented. They too may be open to negotiations with the British.

Jean and Pierre Lafitte were approached and promised commissions in the British navy as well as personal wealth and pardons if they would support the English effort. The British needed intelligence about hidden approaches to New Orleans and the Lafitte's' smuggling operations could prove vital.

Certainly, the British would not have embarked upon such a course unless they believed they could gain the "privateers" support. Hadn't Claiborne recently arrested many of Lafitte's men, seized his property, and destroyed his bayou headquarters? The governor's attack on the "pirates" lair shattered much of Lafitte's wealth as recently as September. Perhaps Lafitte was ready to strike back. Also, since Lafitte's predations had been terrorizing international merchantmen at sea, the promise of pardons might be welcomed. Capture meant death! Why contact the Baratarians with a promise of rewards unless there was reason to suspect success? (more on this later)

It is reasonable to believe, therefore, that Pakenham's command structure justifiably assumed that they could gain local support from an assortment of disgruntled ethnic elements in New Orleans in advance of the invasion. Although they hoped to enlist allies to fight in the British lines; they would accept neutrality.

In fact, when the British did finally appear, governor Claiborne could only rely upon the local services of about 700 regular soldiers and a small force of local militia. Even the Louisiana Militia was divided between city boys and country boys who did not play well together. In early 1814, these two detachments nearly came to blows when called up together at the Magazine Barracks uptown.

Furthermore, the only matter they agreed upon, *". . . none were prepared to serve under American officers and all insisted that they that they should be relieved at frequent intervals."*[109]

As for material support, a flat-bottom frigate designed to carry forty-two guns remained under construction on the Tchefuncta River across Lake Pontchartrain. Fort St. Philip was wholly lacking in the necessities for defense and Fort Petit Coquilles protecting the Rigolets, *". . . was incomplete and only partially defensible."* The old Spanish Fort St. John at Bayou St Jean lacked proper armament.[110]

Defending Louisiana from a concerted attack by a determined and well trained foe presented real cause for concern. Logic dictated that the region was ripe for conquest.

The Baratarians . . . . "*A Widow's Son*" . . . A Masonic Connection?

A notoriously twisted coastline marks Louisiana's southern boundary. It traces an irregular path extending for over six hundred miles. Actually, it is likely much longer because there is no means to accurately measure the contours of its countless inlets, bays, and bayous. Throughout its history, this uniquely irregular coast has provided smugglers with a bountiful opportunity for importing ill gotten goods. First, Jean Lafitte supplied Creoles with a variety of purloined items. Later, Rum-Runners plied their illegal alcohol trade from Cuba during the 1920s Prohibition. More recently, drug smugglers from Central and South America have found similar advantage importing their contraband along this unprotected coastline.

At about a mile above New Orleans, on the west bank of the Mississippi River, flows a small canal. It approaches to within a few hundred yards of the river. Paddling along this canal to the southeast, one runs into Lake Salvador, then Bayou Perot, through Little Lake until one reaches a bayou which flows through the swamps to Barataria

Bay. From here, through a maze of Cypress trees, a small island soon beckons the eye. It nearly blocks the mouth of Barataria Bay, allowing two outlets to the Gulf of Mexico, one to the east and the other to the west. [111]

This small island measures a mere six miles in length with an average of one and half miles in width. Several shell mindens, small mounds composed of piles of discarded sea shells, lie scattered along this isle. These are the remnants of the long gone Native-American cultures that once populated the area. Some consider them tombs while others view them as temple mounds where tribes celebrated the "Great Sun." Perhaps they are merely refuse piles. Their real purpose remains a mystery. A sandy beach stretches along the southern boundary of this island washed by the Gulf of Mexico's waves. Locals call the place "*Grande Terre*".

The island proved to be a valuable asset to Lafitte because of its inaccessibility to vessels of war. The surrounding waters were far too shallow for larger ships, running at only ten feet in depth. This would require any invading force to take to small boats, thus providing necessary protection for anyone living here. More important, the position of Grande Terre and the easily navigated waterways connecting it to the Mississippi River placed it in close proximity to New Orleans markets. Grande Terre arose as the ideal location for smuggling . . . and from the British perspective an ideal access point for an invasion.[112]

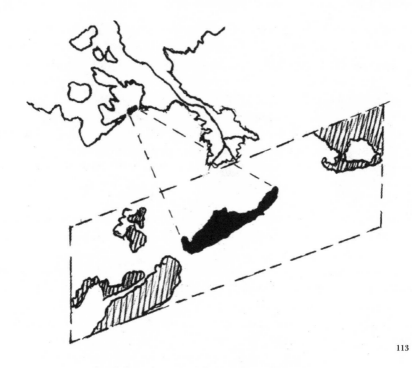

113

Symbol marks spot of Grand Terre. The route from
Lafitte's pirates lair to the city is marked.

This island had become the habitat for a group of men conducting their "business." Some considered them pirates . . . sympathizers called them Privateers. This difference is difficult to ascertain . . . both attacked and seized ships sailing the gulf. Privateers, to their advantage, were issued Letters of Marque, sailed under the protection of a national flag, and thus were not subject to the same punishments as pirates if caught. Pirates were unceremoniously hanged.

In the early 19th century, the Gulf of Mexico and the Caribbean Sea swarmed with pirates and privateers from all nations as a result of the Napoleonic Wars that ravaged Europe. During these years, many were able to receive the coveted Letters of Marque and sailed under the tri-color of France having purchased their commissions through the islands of Guadalupe and Martinique.

However, in 1806, Colonel Edward Pakenham distinguished himself by conducting military operations against both of these French possessions. He sustained serious wounds in his campaign on these islands but succeeded in conquering them. This broke up the favored port of the privateers and cost them their coveted flags. Once Napoleon abdicated, all French Letters of Marque disappeared. [114]

These swarthy sailors averted a crisis when Columbia declared independence from Spain. The rebellious colony sent out a call to all privateers and pirates requesting help to throw off Spain's shackles. Although final victory would not be achieved until 1819, the Columbians immediately issued their own "Letters of Marque" commissioned through the Port of Cartagena on the north coast of Columbia. This city had declared its independence in 1811. Under the flag of Cartagena, Columbia's allies retrieved the status of privateers, not pirates, and could legally ply their trade against Spain once again.[115]

Jean Lafitte and his band of buccaneers operated out of Grande Terre flying the flag of Cartagena from their mastheads. Once secure in their legal status, these mariners roamed the seas plying their bloody and parasitic trade against Spanish merchantmen . . . among others.

By 1814, Lafitte's operation had become entrenched in the local economy and his men had openly declared him their captain. There is some evidence that he plied the gulf waters himself. However, his real value stemmed from his business acumen. Jean Lafitte distinguished himself as a "fence", someone who sold stolen property. These men had the ability to steal cargoes, but not the contacts to sell those goods. Lafitte established a regular organization of privateers, elected officers, and appointed agents in New Orleans to conduct his business.[116]

Romantic legend has it that the brothers Jean and Pierre Lafitte opened a shop on the corner of Bourbon and St. Philip streets called *"Lafitte's Blacksmith Shop"* (It still stands). Most sources, however, agree that they actually operated from a warehouse on Royal Street. No matter what the location, the fact remains that from a French Quarter site they met with their Creole clients and made arrangements to have their stolen goods purchased.

Lafitte provided a vast assortment of valued items. The Baratarians possessed fine silks, rum, hardware, tools, furniture, plate, clothing, anything a plantation owner could possibly desire . . . including slaves. The Privateers smuggled these poor Africans into Louisiana to work on the ever increasing number of prosperous sugar, cotton, indigo, and rice plantations. All were in desperate need of a labor force. Smuggled slaves proved particularly appealing to the growing plantation economy because the United States had officially ended the international slave trade in 1808.

The goods Lafitte traded were not taxed. The Creoles loved the Lafitte brothers; they were practically kin folk. The advantage this trade afforded angered American merchants who suffered under the burden of actually having to purchase goods, pay customs duties, and pay taxes.

The money issue added to the already tense relations between these two ethnic groups. With the New Orleans population in 1810 having grown to 24,552 among whom only 3,200 were American, one can appreciate the cultural dynamics in play here. The resident Creoles and new French speaking immigrants often placed themselves opposed to the Americans in nearly all matters social and political. [117]

Lafitte's Blacksmith Shop

Jean conducted his business with energy and ability. His ships plied the local waterways, and his storehouses were filled with valuable goods his compatriots had gained though their conquests at sea. After Lafitte's Creole customers made their transactions in the French Quarter, they then journeyed to "*The Temple*" (a shell Minden on Grande Terre) where they completed their pre-arranged business and secured their property at considerable discount. This activity afforded Lafitte sizable profits while saving Creole clients much money.

Their predations originating from American territory placed the American government in conflict with other nations. Perhaps, of greater importance, Lafitte's violation of the international slave trade had become a source of serious concern to the American government.

Local Americans expressed specific alarm about the illegal smuggling of slaves. A number of those smuggled into Louisiana originated from the Caribbean islands where growing slave revolts had become a serious problem. The outbreak of a slave rebellion in Point Coupee Parish in 1795 was traced to recently smuggled slaves. Then on January 8, 1811, another more violent rebellion erupted on the plantation of Manuel Andry in St. Charles Parish. This turned into a very bloody affair that some believed was traceable to slaves brought in by Lafitte. [119]

All of these activities placed him at odds with Governor Claiborne and the American authorities who were under considerable pressure by American merchants and the national government to bring Lafitte's reign of piracy to a close.

Jean Lafitte and Governor Claiborne maintained a testy relationship. On numerous occasions Claiborne had sought to break up Lafitte's band and even had placed a reward on Jean Lafitte for his capture. Local Creoles, however, refused to cooperate and never betrayed their beloved Jean. When Governor Claiborne secured a bounty of $500 on Jean Lafitte's head, Lafitte pasted notices around the French Quarter offering a $1,500 reward on Governor Claiborne's head. The Creoles were amused, Claiborne was not! Such behavior served to further undermine an already tattered relationship. [120]

Throughout 1813 and 1814, several efforts had been made to shut his operations down. All to no avail. He enjoyed the protection and support of too many Creoles, many of whom were men of influence, some even elected officials. All too often from the American perspective, rulings from Louisiana's First Federal District Judge, Dominic Augustin Hall, undermined the law. [121]

An international event had an impact on Lafitte's operations. After the defeat and abdication of Napoleon in 1814, Spain became once again a neutral nation. This status required the United States to afford Spanish merchantmen protection from privateers. The local navy commander was thus required to extend such protection to all local Spanish shipping . . . the particular target of Lafitte's men flying the Columbian flag. [122]

In 1814, indictments for piracy were finally lodged against the Baratarians, in particular Pierre Lafitte. Jean's brother, Pierre, was charged as an aide and abettor in these crimes before and after the fact. *". . . to wit: in the city of New Orleans, within the District of Louisiana, knowingly and willingly aid, assist, procure, counsel, and advise the said piracies and robberies."* [123]

Although difficult to locate, American authorities eventually arrested Pierre Lafitte under these indictments. Prosecutors denied bail, so he was incarcerated in the Calaboose (city prison). Creoles were outraged. Tensions were building. Such was the troubled relationship between the local American government and the

Baratarians in the summer of 1814.[124] Knowledge about this gave the British hope.

Claiborne was determined to crush these pirates who infected his territory, and he vowed to destroy their criminal lair. As for Jean Lafitte, he sought to continue his lucrative business activities despite the governor's opposition.

In the midst of this conflict the British decided on their plan to conquer New Orleans. Undoubtedly, they saw an opportunity to take advantage of the sour relations between the Lafitte brothers and Governor Claiborne. This animosity, they believed, could serve their purpose. If anyone knew about secret approaches to the city, Jean Lafitte was their man. Furthermore, if the relations between these two men had deteriorated to such a strong degree, Lafitte just might be willing to welcome British protection.

On September 1, 1814, two weeks before his defeat at Mobile, Captain William Henry Percy of the *HMS Hermes* stationed at Pensacola was senior officer in the "Gulph of Mexico." He learned that some British merchant ships had been detained by Lafitte's men. He then directed Captain Lockyer of the *HMS Sophia* to proceed to Barataria *". . . to demand restitution, and in case of refusal, to destroy to his utmost, every vessel there, as well as to carry destruction over the whole place . . ."* Furthermore, he assured Lockyer of total support from British naval forces operating in the Gulf should he need assistance.[125]

With the stick came a carrot. Percy added to this communication the following:

"I trust at the same time that the inhabitants of Barataria in consulting their own interests, will to make it necessary to proceed to such extremities—I hold out at the same time to them, a war instantly destructive to them, and on the other hand, should they be inclined to assist Great Britain, in an unjust and unprovoked war against the United States, the security of their property, the blessings of the British constitution, and should they be inclined to settle on this continent, lands will be at the conclusion of the war, allotted to them, in his majesty's colonies in America . . . Should any inhabitants be inclined to volunteer their services to H.M. force, either naval or military, for limited service, they will be received, and if any British subject being at Barataria wishes to return to his native country, he will, on joining his majesty's service, receive free pardon." [126]

With these orders in hand, Captain Lockyer sailed to Grand Terre. His mission: intimidate the Baratarians into helping out the British invasion or face the consequences.

On September 3rd, shortly after sunrise, the *HMS Sophia* anchored six miles from Barataria Bay and announced its arrival by firing a cannon. At first, the Baratarians did not know the purpose of the visit, nor were they aware of the ship's origins. Once they recognized the British Union Jack flying from the masthead, Jean Lafitte ordered a boat out to meet his surprise visitors. Under a flag of truce, Captain McWilliams of the British Army and Captain Lockyer of the British Royal Navy approached the home of the Baratarians in their own gig and met Lafitte who had set out to meet them. Escorted by Lafitte's boat, they approached Grande Terre.[127]

Initially, Lafitte did not identify himself to his visitors as the boats met. When the British officers announced that they sought Mr. Lafitte, Jean informed them that the man in question was ashore. Lafitte disclosed nothing until landfall. However, once acquaintance had been made and the peaceful nature of their mission ascertained, Lafitte confessed his true identity. Captain Lockyer then delivered dispatches from the Admiral.

Lafitte invited the British to visit Grande Terre where they received an almost too warm welcome. The Baratarians despised the British and some wished to have their heads taken on the spot. Jean prevailed upon his comrades who had gathered on the beach to give way by reminding them that the British had landed under his protection. He then conducted the officers to his apartments.

John Randolf Grymes, a noted New Orleans attorney and onetime member of the New Orleans City Council, was present at the time. He would later recount that the British were treated to a fine breakfast: *"The best wines of Spain, the richest fruits from the West Indies and every variety of fish and game were spread out before them, and served on the richest carved silver plate. After the repast and when they had all smoked cigars of the finest Cuban flavor, Lafitte requested that his guests proceed to business."* After which the business at hand was discussed. [128]

The British first presented a copy of the broadside they intended to distribute around New Orleans. It was an appeal to Creoles to join the English against the United States:

"Native Louisiana! On you the first call is made to assist in liberating from a faithless and imbecile government, your paternal soil: Spaniards, Frenchmen, Italians, and British whether settled or residing for a time in Louisiana, on you also I call to aid me in this just cause: the American usurpation in this country must be abolished and the lawful owners of the soil put in possession . . . a flag over any door whether Spanish, French, or British will be certain protection . . . . Given under my hand at my headquarters in Pensacola, this 29th day of August 1814."[129]

Properly flag your home and you will avoid destruction, it said, a powerful message to residents when facing an invasion by an overwhelmingly powerful opponent. This note could also be interpreted to imply a repudiation of the Louisiana Purchase. The inclusion of the phrase: "*usurpation in this country must be abolished and the lawful owners of the soil put in possession*" is telling!

After reading this document, Lockyer presented Laffite with a second letter addressed exclusively to him. This one held a promise of considerable reward for his cooperation. It included: pardons for all crimes, a commission of Captain in the Royal Navy, and $30,000 in cash. "*I call on you, with your brave followers, to enter into the service of Great Britain, in which you shall have the rank of captain, lands will be given to you all . . . your property will be guaranteed to you, and your persons protected.*"[130]

Other letters provided instructions for Lafitte and his men should they decide to join forces with the British expeditionary forces. In particular, they were ordered to immediately cease ". . . *hostilities against Spain, and in any case they should have any Spanish property not disposed of that it be restored and that they put their naval force into the hands of the senior officer here.*"[131]

The fourth letter was more direct, first carrots then a stick. The Captain of the *HMS Hermes*, W.H. Percy made it perfectly clear what Lafitte's alternative was: "*I have directed Captain Lockyer of his majesty's sloop Sophia to proceed to that place (Barataria) and inquire into the circumstances with positive orders to demand instant restitution, and in case of refusal to destroy to his utmost every vessel there as well as to carry destruction over the whole place . . . .*"[132]

Lockyer also suggested to Lafitte that Major Nicholls requested permission to land troops on Grand Isle for the purpose of attacking New Orleans from the south. Lafitte replied that he had no intention: ". . . *to fight against the Americans.*" [133]

The prospects were clear, join us or endure the consequences . . . utter destruction. Jean Lafitte's options were narrowing. His alternatives proved to be especially dangerous since he did not enjoy a good relationship with Louisiana's Governor Claiborne. Indeed, an English victory might actually remove Lafitte's greatest tormentors . . . the Louisiana governor and the American authorities. Lafitte had a lot to ponder, so he informed Lockyer that he was not a dictator and must discuss these important matters with his men. He needed time . . . at least a fortnight . . . since a good number were presently "working" at sea.

Once the British had departed, Lafitte immediately penned a letter to French Creole Legislative Representative Jean Blanque. Mr. Blanque's strong reputation for being pro-French stemmed from the fact that he had arrived in New Orleans in 1803 with Pierre Laussat, the designated governor for Louisiana under France before the Louisiana Purchase transferred the region to the United States. When Laussat departed, Blanque stayed, purchased a home on Royal Street, married, and became a political power broker in his adopted home. As an interesting side note, after Blanque's death his wife, Madam Lalaurie, abused his slaves terribly and became the subject of the famous French Quarter "Haunted House" tales.[134]

In his letter to Blanque, Lafitte stated: "*. . . though proscribed by my adopted country, I will never miss an occasion of serving her, or of proving that she has never ceased to be dear to me.*" Lafitte then dispatched one of his men by fast pirogue to Blanque with the dispatches given to him by his British visitors. Included with the dispatches was also a personal appeal from Lafitte to Claiborne: "*I confidently address you on an affair on which may depend the safety of this country. I offer to restore to this state several citizens who, perhaps, in your eyes have lost that sacred title. I offer you them, however, such as you would wish to find them, ready to exert their utmost efforts in defense of the country.*" Lafitte sought to win the confidence and legal pardon of the Louisiana governor.[135] At a minimum he may have hoped to forestall the expected expedition against his Barataria headquarters.[136]

On a more humble note, Lafitte appealed to Claiborne's sense of humanity. He added in his letter to the governor these words: "I *am the stray sheep wishing to return to the sheepfold.*" He further informed the governor of the critical nature of the present situation. "*This point of Louisiana which I occupy is of great importance in the present crisis. I tender my services to defend it.*"[137]

Why Lafitte remained loyal to Louisiana and Governor Claiborne is open to conjecture. The British had made a commendable offer to him, Claiborne promised to destroy his base of operations and his business. Yet he sought succor from the Americans.

Within twelve hours, the letters arrived at their destination. Blanque forwarded them immediately to the governor where they caused deep concern. On the one hand, Claiborne had to consider the source, Jean Lafitte. On the other hand, there was no question that the British were planning an invasion. Could Lafitte be trusted?

Claiborne convened a meeting of his Committee of Public Safety: Major-General Jacques Villere, Commodore Patterson of the U.S. Navy, and Colonel Ross of the Regular Army. Two questions had to be addressed: First, were the letters legitimate? Second, was it proper for the governor to have any intercourse with pirates? Undoubtedly a heated discussion arose between the Creole who love and trusted Lafitte and the American faction who considered him nothing short of a pirate and murderer. Ross offered the suggestion that the mere fact that Lafitte had communication with the British was sufficient evidence of treachery. Claiborne sought an answer from his committee.[138]

The committee voted "No" to both questions with Villere, a Creole, outvoted on both counts.[139] This once again exposed the divisions between Americans and Creoles. The Americans employed the majority position to impose their view.

The conversation then turned to a discussion about what to do about the Lafitte buccaneers. If they could not be trusted, were they in league with the British? Collector of Revenue Dubourg in conjunction with Ross and Patterson pushed Claiborne to employ the forces now available to attack Laffite's stronghold on Grande Terre and end his reign of piracy. The fact that these two military officers could legally claim the riches stored in Barataria as "prizes of war" cannot be lost. They stood to make a tremendous profit by seizing Lafitte's warehouses.

Despite the fact that the information they possessed had come from Lafitte himself, Governor Claiborne took the American side. He framed his orders to the commanders in these words as represented in the Louisiana Gazette. Governor Claiborne addressed letters: "... to George T. Ross of the 44 regiment and Commodore Patterson to have an expedition against this bastion of pirates and smugglers that so long established themselves at Barataria on the island of Grand Terre and infested the waters. Shortly after intelligence received that the British were endeavoring to gain over Laffite and his pirates to their interest, which intelligence since been confirmed by letters into the hands of the commanders of the expedition containing a correspondence between Captain Lockyer of the British gun brig and Lafitte . . . requiring only fifteen days to decide the subject of adhesion."[140]

Negative attitudes toward the Baratarians extended beyond New Orleans and Louisiana. On November 5, 1814, the The Niles Register, published in Baltimore, expressed the feelings of most of the rest of the nation in regards to their activities. "Although we have laughed heartily at the appeal of the gallant colonel [Nicholls] to the people of Kentucky and his story of French influence—the base, villainous and unprincipled application to the celebrated pirate Lafitte, for his alliance—a man for the past two years past has been famous for crimes that the civilized world wars against—who is supposed to have captured one hundred vessels, of all nations, and certainly murdered the crews of all the he took, for no one has ever escaped him."[141]

The periodical added a personal attack on Captain Percy for even considering cooperating with such a loathsome character: ". . . his Britannic Majesty's senior officer indubitably know[s], as such an outlaw, pirate and murderer—is of a character so infamous and detestable, that, *in the strong language of an anonymous writer on other occasions we would* *"with trumpet lungs, call upon heaven and earth to punish for the offense."* Claiborne's actions against Lafitte were in accord with most American feelings towards the infamous Creole.[142]

In the midst of these meetings, Pierre Lafitte, Jean's brother, and several confederates escaped from the parish prison, some argued with inside assistance. The Americans posted a $1,000 reward for his return. Pierre worked his way to Grande Terre to meet with his brother Jean. Jean, for his part, was anxiously awaiting a response from governor Claiborne about the letters he had sent earlier with Blanque.

On September 7, 1814 Lafitte intercepted another letter that contained further warnings about British intentions. He also forwarded this to Blanque with a cover letter stating in part: *"You will always* *find me eager to evince my devotedness to the good of the country, of which I* *endeavored to give some proof in my letter of the 4*th*."* Jean hoped his charm and proven loyalty would win over Claiborne. He did not expect the violent and unexpected response that was soon to befall him at the hands of those whom he had sought to help.[143]

Jean Lafitte hoped that his intelligence gathering for the American cause would have the desired effect. As his letter to Claiborne indicated, his men wanted to become loyal Americans and offered: *". . . to exert their utmost in defense of the country. This point of Louisiana,* *which I occupy, is of great importance in the present crisis. "*[144]

Surprisingly, Lafitte's efforts to inform Claiborne of the impending threat by sending the packet of letters given to him by the British, worked to his disadvantage. Americans chose to view his contact with the British as treasonous. The governor finally gained the funds he needed from the American dominated legislature to organize an armed attack on Barataria. Once Claiborne's committee rejected Laffite's appeal, plans for an attack began in earnest.

By September 11th American Commodore Patterson had complete his operational strategy. Three barges loaded with armed men pushed off from the New Orleans levee and drifted to Balize near the mouth of the river. They met with Colonel Ross and his troops who were accompanied by the schooner *Carolina*. This vessel would play a major role in the campaign against the British six weeks later.[145]

On the evening of September 15th, Patterson, with the schooner *Sea* *Horse* and the six gunboats that would in a few weeks seek to defend Lake Borgne from the British, set sail from Balize for Grand Isle.[146]

As the flotilla approached Barataria, Lafitte's men first assumed that they were the British returning for an answer. However, it didn't take long to discover their error. Once the American flag was unfurled, they realized they were under attack. Nevertheless, they did not fire their weapons, but *"scattered in every direction."* Patterson arrested nearly 80 men. The rest vanished into the surrounding impenetrable swamps.[147]

The Americans destroyed Barataria. Patterson also claimed credit for seizing Jean's fleet of ships including *". . . six fine schooners", one felucca, one brig, cruisers, and a prize."*[148] $500,000 worth of treasure was also taken from Lafitte. It proved to be a splendid victory for Claiborne's forces. Furthermore, his anti-piracy campaign enriched Patterson and Ross. (An extended legal battle would later ensue between the Lafittes and Pattersons over disposition of these prizes).

On September 19th, Colonel Ross wrote a hurried letter to Claiborne announcing the success of his raid. This letter was published in the *Louisiana Gazette* on September 24th:

"We are in possession of all of the flotilla except a schooner that was burnt to the water's edge. They were here say seven fine schooners and feluccas, armed and unarmed. We have this moment returned from taking a fine schooner outside of the island of 1590 tons, armed complete Capt Henley lay off the bar and out-maneuvered her. You will see us soon in town. "[149]

In all, twelve vessels fell into American hands along with a number of prisoners and a large quantity of merchandise. On the 30th, they arrived back in New Orleans to the satisfaction of the American sector who met them at the docks. [150]

On October 20th Governor Claiborne had the *Louisiana Gazette* publish the letters Lieutenant Colonel Nicholls and Admiral Percy had given to Lafitte addressed to the people of Louisiana. These were documents informing non-American residents that they had nothing to fear from a British victory. Likely this was done to justify his actions against the Lafittes and prove that they were guilty of treachery. It may also have served to embarrass Creoles into supporting the American cause. He neglected to mention that the letters were given to him by Jean Lafitte.[151]

This was soon followed by a number of similar official reports of the action. A month later, on October 25th, Claiborne himself penned a similar glowing report to James Monroe announcing his great victory: *"These pirates are at present dispersed, but to prevent their re-assembling, a naval force on this station, in peace or in war, will be indispensable. "*[152]

In light of the fact that Claiborne was facing a massive invasion from the British with a paucity of defensive support, it is surprising that he would deplete his resources by committing men and material to such a military expedition against a potential ally. Nevertheless, he did.

Now he had to consider maintaining a sizable compliment of troops and naval assets to secure Barataria.

As for Jackson, on being informed about Claiborne's planned attack he stated: *"The Baratarians are now being prosecuted by civil officers of the United States . . . I cannot and will not do anything in the matter."*[153]

Claiborne wrote to General Andrew Jackson to announce the success of this expedition. At about the same time, Lafitte's letters, documents, and his bid to help the American cause arrived in Jackson's hands. How is a matter of conjecture, but it is probable Lafitte's attorney, Edward Livingston may have acted as conduit. Jackson: *"rejected them with scorn [and] denounced the British for their overtures to 'robbers, pirates, and hellish banditti."*[154]

Despite Claiborne's attack, surprisingly, Lafitte persisted in offering both Claiborne and Jackson his support. At first, many members of the American faction in the legislature persisted in questioning Lafitte's motives and doubted his sincerity. Others, especially the Creole legislators, extolled him as a great asset and advised acceptance of his offer. With the British practically at the city's gates and the demand for every man to take up arms, the issue of what to do about Lafitte grew in importance.

On the legal front, the Lafitte's were well represented. John Grymes and Edward Livingston, two of the most renowned attorneys in New Orleans, took their cause. Both had close relations with the Lafittes. Grymes, in particular, reportedly spent considerable time at The Temple gambling and socializing. He was there when the British arrived.

Andrew Jackson despised these pirates and persisted in his refusal to meet with them. He was not a man known for changing his mind. In fact, those who knew him acknowledged his renowned stubbornness.

An American soldier captured by the British after the December 23rd action had this to say about Jackson when questioned: *"He has been my attorney for some years and I have found it an impossibility to alter any arrangements of his, when once he had made of his mind. His determination in many cases, amounts to obstinacy and has gained for him the name Old Hickory, that being the wood more difficult to manage than any other."*[155]

Jackson even made the boast in New Orleans that he had only changed his mind once during his lifetime. Nevertheless, within five weeks Jackson would alter his position by embracing Jean Lafitte and his men as comrades in arms.[156]

What then, could possibly have transpired to have caused Jackson's strong attitude opposed to the Baratarians to soften and even become a flourishing relationship of mutual respect which some might even interpret as friendship. After the Battle of New Orleans, Jackson would say of Lafitte's Baratarians:

"The general cannot avoid giving his warm approbation of the manner in which these gentlemen have uniformly conducted themselves . . . and of the gallantry with which they have redeemed the pledge they gave at the opening of the campaign to defend the country"[157]

Note the use of the word "gentlemen" in place of "banditti." Whatever the cause, Jackson altered his opinion of Jean Lafitte and his companions in short order, provided them with the requested pardons, and highly commended them at the conclusion of hostilities. Somehow Jean Lafitte had gained the confidence of General Jackson. Certainly, it could not be Jean's charm alone. How was this meeting arranged? Who engineered it? What was said once they met?

Several popular sources mention a meeting on the *". . . second floor of Exchange Coffee House at Charters and Saint Louis Streets."*[158] Others note that the meeting took place in the Cabildo. Perhaps, it was at Jackson's headquarters on Royal Street. The location is of no import. What matters is that they did meet and became friends. But, one may still wonder: How did it happen?

The answer may lie in a society of men sharing mutual beliefs. A strong association of brotherhood existed that required these men from varied backgrounds to accept one another on level footing and respect. Freemasons considered themselves a brotherhood. No Freemason can deceive another. It is a bond that transcends all boundaries.

Among Laffite's men was Dominique Youx, a gifted artillerist and close ally of Jean. Sources identify him as having been born in 1775 in Port-au-Prince, Haiti. Drafted into the service of the French Republic in 1800, he was later found fighting for Napoleon soon after. He was one of the troops Napoleon dispatched to Haiti to fight Touissaint Louverture, leader of the slave rebellion on that island.

According to legend, his deployment there proved to be unfortunate. He was wounded in a gunpowder explosion and later was forced to flee for killing an officer in an altercation. He left Haiti and ran to Jean Lafitte. Dominique Youx was an assumed name to cover his activities in Haiti. His real name, according to some sources, was Alexandre Fredric Lafitte, half-brother to Jean and Pierre Lafitte.

Dominique Youx was a Mason. Existing records identify him as a member of the Lodge la Concorde #117 as early as 1811[159]. He may have been a founding member since refugees from Santo Domingo received the charter for Concorde #117 in 1810 from the Grand Lodge of Pennsylvania.[160] Some have stated that Jean Lafitte himself was a

Mason, but there exists no firm evidence to confirm this assertion. In fact, very little is actually documented about Jean's life, despite many attempts to portray it through biographies and what has come to be revealed as a fraudulent journal. Dominique, on the other hand, was active in his Masonic lodge and retained membership throughout his life. His tomb in St. Louis #3 cemetery bears Masonic symbols.[161]

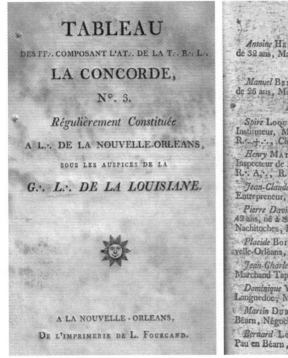

Dominick You [Youx], Jean Lafitte's purported brother, was a member of La Concorde Lodge from 1811 to at least 1815.

Dominic Youx's Grave site. Note circle around Masonic Symbol.

Andrew Jackson was a Mason as well. According to historian Robert Remini, Jackson reentered private life after failing to win appointment as governor. At this time, he became more active in the operations of the local Masonic Lodge in Greenville, Tennessee under the dispensation of the Grand Lodge of North Carolina, his place of birth. Jackson would become an honorary member of the Harmony Lodge #1 in Tennessee in 1800. Later he would be made Master of the Tennessee Lodge. Jackson enjoyed a long association with Freemasonry.

Edward Livingston, brother to Robert Livingston who had arranged the Louisiana Purchase in 1803, acted as negotiator between Jackson and Lafitte. He was Jean and Pierre Lafitte's attorney and would soon serve Jackson as his military secretary. He would also later serve as President Andrew Jackson's Secretary of State from 1831-33.

Livingston knew Jackson well. They served in Congress together and were two of the three members of Congress who voted against a bill giving thanks to George Washington as a "Great Man" at the conclusion of his second Presidential term. Furthermore, like Jackson, Livingston was a Mason.[164]

"Edward Livingston was not ashamed publicly to declare his acceptance of that same office of Grand Master of the Order."[165] This was penned by John Quincy Adams in his criticisms of the Masonic Orders. Livingston was

Master of his lodge in New York and addressed the members of the Erin Lodge in 1802.

Livingston brought his Masonic connections with him when he arrived in New Orleans. In 1807, the Grand Lodge of New York chartered the first English speaking lodge called Louisiana Lodge #1 in New Orleans. Livingston became Grand Master. There is reason to believe that Livingston was instrumental in arranging the charter for this lodge.

It may be argued that since Jackson, Livingston, and at least one Lafitte brother were Masons, this connection could have served as the basis for their growing trust and later affection. Masons hold one another in the deepest regard and speak to one another "*on the level*" in matters of importance. Lying and disrespect are considered unacceptable behavior among Masons. Taking all of this into consideration, a Masonic bond may have played an important role in opening the lines of communication between Andrew Jackson and Jean Lafitte. Perhaps this connection provided the essential bond of trust between these different men at a critical juncture in history. If nothing else, it provides a useful basis for speculation.

What is known is that the situation became so desperate that Jackson put aside all former objections and saw advantage in conferring with Lafitte to learn what the British had planned. He would also learn from Lafitte that despite the attack on Barataria, the American forces had not raided his military storehouse where he had secreted cannon, gunpowder, shot, and flints. All of these items were in short supply for Jackson. Lafitte made them available.

Pardons were forthcoming. Friendly exchanges were soon established between the great general and the notorious pirate. Their differences dissolved, and it appears a legitimate friendship evolved.

Lafitte's men would play a major role in the Battle of New Orleans. They not only made a vast store of materials available, but Baratarians, like Dominique Youx and Beluche, were master gunners. These artillerists delivered some of the most effective artillery exchanges during the ensuing battles. The Baratarian's accuracy destroyed many of the British gun emplacements hampering their plan of attack. The Baratarians conducted themselves with distinction.

As for Jean Lafitte himself, little is known about his whereabouts during the battles that raged from December 23 to January 8th. According to Lyle Saxon (not the best source), two documents exist that demonstrate that Jean served Jackson on the West Bank. The first is a pass to allow him and General Humbert to cross the river. The second is a letter signed by Jackson dated January 8, 1815: "This *will be handed to you by Mr. Lafitte whom I have sent to you as a man acquainted with the geography of the country on your side of the river, and will be able to afford you any information you may want with respect to canals and passes by which the enemy may attempt to penetrate.* "[166]

What little evidence exists indicates that Jean Lafitte served in an important capacity close to Jackson. It must be recalled that Jackson always believed that the British would open a second front. The earlier contacts with Lafitte would indicate that the enemy sought another approach to the city besides that from below the river in Chalmette. Perhaps Jean served Jackson by protecting his vulnerable flank. Lafitte may have secured the approaches through Barataria to prevent a British invasion from that quarter.

Whatever the circumstances, the underlying fact remains clear that Captain Percy had failed to detach Jean Lafitte and his band from the American cause in the War of 1812. The Baratarians provided material and physical support to the defense of New Orleans. Had the British succeeded in turning them, the outcome of the expedition against New Orleans would have turned out quite differently.

As further proof of the important role of Masons during the Battle of New Orleans, there are two Masonic Lodges in Chalmette, Louisiana. The Andrew Jackson Lodge #428 found its home in Arabi and the Dominique Youx Lodge #468, located in Reggio, was established in 1968.[167]

Andrew Jackson Lodge #428 Arabi, Louisiana

Dominique Youx Lodge #468 Reggio, Louisiana

Besides the issues relating to the Baratarians, New Orleans itself seemed hopelessly divided by the various ethnic groups that populated the city. Efforts to coordinate these uncooperative elements would plague efforts to forge an effective defense.

Home Front . . .

The New Orleans population celebrates January 8th as "victory day" for the Battle of New Orleans. Commemorating that one day leaves many people with the impression that one battle on one morning decided the fate of the city and caused only slight casualties on the American side.

The January 8th "Battle of New Orleans" actually culminated a four-month long campaign by the British to gain control of the city and the gulf region. Six separate battles were fought in the immediate area resulting in the death of many Americans. Victory did not come easy or without cost.

The first problem facing the city's defenders was overcoming their personal rivalries. Initially, it appeared to be a hopeless task.

When the citizens of New Orleans learned the British fleet had targeted their city for invasion, Edward Livingston, a leading lawyer in the state, called a meeting on September 15, 1814, at Tremouilet's coffee-house to address the city's defense. Once assembled the

Committee of Public Defense, composed of nine members, heard a speech by Livingston in which he invoked the spirit of nationalism so needed at that time. They then commissioned a saber to be presented to commander Lawrence of Fort Bowyer in Mobile Bay for his successful defense against the British.[169]

On Saturday, September 24th, the Committee of Public Defense warned of the enemy's attempts to undermine morale: *"Your open enemy is attempting to attack you from without. And by means of his vile agents dispersed through the country, endeavors to excite to insurrection a more dangerous and cruel one in midst of you."* This is a reference to the British handiwork in support of a slave rebellion and an Indian war as well as efforts to divide Louisiana along ethnic lines.

It should be kept in mind that the British had employed both Indians and former slaves in their plans. The committee announced: *". . . listen to the voice of honor, duty and nature."* This announcement was signed by the committee's members: P. Foucher, Boutigny, Destrehan, Benjamin Morgan, Edward Livingston. August Macarty, and D. Le la Croix.

Complicating matters, Roffignac organized a similar body for public defense. Once again New Orleans demonstrated its inability to coordinate efforts even in so simple as a matter of setting up a Committee of Public Safety. These two organizations were soon embroiled in pointless disputes of foolish questions of *". . . precedence and authority, and checkmated each others plans for usefulness."* Their focus seems to have turned from defense against British aggression to fighting among themselves.[170]

In the midst of this tension, Governor Claiborne sought to bring attention to the immediate problem at hand. He issued his Militia General Orders on September 28th. Accordingly, he called attention to the dangers which: *". . . menace the state to order each and every corps to hold itself in readiness for service . . . . but a knowledge of the enemy's advance will be of little value unless we are prepared to meet him."* This appears to be a direct response to his frustration with the infighting.

He added*: "Let every man then hold it a sacred duty to keep his arms and accoutrements in condition for immediate service and be himself ready to rally on a moments notice for a call of his chief"*[171]

In response to this call to arms, on October 4, 1814, the "Louisiana Blues", a famous local militia group, published an advertisement in the *Louisiana Gazette* addressed to its members. Militia members were ordered to assemble: *"The company will parade completely equipped at their usual place of rendezvous on Wednesday the 13 October at 3 o'clock PM in order to join their regiment on Washington Square Faubourg Marigny at half past three o'clock in obedience to regimental orders, by order of the captain September 27*[th]. " [172]

Caliborne then convened the State Legislature on October 5th to take action on the request of Jackson who was expected to arrive. But they soon became involved in ". . . *interminable controversies, and frittered away precious time without accomplishing anything.*" The state legislature once again degenerated into a rabble . . . "*Factious, and Incredulous of danger it did nothing, it attempted nothing, for the defense of the city. Disputes of the most trivial character engrossed the minds of the members*". [173]

Representative Louallier, of Opelousas, became indignant and reproached his fellow members: "*Are we so situated that we have no dangers to dread? . . . Shall we always confine ourselves to letters and proclamations? Are we always to witness the several departments entrusted with our defense languishing in a state of inactivity . . .*"[174]

On October 25, The Louisiana Gazette published numerous letters and articles about the war as it was ravaging Washington, D.C., and the British withdrawal from Baltimore. The paper then states: "*Among these which generally are the news of the day, will be found some seriously admonishing us of our danger and the necessity of prompt and extensive preparations. Some pointing out the line of conduct proper to be pursued when the danger is certain and imminent . . . .*" The newspaper sought to enlighten the population about the imminent dangers confronting all Americans; hopefully the news would reach New Orleans.[175]

The New Orleans population persisted in their internecine infighting despite their fears of imminent invasion. Was there no one in New Orleans to whom the people could turn? [176]

Chapter 4

WEAPONS OF WAR

As in all conflicts differences in weapon technology existed between the opposing armies on the battlefield. As combatants meet, the unique weapons they carry help to determine the outcome.

The Americans employed cannon and carronades (small canons) in their artillery batteries. Although the Americans possessed a limited number of cannons, what they had were designed for operations on land. Large wheels supported the gun carriage which allowed cannoneers to easily swivel the barrel from left to right to establish windage while an elevation screw permitted raising or lowering the barrel for accurate ranging. These elements made aiming at specific targets easy.

Land Artillery Piece

The British had an advantage in the number of guns deployed, but much of their compliment was made up of naval guns taken from the ships anchored off Ship Island. However, getting the weapons to the field, supplying them with ammunition, and then managing them once deployed, created problems.

Furthermore, every gun and all of the powder and shot had to be ferried from the fleet stationed at Ship Island to the scene of the battle, a distance of nearly 80 miles, by rowed barge! It is reported that each British soldier, when disembarking at Ship Island was given either a cannon ball or a canister of powder to carry to the front.

The carriage design caused the greatest disadvantage when using "naval guns" on land. The gun carriage was supported with four small wheels designed only for recoil on the hardwood gun deck. Unlike land artillery, which is designed for swiveling to gain windage, naval guns depend upon the ship changing course to align with a target. Elevation is achieved with naval guns by timing firing to the roll of the ship.

When on land, a naval gun is almost impossible to manage, especially when embedded in soft, wet soil.

Unfortunately for the British, just such conditions prevailed on Louisiana's sugar plantations in late December. The sugarcane had just been harvested in preparation for the grinding season. The land was bare and the stubble burnt. Late winter rains and cold weather had made the ground soft and soggy.

Naval Gun

The British made other critical errors in this regard. Following their overwhelming victory at the Battle of Bladensburg outside of Washington D.C., they underestimated the willingness of western Americans to stand and fight. With this in mind, the officers in charge decided that naval guns would prove more than sufficient to meet their needs at New Orleans. They believed merely a show of force would frighten their foes and carry the day.

However, the limitations imposed through the use of naval guns in land warfare would prove disastrous. The aforementioned disadvantages made it nearly impossible for the British to accurately target a specific object. In an artillery duel, the inability to focus fire against the opposing batteries prove to be a critical problem. The British could not destroy the American gun emplacements prior to the planned infantry advance.

British artillerists became immediately aware of the problems when they constructed their redoubts in the soft, damp ground on the Chalmette Plantation. The small wheels became clogged with mud, and every time a gun was fired it sank deeper into the muck and rolled to the side. After each firing the guns had to be muscled back into position. The difficulties became especially unnerving when elevating the guns or attempting to establish windage. There were no mechanical mechanisms to achieve that so accuracy became illusive.

Needing protection for their gunners from the American guns and riflemen raised another problem. They resorted to using barrels of sugar taken from the surrounding plantations. These were placed under and around the cannons in an attempt to provide shelter for the men servicing the guns and to establish some stability. Unfortunately, when these barrels were struck by opposing fire, the British found themselves wallowing in what can only be described as simple syrup . . . a sticky mess of water soaked sugar.

Additionally, the British lines of supply were so long that at no time was a sufficient number of shells and powder brought to the front. Thus the British artillery could never bring effective fire-power to an engagement.

Problems did not end there. Perhaps of greater importance were the differences in infantry muskets. The British army had been depending upon the Brown Bess for years. It was ingrained in the traditions of the British Army and always had served the purpose. In 1797, the Board of Ordinance introduced the 3rd Model (India Pattern) which offered a few improvements, in particular a shorter, lighter 39 inch barrel.

Use of the Brown Bess was cardinal to British warfare, and its production was licensed by the king. The manufacturer earned the designation of Royal Armorer. A change in technology would have to fight the political currents of the times . . . their own "military/ industrial complex." Entrenched preference for preferred arms manufacturers prevented any change. This persisted despite the fact that some British officers had recognized the advantages of rifles over muskets during the American Revolution.

The Brown Bess was a smooth bore musket of .78 caliber with the ability to affix a bayonet. Its length overall was 42 inches and weighed 10 pounds without its bayonet. As for the origins of the name "Brown Bess", that is lost in the lore of the early 18th century British Army. It grew though the ranks of the common soldier.

The Brown Bess was designed around the principle of quick reload . . . not accuracy. It even lacked sights! A good soldier could deliver one shot every 15 seconds. That served well in European warfare where men faced one another across an open field in fixed, advancing, closed ranks. Accuracy was not even an issue in such a situation. One need merely pull the trigger; opponents were close enough that the bullet would likely hit someone somewhere. Besides, the battle's outcome was more often determined by tactics and the bayonet charge then the firing line.

179

Brown Bess

"On account in the inaccuracy of the smooth-bore musket, the attackers were relatively free from casualties until they reached a point eighty to one hundred yards from their objective.

In this manner of warfare, rate of fire became more valuable that accuracy. A soldier's musket will strike the figure of a man at eighty yards; it may even at 100; but a soldier must be very unfortunate indeed who shall be wounded at 150 yards . . . that no man was ever killed at 200"[180]

In contrast, the Americans exhibited an eclectic mix of shotguns, muskets, sporting arms, and antiques handed down for generations. Whatever many could find they brought to the front. In fact, some even appeared eager to fight weaponless.

However, many of the Kentuckians and Tennesseans arrived with their prized Long Rifles. These weapons were carefully manufactured hunting rifles designed for long distance and accuracy. The key lay in the rifled barrel.

Kentucky Long Rifles, having evolved from the Pennsylvania Long Rifle, were originally designed by German immigrants who moved into Pennsylvania with their German Jaeger Rifles. These carefully crafted guns proved to be the most accurate firearms manufactured for decades. The Long Rifle fired a .50 caliber ball traveling through a rifled (grooved) 46 inch barrel. Each weapon had front and rear sights.

181

Kentucky Long Rifle

How accurate were they? Colonel George Hanger of the British Army studied the weapon at the conclusion of the American Revolution. He was amazed to witness a horse killed at 400 yards and heard from experienced riflemen that they could strike a man's head at over 200 yards.

As children, American frontiersmen learned how to make the variably sized hand-made balls fit snugly. The secret to the accuracy was the use of an oiled piece of linen cloth patch wrapped around the bullet before it was driven down the muzzle when loading. This acted as a gasket and allowed relatively fast loading with a tight fit . . . two key elements for accuracy. The patch imparted rotation to the bullet as it traveled down the rifled barrel while preventing expanding gasses from escaping around the projectile. These patches were stored in a "*patch box*" carved into the rifle's stock and covered with an engraved brass cover.

A phenomenon called gyroscopic effect came into play. The Long Rifle was not a smooth bore like the Brown Bess, it was rifled which stabilized its bullet's trajectory. When a tight fitting ball was rammed down the barrel and fired from the rifle, the ball started rotating because of the twisted grooves (lands) cut inside the barrel. Rifling imparted one full revolution in 33 inches. Once the projectile exited the gun, the imparted spin continued, physics keeps the ball traveling straight over a long distance. This made the Long Rifle extremely accurate.

In contrast, the Brown Bess was smooth bore. The inside of the barrel resembled a shotgun. When a ball was rammed down this barrel and the weapon fired, the exiting ball moved about in the free space between the bullet and the barrel. When it left the barrel it traveled an unpredictable path determined by the surrounding air . . . much like a knuckle ball. Hitting a target was not a result of accurate aim . . . only close proximity, fast reloading, and luck!

The British cartridge was made of paper with the ball to the front and powder in back. The soldier bit off the back of the paper, poured the gunpowder down the barrel then used the paper as wading to snug up the ball. It was not a tight fit, so the ball was relatively loose in the barrel. This was in contrast to the American use of bear greased linen for tight packing.

The British method was acceptable so long as a battle was determined by lines of men facing one another at short range. The point here was not accuracy, but speed of reloading which results in high firepower. Soldiers shooting at densely compacted lines of opposing soldiers made aiming unnecessary. Some argue that the phrase "*that's the way the ball bounces*" was coined from the acknowledged inaccuracy of muskets of that era.

The fact that the Brown Bess delivered a ball of .78 caliber while the Kentucky Long Rifle fired a .50 caliber ball is of consequence as well. One would think the larger round would be more effective . . . wrong! The lighter smaller ball traveled farther, faster, and straighter . . . thus it was decidedly more deadly at a far greater distance.

The differences among the weapons brought to the battlefield were matched by the contrasts in military tactics.

Many of the Americans were untrained urban dwellers. However, the men coming from Tennessee and Kentucky were seasoned Indian fighters. They used their guns to hunt for food and defend homesteads. They could not afford to miss a shot. These frontiersmen picked a target, took careful aim, and struck accurately from a great distance. The number of rounds fired in a given amount of time was of little consequence. What mattered most was hitting the target the first time, every time. These Americans were hunters. Accordingly, the term "*they went hunting*" applied to the westerners' sniping tactics during the Battle of New Orleans

The British would become particularly appalled by this practice of "sniping" from behind trees and attacking at night. It allowed no rest for shivering, weary, hungry warriors and generated a sense of vulnerability never before experienced. Woe to the Brit who started a fire at night.

During the conflict on the Chalmette plain, some of the rifleman set "range sticks." They stepped off the distance in the open battlefield prior to the engagement and marked the position with sticks driven into the ground. At the exact moment when the opposing target reached the "stick" which was the point at which the weapon was "sighted in" . . . they fired! No time need be wasted on calculating distance to target. That had been already done. The American riflemen merely aimed and fired!

The accuracy had a strategic impact far beyond that of hitting nearly every soldier targeted. In Europe, protecting the lives of young noble officers was proper sport. They were too valuable to be killed and thus wore highly decorated uniforms so as to be readily seen from afar and avoid injury. In America, taking out the officer class was considered reasonable . . . proper form. Without commanders and field officers a highly disciplined infantry became disoriented. It was not only proper to target officers . . . it was necessary if you intended to win. Their distinctive dress made them an easy target.

This difference in infantry weapons and tactics had a measurable impact on the outcome of this campaign. The tactical advantage of the long rifle, coupled with the strategy of stripping away the officer class, helped secure an American victory.

Other factors came into play as well. Americans had honed their skills fighting Indians and had adopted some of the weapons of these worthy opponents. American woodsmen carried a tomahawk. In close hand to hand fighting, westerners quickly drew their tomahawk from their belt and began slashing with it. The results of the butchering became apparent after the night battle of December 23rd. British reports of the wounds found on bodies the following morning revealed a scale of butchery never before seen in civilized combat.

182

Native American Tomahawks were standard weapon of backwoodsmen.

The British, for their part, deployed a relatively new weapon, the Congreve Rockets. Forerunners of modern missiles, they amounted to little more than today's fireworks. Their impact proved to be more psychological than practical . . . *"The rocket's red glare."* Nevertheless, many were fired at the American lines accounting for a lot of noise, visual effects, and some minimal damage. But the sound and spectacular show could only generate fear among opponents. They did little real damage. Jackson had to reassure his troops that these missiles merely produced sound and fury amounting to nothing. They posed no reasonable threat.

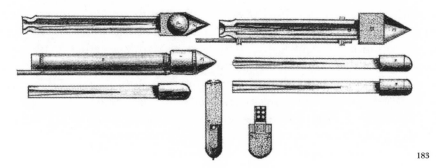

183

Congreve Rocket

Artillery shells were another matter. Besides solid round balls of varying weights, both sides employed grapeshot and canister which were nothing more than varying sized round balls of several inches in diameter fired into the ranks much like an oversized shotgun blast. These types of shot had a withering impact on lines of troops and proved an effective anti-personnel weapon.

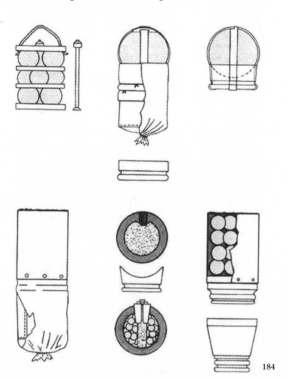

184

These are the types of ammunition fired from the cannons
by both sides at the Battle of New Orleans.

Thus, both sides employed basic early 19th century weapons: swords, bayonets, black powder, flintlock styled weapons, and artillery. But the differences between weapons used by the opposing armies were significant and had much to do with the final outcome of the battles.

Sometimes a new technology arises that, although not a weapon, has significant military applications. The Americans in the Battle of New Orleans benefited from just such an innovation.

River travel had historically been conducted by flatboats and keelboats. These vessels merely followed the current downstream carrying their trade goods. Flatboats generally were sold and dismantled so the wood could be used for other purposes. Keelboats were laboriously pulled upstream by cordelling, bushwhacking, or polling. All that suddenly changed in 1811.

On October 20, 1811, Nicholas Roosevelt, a partner with Robert Livingston and Robert Fulton, left Pittsburg in the steam-powered riverboat *New Orleans*. After an adventurous trip, he arrived in the boat's namesake, the city of New Orleans, on January 10, 1812. This opened a new era in river travel.[185]

The Livingston-Fulton Corporation gained a legal monopoly on steam travel on the western rivers and intended to enforce it. Although the Ordinance of 1787 opened the rivers throughout most of the Mississippi valley, the Territory of Orleans (present state of Louisiana) licensed the monopoly through the influence of the powerful local attorney, Edward Livingston. New Orleans was closed to all but them.

Unfortunately, the boats they designed were better suited for ocean travel than shallow inland waters. Result: the riverboat *New Orleans* hit a snag near Baton Rouge, the *Vesuvius* later ran aground above Natchez, and the Daniel French's competing *Comet* had to be scrapped. They had a monopoly, but no boats. Nevertheless, they intended to maintain their legal domination of the trade, despite these setbacks.

The partnership did not anticipate the bold spirit of another river man by the name of Henry Shreve. The biographer of Mr. Shreve provides this account of events.

Shreve recognized the value of steam travel. He operated one of the largest keelboats in the river and fought tirelessly every season to bring his vessel back upriver. Steam promised an easy, fast, and cheap means of taming the Mississippi. Henry Shreve decided to challenge the monopoly and open the western waters to all comers. To achieve this goal he had to steam to New Orleans.

Henry Shreve contracted with Daniel French who had built the *Comet* and was about to complete a new boat with an improved engine, the *Enterprise*. This was a small boat of only 75 tons. Shreve talked

French into letting him challenge the monopoly. He gave French $500 down with a personal note for an additional $1,500 more. Shreve also retained New Orleans attorney Al Duncan to represent him in a legal challenge to the Livingston-Fulton monopoly. The *Enterprise* would be the fourth steamboat to operate on the Mississippi River. [186]

187

Riverboat Enterprise

On December 1, 1814, Henry Shreve sailed the *Enterprise* from Pittsburg with *"a cargo of ordinance and ammunition for New Orleans."*[188] On December 14, 1814, a mere two weeks later, Shreve pulled up at a wharf in the frightened city of New Orleans. The population at the time was overwhelmed with fears of a British occupation. The arrival of this exotic new vessel with its cargo of much needed armaments captured everyone's attention.[189]

News of the *Enterprise's* arrival sped throughout the city and it was only a matter of time before Edward Livingston learned of the event. Livingston took immediate steps to have the steamboat seized for violating the monopoly.

However, another, more powerful man also heard about Shreve's unique vessel . . . General Andrew Jackson! New Orleans was under martial law. Jackson sent for Shreve and ordered him to take his vessel upstream in search of three overdue keelboats carrying small arms.

As Shreve prepared his boat for this duty, Livingston's representatives also arrived and ordered Shreve to turn the boat over to the Livingston-Fulton Company. With a smile, Shreve informed these men that they would have to take that up with General Jackson, because his boat had been commandeered for government service.[190]

Shreve left New Orleans, steamed upstream, and found the keelboats north of Natchez on the Mississippi River ". . . *dawdling along, doing a little trading by the* way." Shreve took the keelboat masters aboard and informed him that he had orders: *"Taking their cargoes and masters aboard the steamer, he tied the boats on behind and returned to New Orleans, the first instance of steam towage in the valley."*[191]

It took Henry Shreve just six and a half days to run six hundred and fifty-four miles in his round trip rescue. Once he returned Jackson pressed the *Enterprise* into further service. Shreve carried men and supplies down to the Chalmette battlefield. He even made a dangerous night run passed the British batteries down to Fort St. Philip with much needed supplies and ammunition after covering the sides of his riverboat with cotton bales to protect it from cannonballs. The *Enterprise* would also be used to evacuate some ladies from the city and then be later employed bringing 406 captive British soldiers up to Natchez. [192]

Once hostilities opened in Chalmette, Henry Shreve asked permission of Jackson to fight. Jackson hesitated because he recognized the value of the brave master river man. However, he relented and allowed Shreve to take a position working the gun at Humphrey's battery . . . a long twenty-four pounder.

Following the January 8th battle, Jackson again turned to Shreve. He was ordered to transport stores from the battlefield and bring British prisoners down to the Balize at the mouth of the river for a prisoner exchange. He made five trips to the Balize and nine to Natchez. He even returned American troops to their post on the Red River, a place were no steamboat had gone before.[193]

All told, according to Henry Shreve's biographer, he took the *Enterprise* on fifteen trips on behalf of the American cause at considerable risk to himself and his vessel.

As for the Livingston-Fulton monopoly, Livingston waited until all of Shreve's duties for Jackson had been completed before he attempted to seize the *Enterprise.* Litigation followed. Henry Shreve eventually won in court ending the monopoly, thus opening the western rivers to free navigation by steam.

A second steam boat also contributed to the war effort. The aforementioned *Vesuvius* was constructed by Robert Fulton for the Louisville-New Orleans trade. She first arrived in New Orleans in April 22, 1814. She was 146 feet long with a beam of twenty-five feet. Her captain, Samuel Clement, composed a pamphlet in 1827 in which he described his actions on behalf of the American effort in Battle of New Orleans.[194]

Clement reports that while taking on wood above Natchez on December 9, 1814, he was passed by a group of flatboats containing nearly 3,000 American militia under the command of General Carrol. He sped downriver to intercept the flotilla and received on board Colonel Andrew Hynes as a passenger. He would later take on an additional 120 recruits and headed to New Orleans.

When he arrived in Baton Rouge on December 15th he learned from the excited population there about the destruction of the American gunboats and the close proximity of the British invaders to the City of New Orleans. *"They were fully of the opinion that the city of New Orleans would be taken before I could get there."*[195]

Clement then reports that after arriving in New Orleans, Jackson ordered him on the evening of December 18th to steam upriver to meet with General Carroll and to take as many men onboard as his vessel could safely manage. Carroll, however, refused the offer and within a day had his entire contingent in the city.

On the morning of the 27th, Clement mentioned that Charles Harrod, deputy quarter master, requested that he take his steamboat to pick up a large quantity of *". . . thick plank and scantlings which were in a sawmill yard above town"* down to Chalmette likely for use in reinforcing Jackson's defensive line at the Rodriguez Canal.[196]

Although not technically a weapon of war, no one can question the value derived from applying steam technology to the riverboat on the war effort. It could be argued that the timely arrival of steam travel had as much impact on the outcome of the Battle of New Orleans as railroads had for Lincoln during the Civil War. Henry Shreve's *Enterprise* and Samuel Clement's *Vesuvius* provided a critical logistical advantage to Jackson during the campaign that cannot be minimized.

Although some question the accuracy of these stories, there appears sufficient evidence that riverboats did play some role in Jackson's defense. In fact, in one of his reports to his superiors Jackson expresses anger that the Quartermaster sent arms by means of flatboat rather than steamboat.

Consider for a moment what might have occurred had the British enjoyed a similar advantage of steam power to sail upriver. How might that have changed the outcome of the invasion? The geographic protection of English Turn would have been nullified, Fort St. Philip easily passed, and Admiral Cochrane would have been able to coordinate his naval forces with Pakenham's land army to achieve a British victory.

Technology plays a critical role in every war. The Battle of New Orleans was no exception.

Chapter 5

FIRST BLOOD

Contrary to popular belief and many published accounts, the Battle of New Orleans was not limited to one conflict on the Chalmette Battlefield or to the single date of January 8, 1815. The British launched a massive expeditionary force to take this major port city and perhaps to continue operations northward to unite with other British forces coming down from Canada. They sought to cut the United States in half.

The actual military engagements began with an attack on Fort Bowyer, Mobile. Actions in close proximity to New Orleans opened with the assault on the American gunboats on December 14, 1814. It did not end until the final shots were fired as Admiral Cochrane retreated from his assault on Fort St. Philip on January 18, 1815. A total of eight different battles marked this historic gulf campaign any one of which could have decided the fate of New Orleans. The field of battle extended through most of what is called the "*Isle of Orleans*" . . . all areas east of the Mississippi River and below the lakes.[197]

Many factors contributed to the British defeat and the American victory: weather conditions, choice of battlefield, types of weapons, miscalculations, lack of determination, deficiency of courage, impatience, failure to follow orders, extended supply lines, frustration, exhaustion, diminished morale, and that all valuable companion of victory . . . luck. [198]

As the story of this epic conflict unfolds, each of these factors will come into play. The invasion begins with planning in late Spring of 1814 when the British Admiralty cut orders to assemble a fleet in Jamaica.

The Weekly Chronicle published in Halifax, Nova Scotia, reported the formation of a large fleet in the Caribbean. On December 3, 1814, a report from St. Jugo de la Vaga listed some of His Majesty's ships on station in Negril Bay assembling and preparing to depart for the Gulf of Mexico. The navy was under command of Sir Alexander Cochrane, K.B. and the army under temporary leadership of Major-General Keane.[199]

Although command of the army belonged to Major-General Sir Edward Pakenham, he was in route from London and did not arrive at the scene until December 25th. The concern here was that Pakenham would arrive too late to partake of the victory. Colonel Dickson, artillerist, reported that Cochrane ". . . *sailed the 27*[th] *November, he is 16 days ahead of us, I fear, therefore, we shall not arrive in time to partake of the operation, unless he has been retarded by some adverse circumstance.*"[200]

Some argue that Cochrane left early because of a desire to gain the glories and treasure for himself. Others believe he feared waiting in Negril Bay out of concern that the fleet might contract disease. He had legitimate concerns that the army could be decimated by malaria, Yellow Fever, or some other sort of malady endemic to Jamaica's tropical environment. Whatever the case, Pakenham sailed past Jamaica directly to the mouth of the Mississippi River where he arrived on December 22nd hoping to catch up with his army.

Interestingly, Dickson reflects again on the overwhelming expectation of success: *"From all this I imagine the operation has been delayed for want of craft, but don't imagine there will be great resistance made, and I expect when we reach the Flag Ship to hear that New Orleans is already in our possession."*[201]

Judging from the number and types of ships employed, the British planned this invasion with intentions far greater than merely taking the City of New Orleans. By mid-December, the number of vessels anchored off Chandeleur Island would reportedly number nearly one hundred.

As the fleet gathered in Jamaica, the British sent vessels into the Gulf of Mexico to collect the necessary intelligence about geography and water depths. This mission permitted the British to determine the extent of America's naval defensive assets. An 1814 British document lists all of the ships available to the Americans. New Orleans is listed as having: *". . . gunboats and small craft only."*[202]

Early on, the British noted that Ship Island afforded the best anchorage. Water depth was five to six fathoms on the south side of the island and two to three to the north. This depth allowed plenty of water to meet the demands of most of the British navy. However, water depth soon dropped to under eleven feet at Passes Christian and Marianne, which made it impossible for ships to enter the lakes beyond. Any attack had to be achieved with the use of rowed barges.[203]

As mentioned earlier, the British first sought to establish a base in Spanish Pensacola. General Jackson put a stop to that plan. Their efforts to take Fort Bowyer at Mobile Point met a similar fate. The British lost one ship and suffered over two hundred casualties before finally being forced to retire.

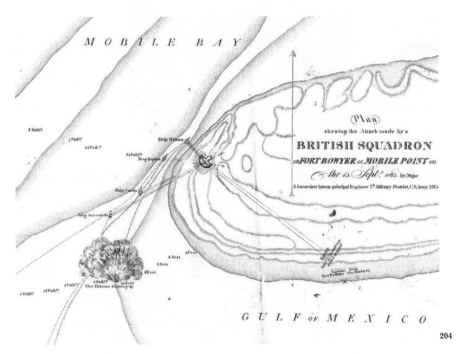

204

The Location of Fort Bowyer at the mouth of Mobile Bay

Following the failed attempt on Mobile and loss of Pensacola, the British seized their only option. They moved directly against their main target, New Orleans. The inability to establish other bases along the coast would prove critical because they needed the fresh food and supplies their Spanish ally could provide. Like Iberville and Bienville 120 years before, they recognized Ship Island as a perfect base to amass their forces. It offered a convenient natural harbor and close proximity to Lake Borgne.

On December 5, 1814, a letter signed "N" arrived from Pensacola. In it this informer notified Master Commandant Daniel Todd Patterson, Commander of the New Orleans Station, about the British activities in the area. The note reported: *"It is my duty to inform you of a very large force of the enemy off the coast, and it is generally believed that New Orleans is the object of attack."* The source continued by stating that *"It amounts at present to about eighty vessels and more than double that number are momentarily looked for to form a junction, when the immediate commencement of their operations will take place."*[205]

Commodore David Todd Patterson

Patterson immediately forwarded this intelligence to Jackson, who ordered five gunboats manned by 182 men to guard the seaward approaches to the east. He had to protect New Orleans from assault from Lake Pontchartrain and Lake Borgne. Later, the schooner *Seahorse* with one six (6) pounder and 14 men and the sloop *Alligator* armed with one four (4) pounder and eight men were added. This small flotilla was all Jackson possessed to confront a major British naval invasion.

Patterson notified Lieutenant AP Catsby Jones to report to him for orders. [207] Patterson had access to limited naval assets: the 16 gun *Louisiana,* the 18 gun *Carolina,* and the small flotilla Jackson had ordered into action at Lake Borgne. [208] Jones was ordered to the Mississippi Sound to command the defense force stationed there and to scout for the enemy's arrival.[209]

The British intelligence report of New Orleans having *". . . gunboats and small craft only"* proved to be accurate! Cochrane was confident of a quick naval victory having such minimal opposition.

Gunboats had become the preferred weapon for the American navy. President Jefferson ordered that they be constructed to protect the coastal waters of the nation, defense being his main concern. Each vessel measured between 60-71 feet in length with a beam of 16-18 feet. They were armed with two 18-24 pound long guns, a six pound long gun, and smaller carronades for close in work. Smaller portable swivel guns could be located at various positions along the rail for fending off attacking sailors.[210]

Lieutenant McKeever's gunboat #23 was fortunate to be equipped with a 32 pound gun. This provided his boat with considerable punch, but would prove of little value when confronting small, fast moving barges.

Jones took the five gunboats (#5, #23, #156, #162, and #163) and his two smaller craft eastward. He stationed them between the mainland and Ship Island near Bay St. Louis. Jones then ordered two gunboats to sail eastward between the islands and the mainland toward Dauphin Island in search of this reported British armada and to return with any sightings without engaging.

On December 9, 1814, these scouting ships discovered three British warships sailing west in the gulf waters outside of the barrier islands: the *Seahorse, Armide,* and *Sophie.* The American vessels turned and shadowed them tracking a parallel course on the bayside of the barrier islands sailing westward to report their discovery to Jones.[211]

Aboard the British ships, Post-Captain James Alexander Gordon and his officers gathered on deck after sighting the American sails. They also took note of the shallow water between the islands and the fact that their opponents were out of range. The game of cat and mouse continued for hours.[212]

The small American scouting boats continued to shadow the British vessels in the shallow waters between the gulf coast and the barrier islands. Although out of reach of British gunners, they were able to note the movement of the enemy flotilla's movements.

As the British ships closed on Ship Island, they noticed several of Jones' other gun boats on the gulf side of the island. They gave chase, but the Americans retreated to the protected shallows firing several salvos as they sailed for safety. The British took note of the size and range of their guns.

Captain Gordon then ordered his ships to join the rest of the gathering British fleet anchored just off of Chandeleur Island. Nearly 65 vessels carrying over 10,000 troops had already arrived. Within days the remainder of the fleet, which would eventually total nearly 100 ships, would drop their hooks.

In the early morning hours of December 10th, the American gunboats reported that an entire fleet of the enemy's vessels had arrived and dropped anchor. They were so situated to offer a sustained attack in the channel between Cat Island and Ship Island."[213]

The British invasion force, minus its commander Major-General Sir Edward Pakenham and his reinforcements, was in place. Admiral Cochrane ordered his officers to meet on his flagship, *HMS Tonnant*, to plan the attack. His first order of business was to order the waterway cleared of the American gunboats and he devised a plan to accomplish that task.

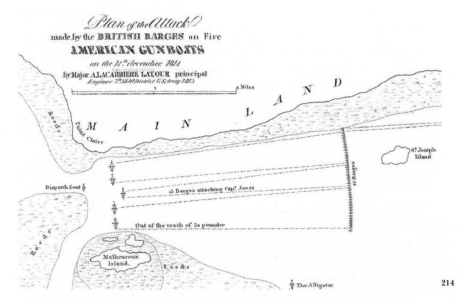

Alignement of American and British Vessels at Battle of Lake Borgne

To confront a small armada of gunboats, the British would embark 1,200 men on 43 (some report 42) barges armed with a carronade mounted on the bow. Each barge would hold 26 men accompanied by a coxswain and a helmsman. This provided two shifts at the oars, necessary because they would be nearly twenty hours rowing. The barges were large enough for a larger crew, but the need to man the carronade demanded a smaller compliment of men.[215] These same barges would later transport fifty to seventy-five men each to the front once the American gunboats had been eliminated.

Admiral Cochrane placed Captain Lockyer in command. This was the same Lockyer that had been sent to entice Jean Lafitte to defect back in September. The first order of business was to prepare one barge and take it out for training. Rowing and firing a carronade proved a formidable task. With training, the gunners soon achieved the necessary expertise which could then be shared with the other boat crews. This exercise, however, consumed valuable time.[216]

On the 12th of December, Jones observed that the enemy's armada off of Ship Island had grown to immense proportions. This forced him to withdraw to a more defensive position at the Isle Mallheureuse. There he established a defensive line blocking the entrance to Lake Borgne and prepared for whatever the British would throw at him.

On the 13th at 10:00 A.M., a large number of barges disembarked from the British fleet and moved toward Pass Christian. They had been divided into three commands: one under Robert, another under Pratt, and the final under Montressor. Once the barges were loaded, they began a coordinated advance. Jones knew their destination was his small fleet.

The first actual combat occurred soon thereafter when Jones ordered Sailing Master Richard Johnson of the *Sea Horse* to dock at Bay St. Louis and secure supplies stored at the depot located there. Johnson was told to take what he could and destroy the rest so that they would not fall into enemy hands.

After arriving there, Johnson noticed that the supply house was on a small hill overlooking the bay and had been armed with two small 6 pound cannons for protection from pirates. Johnson sent some of his crew to man those guns while he "beat to battle stations" on his own vessel.

For his part, Captain Lockyer ordered a detachment of barges to break off from the main force and attack Bay St. Louis. As these troops approached, they met the combined fire of the *Sea Horse* and the two cannons on the hill. The British assault came to a halt when one of the barges was hit sustaining damage and injury to the crew. [217]

The British withdrew out of range and clustered together. They awaited reinforcements. When those arrived, a second assault was ordered. It too failed. For twelve hours the approaches to Bay St. Louis were contested. When night fell the Americans determined that a night assault might well succeed. With that in mind Johnson ordered the supply house and the *Sea Horse* destroyed to prevent their capture. The Americans retreated inland.[218]

The explosions caught the attention of all combatants. The Americans knew that Johnson had followed his orders; the British at first believed their attack had been successful. Only when the barges returned did they learn what had actually occurred. Lockyer gathered his now re-combined forces together, formed a line, and started rowing methodically toward the American gunboats.

The matter now fell to circumstances beyond the control of any mariner . . . tides and wind. The narrow opening of the Rigolets drains all of the inland lakes: Marapaus, Pontchartrain, and Borgne. East winds and tides build up water in these lakes, and contrary western winds and tides empty the excess water from these lakes. An east wind pushes water in; a west wind drains it out.

Once Jones realized the extent of the approaching danger, he sought protection under the guns of *Fort Petite Coquilles* (Small Shells) at the Rigolets. This would provide necessary support. Getting there, however, would prove a challenge. Jones had to await the incoming tide and easterly wind so he could work to the west where the fort lay. In the meantime, these same winds and tides benefited the British advance. The cat and mouse game was on once again.

As night fell the winds shifted and the tide turned. Jones took advantage of this change in circumstances to sail west to the protection of the fort. Lockyer also gained an advantage and continued driving his barges toward the retreating gunboats.

But Lockyer's men were tired after having rowed for over twelve hours. The fear of having his barge formation become misaligned in the dark became a growing concern. He slowed his approach during the moonless night.

By midnight the wind slackened . . . by 1:00 A.M. it stopped. The tide began to turn again, this time flowing out of the lakes through the Rigolets, slowly at first then it quickened. This left Jones a mere eight miles from the protection of *Fort Petite Coquilles* and now drifting back to the east . . . towards the British. Since he failed to gain protection of the fort, he had to act quickly![219]

Jones beat his men to quarters. He ordered his gunboats to anchor forming a line blocking the entrance to Lake Borgne. Boarding nets were set, guns charged, carronades set on the rails, and armed sailors sent into the rigging. As a safeguard, Jones ordered a sailing boat cast over the side with a small crew. Their job was to monitor the situation from further west of the action and be prepared to report expeditiously to General Jackson the outcome of the coming battle.[220]

For his part, Lockyer welcomed sunrise with relish. His barges had maintained their positions throughout the dark night. Furthermore, he realized that the Americans opportunity for flight had passed with the turn of the tide. He saw they had anchored and positioned themselves to repel his attack.[221]

On December 14th, the British barges were nine miles from the Americans. The British had 43 launches and barges with 43 cannons and 1,200 men. They maintained their battle line. Rowing in unison they methodically advanced. One group had earlier cut off the schooner *Seahorse* at Bay St. Louis, whose captain was forced to blow up his ship. Within a short time a second vessel, the *Alligator*, a small dispatch sloop, had likewise been captured.[222]

Lockyer breathed a sigh of relief. The stage was set and the initiative belonged to him. He ordered his barges to halt just out of range of the anchored American gunboats. He took this opportunity to have his men eat, rest, and refresh themselves. His men had to be prepared for a brutal and bloody battle. In the meantime, officers Lockyer, Pratt, Roberts, and Monrressor gathered in the stern sheets of the command barge to discuss a coordinated plan of action.

Jones, for his part, positioned himself to his best advantage and waited for the assault. Soon he perceived the entire line of British barges advancing. When he judged them in range, he ordered his men to "open fire!" The roar of cannons shattered the morning calm, rolls of black powder smoke engulfed the gunners, and towering columns of water arose from splashing cannon balls . . . but the bombardment inflicted little damage.

The British barges were too small, too fast, and too far away for the gunboats to effectively target them. With impunity bordering on arrogance, the British mightily manned the oars pulling their boats as quickly as possible to their American opponents. They knew the sooner they closed with the American gunboats, the less time they would spend under the barrage.

As for the Americans, things could not have gone worse. The easterly set of the tide increased and the recoil of the guns caused the anchors of two of Jones' gunboats, # 156 and #163, to drag pulling these two gunboats out of position and toward the approaching enemy.

Were that not enough, once the anchors had been reset, these two gunboats found themselves stationed further to the east than their compatriots. This changed position left the American line vulnerable.

The forward two vessels became easy targets for the approaching British. The three gunboats behind them could not fire to aid their comrades without hitting their own ships. The effective line of defense Jones has so carefully prepared collapsed because of his ships untimely drift out of formation. This is just one more unexpected event of many to come that would have major consequences throughout the campaign.

At 10:50 A.M. the British barges had neared the Americans and opened fire along their entire line. Lockyer immediately recognized the advantage gained by the misplaced American gunboats. He ordered his troops to concentrate on these two misaligned vessels. When they gained range they opened fire with grapeshot from their carronades. The first three British boats attempted to board Jones' ship, but were repulsed at considerable loss of life. A second attempt by four other boats met the same fate. The Americans fought valiantly. But within a short period of time, the British had pulled alongside, lashed themselves to the Americans, and began the bloody task of boarding with cutlass and blunderbuss.[223]

It did not take long for the seasoned British sailors to overwhelm the Americans and take control over their vessels. Having accomplished this, the British turned the captured American guns against the remaining three American ships. The barges again launched coordinated attacks with similar violence and bloodshed on the remaining American gunboats.

[224]

British overwhelm American Gunboats in Lake Borgne

Being outnumbered, the Americans would eventually succumb to the heavy assault. A change in wind and current had given the more maneuverable small British barges the advantage. The engagement lasted barely two hours. By 12:40 P.M. the battle had ended. The Americans lost six men killed and 35 wounded among them AP Catesby Jones. He was rowed to the British armada for medical attention and detained as a prisoner of war. The Americans sustained nearly 25% casualties . . . 41 of 182 men . . . an unheard of number in naval combat.[225]

Lieutenant Robert Atchison described the action: *"Our boats pulled up with a strong tide against them, but the Commodore was boarded by Lockyer in his gig, who was cut down, as well as almost every man in his boat . . . my poor shipmate, Rob Uniacke, lost a leg, and died after amputation, O'Rielly lost an eye."*[226]

The British losses are more difficult to calculate. Many were wounded and would later die. Captain Lockyer wrote an immediate report that did not list these losses. Likely, he was driven by the need to underreport casualties for political purposes. He reported 21 killed and 74 wounded, when actually most accounts list the "Butchers Bill" at not less than 300. [227]

The small dispatch boat launched by Jones prior to the battle immediately set sail and charted a course toward Lake Pontchartrain and the entrance to Bayou St. John. From there they anxiously reported what had occurred to General Jackson at his headquarters on Royal Street.

The first engagement between American and British forces in the battle for New Orleans was over. Although the Americans failed to fend-off the British onslaught, they did send a clear message that they would stand and fight. American soldiers fled at the Battle of Bladensburg outside of Washington, D.C., which left a clear impression of their lack of courage. The "Westerners" descending the Mississippi to defend New Orleans were cut from different cloth. They were a tough breed who lived a hard life of independence and possessed highly honed survival skills. The British would soon become better acquainted with the difference.

The attacking British expedition welcomed this early victory. However, it did come at a strategic cost. Although the American gunboats had been defeated within a few hours, it took nearly five days to set up and conduct the operation. Valuable hours were lost when moments would prove to be precious later.

As for the Americans, General Jackson had just returned from a tour of Chef Menteur, when the intelligence of the loss of the gunboats reached him.[228] This news undoubtedly troubled him, but was likely expected. Certainly, he did not believe that a small detachment of gunboats could possibly forestall a British invasion fleet of this magnitude.

On December 15th, Claiborne notified the legislature of the disaster that had befallen the fleet. The British had tightened the noose.

Now that the Americans had been removed from the approaches to the lakes the way was opened for the British to begin their invasion. The question for them was . . . what next? How best to take the city?

As for Jackson, although he now knew where the British were, he did not know their ultimate route. Would they enter Lake Pontchartrain and strike New Orleans by way of Bayou St. John? Would they cross Lake Pontchartrain to the Mississippi River near Bayou Manchac then float down the Mississippi River to assault New Orleans from the north? Would they use their position by Lake Borgne to mount an attack up through Chef Menteur and attack the city from the east along that bayou? The city was vulnerable from countless directions . . . which would be used?

Seeking an answer to his questions, Jackson ordered Commodore Patterson to send a Purser and doctor to the British fleet under a flag of truce on December 15th to inquire about ". . . *obtaining correct information as to the situation of the officers and crews made prisoners on board the gunboats, and of endeavoring to obtain their being suffered to return to town on parole.*" He also sought to have these emissaries learn whatever they could about British intentions. [229]

Admiral Cochrane received them courteously but informed them that: "*their visit was unseasonable, and that he could not permit them to return, until the intended attack was made, and the fate of New Orleans decided.*" The Americans were outraged by Cochrane's "inhumane" treatment of envoys despite the fact that there was no question that they had arrived with a dual mission in mind.

The Americans wanted critical information about British plans, and the British had no intention of providing any intelligence of any sort. The next day, December 16th, British soldiers began to disembark of Isle aux Poix, a small swampy islet and an interim assembly point about thirty miles from the entrance to Bayou Bienvenue.

Atchinson describes the scene:

"*Well I went to Pearl Island [Isle aux Pois] also, and although we had roughish work of it, sleeping in open boats, with only our sails for covering, and salt provisions, which hunger sometimes compelled us to eat two day's dinner at once . . . The weather the whole of the six weeks I slept in an open boat was bitterly cold, and many of the Blacks who came from the West Indies with us died of cold. That winter December 1814 was unusually severe.*[230]

General Jackson had to move fast. With limited resources he had to guard all approaches to New Orleans. His main concern became: would he learn about the point of attack in time to concentrate his forces to meet the threat?

Chapter 6

THE BRITISH MAKE A LANDING

As the British worked their way to the west and closed on New Orleans, the rush was on to prepare for an invasion.

Prior to Jackson's arrival Governor Claiborne sought to forge an effective fighting force from among the local population. New Orleans lacked the necessary preparations to defend itself against the number and quality of forces about to invade. The forts were undermanned. They lacked sufficient ammunition for the large caliber guns to effectively serve the function. The militia was divided and ill equipped, and the citizens themselves were a mixed blend of different and conflicting ethnic groups who often refused to cooperate with one another and lacked weapons.

Many of the men called upon to fight possessed only shotguns and hunting weapons . . . "*fowling pieces.*" They did not own the type of arms needed to fight a war or to defend a city. Furthermore, they lacked the training and discipline needed for fast reloading and directing effective fire-power. Jackson fortunately had some U.S. Marines and army among his forces. But his volunteers were a hodgepodge of Free Blacks, Creole planters, city merchants, slaves, fisherman, Choctaw Indians, Islenos, businessmen, and even an assortment of pirates. Some had served in the local militia, others had not. Other than the Tennessee and Kentucky militias, most of whom had not yet arrived, the vast majority had no regular military training.[231]

As mentioned earlier, the militias themselves were hopelessly divided. Adding to the problem, Claiborne had one more particularly perplexing problem. Free Men of Color populated numerous Louisiana militias. These brave men had always played an important role in the defense of the Louisiana colonies throughout both the French and Spanish periods.

Free Black militias had in fact played a decisive role fighting with Galvez in the southern campaign against the British during the American Revolution. They helped capture Manchac, Baton Rouge, Natchez, Mobile, and Pensacola. They were used to hunt down and arrest escaped slaves. Black Militias were particularly adept at attacking the "maroons," bands of escaped slaves, who sometimes assembled in the marshes and swamps and plagued outlying plantations by attacking them, freeing other slaves, and stealing supplies. These Black Militias were even employed to put down slave revolts. As late as January 8, 1811, the Free Black Militia rendered distinguished service in putting down a slave revolt on Andre' Plantation in St. John the Baptist Parish.[232]

Claiborne had two companies of Black Militia upon whom he could rely, and depend upon them he would. They had proven themselves in past conflicts and were desperately needed for the defense of the city. Furthermore, they willingly offered their services.

However, the Latin perspective toward race stood in stark contrast to the more racist and closed system imposed by the United States since statehood. The new Black Codes were onerous. Indeed, many Free Blacks would soon leave Louisiana because of the new restrictions imposed upon them by the American Black Code. Their rights were being significantly reduced and they felt humiliated by their treatment. For their part, Americans entering the Louisiana Territory could not fathom the notion of armed Black men organized into militias. The idea troubled them greatly.

Governor Claiborne was faced with the determination of the Black Militias to fight for New Orleans and the equally determined attitudes of a growing American population seeking to break up their companies. Claiborne, needing all of the support he could muster, sought to find some solution to this perplexing problem. He dashed off letters to Jackson seeking his counsel. Should Governor Claiborne acknowledge the Black Militias, or should he disband them as some suggested?

Andrew Jackson entertained no such constraints. He needed an army. Even before he arrived in New Orleans the general established his tone. Jackson met with the militia leaders and promised to treat his Black soldiers on equal footing as the Whites. He dared anyone to make an issue of it. He promised the same pay, equipment, and consideration after the conflict. He placed them on full equality with the Whites in his ranks.[233]

He was so pleased with the battalion of Free Blacks under Major Lacoste and General Plauche that he levied a new battalion of the same description under the command of Savary which was attached to Major D'Aquin's regiment of militia. The general recognized them as a crucial reservoir for talent and addressed them on December 18th accordingly:

"Soldiers: from the shores of Mobile I collect you in arms—I invite you to share in the perils and to divide the glory of your White countrymen. I expected much from you for I was not uninformed of those qualities which must render you so formidable to an invading foe. I knew you could endure hunger, thirst, and all the hardships of war . . . but you surpass my hopes . . . I have found in you, united in those qualities, that noble enthusiasm which impels to great deeds." Although directed by Black officers, overall command was given to Colonel Fortier.[234]

Juzan even enlisted all of the local Choctaw Indians to defend the city, and Maunsell White raised a company of Irishmen to fight. A Virginian named Beale, a socially prominent man and a noted sharpshooter, formed a volunteer company of riflemen: *"Beale's Rifles".* [235]

With this as a background, Governor Claiborne began to build his army. Despite his continuing problems and lack of federal support, he expressed a measure of confidence in a letter to Jackson dated November 5th. It also articulated some of his reservations:

"In this city there are several uniform militia corps of much promise, and my impression is, that on these, with their companies of militia, much confidence may be reposed in the moment of trial. There are individuals who believe otherwise, it may be that I am in error, but there certainly has been a sensible change in the public mind. There is not to be displayed by the people at large that enthusiastic ardor which is to be found in the Western states."[236]

When Jackson was convinced that New Orleans was the next English target, he moved decisively. After brutally defeating England's Indian allies in the Alabama territory, defending Mobile at Fort Bowyer, and having taken Pensacola by a bold surprise attack, Jackson rushed to New Orleans arriving on December 2nd, 1814.

Anyone seeing this small detachment would never have imagined the importance of their composition or the critical nature of their mission. *"Though devoid of all military display and even of the ordinary equipments of soldiers, the bearing and appearance of these men betokened their connection with the profession of arms. The chief of the party, which was composed of five or six persons, was a tall, gaunt man, of very erect carriage, with a countenance full of stern decision and fearless energy, but furrowed with care and anxiety.* "[237]

Upon first entering the city, Jackson did not impress the locals. The general had ridden hard for eleven days while suffering from severe dysentery or possibly irritable bowel syndrome. His diet consisted of rice and hominy grits and he still nursed the shoulder wound suffered in a duel with the Benton boys just a year before. He was dirty, tired, and emaciated. He looked more like a bedraggled, refugee soldier than an astute, commanding general. *"His complexion was sallow and unhealthy; his hair was iron grey, and his body thin and emaciated, like that of one who had just recovered from a lingering and painful sickness."*[238]

The manner of his dress further illustrates this sorrowful first impression: *"His dress was simple, and nearly threadbare. A small leather cap protected his head, and a short Spanish blue cloak his body, whilst his feet and legs were encased in high dragoon boots, long ignorant of polish or blacking which reached to his knees."*[239]

Jackson rode up Bayou Road along Bayou St. John and stopped near its junction with the Carondelet Canal. He arrived at a plantation house belonging to J Kilty Smith, a leading New Orleans merchant, who was absent from his home at a meeting with the Defense Committee. Acting as hostess, Smith's neighbor provided a sumptuous meal. She ushered them into the marble hall of Smith's old Spanish Villa where they were made comfortable. *"Soon the company were all seated at the breakfast table which fairly groaned with the abundance of generous viands prepared in that style of incomparable cookery for which the Creoles of Louisiana are so renowned."* The younger members of his party partook of this great bounty; however Jackson satisfied himself with some boiled hominy indicative of the effect of his illness.[240]

The Creole lady who had been retained to prepare the repast for these distinguished guests was not impressed. A servant whispered to Smith upon his late arrival home after his meeting that he was wanted in the anteroom. There his Creole hostess quizzed him: *"How could you play such a trick on me? You asked me to get your house in order to receive a great general. I did so. I worked myself half to death . . . and now I find my labor is thrown away upon an ugly, old Kaintuck-flat-boatman, instead of your grand General."*[241]

By the next day, however, his recovery after rest and refreshment proved to be amazing. Jackson adorned his dress military uniform to meet New Orleans dignitaries. He cut the dignified image for which he was known. That alone did much to instill confidence in the people of New Orleans. His will and determination caused men to accomplish things they never would have thought possible.

The general traveled to the New Orleans residence of the late Daniel Clark, the first representative of Louisiana to the United States Congress, who died 1812. Here he met with a committee of city and state authorities. Among them were Governor Claiborne, Commodore Patterson, city mayor Nicholas Girod and attorney Edward Livingston. The group then moved to 106 Royal Street where they established General Jackson's headquarters.[242]

Jackson lived up to his reputation as a somewhat crude frontiersman: *"Rough of speech, fond of telling stories that would go better around a soldier's campfire than in an aristocrat's drawing room and given to express himself in language that shocked the gentle members of his committee of defense . . . the Creoles of New Orleans, contrary to their usual course of action . . . did not invite the gaunt, swearing and crude major general to their homes."*[243]

As legend has it, Edward Livingston, having learned that his Creole wife had invited some of the better bred belles of New Orleans to a dinner party at his home, informed her that he had invited General Jackson. Her reaction could have been predicted: *"You invited that wild Indian-fighter from Tennessee to a dinner party of young ladies!"* Livingston's response: *"He will capture at first sight!"*

Livingston afterwards loved to tell the story of Jackson's reception. With the greatest detail he would gleefully portray the scene: *"The general was in full dress uniform of his rank . . . To my astonishment it was new and spotlessly clean. I had also observed that he had two sets of manners: one for headquarters, the other for the drawing room."* When he left, the ladies were shocked: *"Is this your rough frontier general? Shame on you!"*[244]

As Livingston would later proclaim, General Jackson had the capacity to capture the hearts of the women of the city as effectively as he could motivate the men he commanded at the front.

245

A dignified General Andrew Jackson soon impressed the residents of
New Orleans and generated a spirit of confidence about the city's defense.

Jackson immediately began a tour of the city's defenses. He met
with uniformed companies of the city which consisted of men of means
coming from the city's business quarter, professionals, clerks, and the
sons of planters. They were all armed and proud of their appearance.
Jackson took time to talk to these men and learn of their organization,
history and general martial spirit. He left them confident in their
commander.[246]

The general arose early the next morning and set out in a barge
to continue his inspection of Fort St. Philip in Plaquemines, which
protected the river approach to New Orleans. He ordered additional
cannons and mortars as well as establishing a second battery one-half
mile above the fort and another across the river. Any attempted passage

up the Mississippi River had to be stopped. Jackson also cleared the trees from along the river's batture. This allowed an unobstructed view and a clear shot at any naval movement coming up the river. He also dispatched Colonel A.P. Hayne from Mobile to the Balize to appraise the fort located there. Hayne reported it insufficient for defense. Jackson abandoned this site and recognized that he must depend upon Fort St. Philip as his first line of defense on the Mississippi River.[247]

After a six day examination of the lower Mississippi River, Jackson concluded that the swift current and the geography of English Turn would make an advance from this quarter highly problematical.

Upon his return, Jackson examined the back of the city near Lake Pontchartrain. Two forts were there: the old Spanish Fort at the mouth of Bayou St. John and fort Petite Coquilles guarding the approaches to the Rigolets the entrance into Lake Pontchartrain. Both were considered inadequate. His engineer Latour described it best:

"Such was the inconsiderable defense that protected the shores of Louisiana and covered a country that has an extent of coast upward of 600 miles, of which even a temporary possession by an enemy might be attended with consequences baneful to the future prosperity of the Western States"[248]

One main concern was Chef Menteur. Here he ordered Major Lacoste and a battalion of Free Men of Color along with some dragoons from Feliciana to take two cannons with them and construct a defense at the junction of Bayou Sauvage and the bayou Chef Menteur.[249]

Captain Newman in command of *Fort Petites Coquilles* at the Rigolets was ordered to hold his position at all costs. If forced to abandon the fortification to spike the guns, blow up the fort, and join with Lacoste at Chef Menteur.

General Jackson would also be pleased to form a second battalion of Free Men of Color under the direction of Captain Savary who had served honorably in the battles in Santo Domingo during the slave insurrection there. His corps was formed from exiles from Haiti. Overall command of this new corps was given to Major Daquin.[250]

Jackson ordered Captain Pierre Jugeaut, his long loyal Choctaw mixed-blood ally, to gather all the members of his tribe he could and await further orders. [251]

The approaches to the city were many and varied. It soon became apparent that Jackson lacked the manpower and material to adequately protect New Orleans from any attack on two fronts. This was his greatest concern! As late as mid December, Jackson's troops amounted to two half-filled newly raised regiments of regular troops of about 800 men, Major Planche's battalion of uniformed volunteers of about 500, two regiments of state militia badly-equipped and undisciplined, and a battalion of Free Men of Color highly regarded by all who knew them. In total his force amounted to about 2,000 men at arms.[252] His naval defense comprised the schooner *Carolina* and the ship *Louisiana*. His gunboats had already been taken by the British.

Other reinforcements were soon to arrive. General Coffee arrived from Pensacola with 300 weary but experienced men and General Carroll was anxiously rushing to his friend's assistance, but desperately short of arms and ammunition. Tennessee has practically been stripped of fighting men. Peter Cartwright of the Tennessee's Methodist Church found his congregations thinned because: *". . . so many of our members went into the war, and deemed it their duty to defend our common country under General Jackson."*[253]

As if by divine intervention, General Carroll while taking advantage of the swollen Cumberland River to make a speedy approach to New Orleans happened upon: *"a boat load of muskets"* which he seized and trained his men on the topsides of his flatboats as they traveled downriver.[254]

An additional 2,000 Kentuckians under command of General Thomas and General Adair were also in route. Unfortunately, these men were desperately short of weapons, clothing, and supplies. This would account in large measure for their performance during the coming battle for the West Bank of the Mississippi River on January 8th. The only good luck that accompanied these men was overtaking a boatload of flour which at least allowed them to eat on the way down river.

Thus, taking all assets into consideration, General Jackson had at his disposal as of December 14th: 2,000-3,000 men in the city, 4,000 more reinforcements within fifteen days march, some Choctaw Indians, a detachment of Islenos from St. Bernard Parish, two armed vessels in the Mississippi River, a small garrison at Fort St. Philip, a small detachment at Fort Coquilles to guard access through the Rigolets, and the continued process of blocking all the bayou approaches to the city.[255]

With this strange assortment of defenders, Jackson prepared to confront a major British expedition, men who had honed their martial skills during the Peninsular Campaign in Europe. The British approached New Orleans with an effective force of 14,000 men (not counting over 3,500 naval personnel), a fleet of 50 fighting ships, carrying over 1,000 guns, additional empty cargo vessels, and officers of the highest quality. The entire force all fully equipped for battle as one would expect for any professional army mounting an invasion. [256]

After three weeks of fair weather sailing through the deep azure blue Caribbean waters, this massive flotilla arrived at the entrance of Lake Borgne and, having dispensed with the American gunboats, began preparations for land operations.

On December 14th, Governor Claiborne announced to the legislature the intelligence he had just received from Commodore Patterson which informed him of the imminent arrival of the ". . . *enemy in considerable force.*" Jackson followed with a request that he be in readiness to ". . . *take to the field the whole militia of the state.*"

At this time, Jackson addressed the need for domestic order. Since he considered the city in imminent danger of invasion from a superior enemy force, he felt it critical to prevent any communication with the enemy. He urged Claiborne to take the necessary measures. He incrementally began the process of establishing martial law: "*Among the measures which our safety requires, permit me to recommend the suspension for a limited time of the Writ of Habeas Corpus. This will, as the commodore suggests, enable him to press hands for manning the vessels of the United States under his orders*". [257]

Deep concerns continued to plague Claiborne and Jackson. The rush was on to defend New Orleans. A part of this "rush" was the imposition of Martial Law on December 16th. This gave the general the authority he needed to move men and resources to meet any need. Anyone who opposed his orders faced arrest and imprisonment.

Martial law provided him with the tool he needed to achieve his ambitious ends. He imposed a curfew at 9:00 P.M.; anyone found outside beyond that time was subject to arrest. Every person entering the city had to present himself/herself to headquarters. Anyone leaving had to be issued a pass. All persons capable of bearing arms must volunteer or be impressed into military service.

Thomas Butler, Jackson's Aide-de-camp, issued the order. He then expressed Jackson's concerns about the fear that seemed to permeate the city. Butler sought to reassure the population: "*It is true the enemy is on our coast and threatens to invade our territory; but it is equally true that, with union, energy, and the approbation of Heaven, we will beat him at every point temerity may induce him to set foot on our soil.*" [258]

Jackson further added that although the British have promoted the notion that Louisiana would be returned to Spain that will not happen because America is at peace with Spain. Having said that, Jackson issued a warning: "*The rules and articles of war annex the punishment of death to any person holding secret correspondence with the enemy, creating false alarm, or supplying him with provision. The General announces his determination rigidly to execute the martial law in all cases which may come within his province.*"[259]

The general had already executed several of his own men during the Creek Indian War for disobeying direct orders. No one doubted his willingness to do the same here.

Having issued his proclamation on Martial Law, Jackson then reviewed his troops in preparation for meeting his enemy. *"A considerable force is now assembled under the orders of General Jackson, which will speedily receive large reinforcements from the militia of the western states, but it is nevertheless true that the principal avenues to our capital are not in a situation to insure its preservation . . ."* [260]

Members from all classes of society responded to the call to arms and welcomed the opportunity to serve *"animated with the most ardent zeal."* Although many continued their regular private responsibilities they took what extra time they had to contribute to the defense of their city.

"The citizens were preparing for battle as cheerfully as if it had been a party of pleasure each in his vernacular tongue singing songs of victory. The streets resounded with Yankee Doodle, the Marseilles Hymn, and Chant du Depart all while burnishing their arms and accoutrements."[261]

Nevertheless, both Jackson and Claiborne believed that the country was filled with spies and traitors. They were aware of the numerous British attempts to spread social discord and were personally acquainted with the ethnic tensions that had grown as Americans flooded into the former Spanish and French colony. Would any of these seeds take root? Were there elements present that sought to undermine General Jackson's efforts and support the ambitions of Great Britain? Unbeknownst to them, their fears were well founded.

On top of these domestic concerns, the general still had to focus on the matter of an anticipated invasion. Jackson knew that the city was threatened, but from what direction would the enemy come?

Jackson dispersed what troops he had available to all of the city's approaches. He then ordered that all bayous be blocked to prevent access. This is of particular importance because it was the direct violation of his order by Major Jacques Villere in St. Bernard Parish that allowed the British entry below New Orleans at Bayou Bienvenue.

Why Major Villere would defy General Jackson's order has always been a mystery. Perhaps the British interpretation for the reason might provide some insight. Since they were in league with the Spanish fishermen, they knew them well. The British believed: *"The fact that the route through the bayou eventually merged with the Villere Plantation . . . seems too striking to be coincidental. Obviously, the bayou was a secret smuggling*

route, kept open by the Villeres for their own benefit. " Smuggling is endemic
to St. Bernard Parish because of its many waterways. [262]

Jackson ordered forts to be manned and fortified as best as
possible. He sent men into the Rigolets, Chef Menteur, Lake
Pontchatrain, and others to the mouth of the River. He deployed forces
up river in the event that the British would move north and float down.
Jackson tried to anticipate every potential threat and sought to provide
sufficient men to, at least, monitor the situation, even if they lacked the
ability to defend it.

Planters and businessmen sent their slaves to Jackson to build
whatever fortifications the situation required. The City was a buzz of
activity. There was no doubt that war was about to break upon New
Orleans, and the city was not ready.

New Orleans was unprepared for a major invasion. Divisions
within the population, lack of military preparation, limited manpower,
concerns about spying activities, and uncertainty about where the
enemy might attack created a dire situation in New Orleans.

General Jackson had his work cut out for him and little time
to accomplish his tasks. One can only imagine the stress he felt as
he organized his limited defenses from his headquarters on Royal
Street. Living with little sleep, being continually interrupted by aides,
subsisting on a bland diet of grits and rice because of his illness, the
general waited . . . when and where would the hammer fall. Soon they
would all find out.

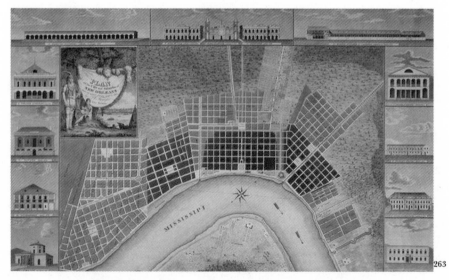

[263]

Map of New Orleans in 1815 at time of Battle of New Orleans.

The Invasion Begins . . .

Jackson and Claiborne's fears of traitors were justified. As events would unfold, betrayal opened the door to the British invaders.

On December 15th, Claiborne notified the legislature of the disaster that had befallen the fleet. This referenced the American loss at the Battle of Lake Borgne. The noose was tightening. He informed them that: *"The enemy menaces this capital, and we know not how soon he may affect a landing."*[264]

Jackson's Martial Law allowed him to arbitrarily arrest anyone opposing his command. It also permitted him to impress any person or item he might need for defense of the city. On the 18th of December, Jackson reviewed his troops and waited impatiently for promised reinforcements from Tennessee and Kentucky.

The expedition against Louisiana was composed of 14,450 men forming three divisions. Sir Edward Pakenham was Commander-in-Chief, Major-General Samuel Gibbs commanded the first division, General Lambert the second, and General Keane the third. The fleet was under command of Admirals Cochrane, Codrington, and Malcolm.[265]

Bayou Bienvenue, once called St. Francis River, flows into Lake Borgne. Its principle branch was called Bayou Mazant which flowed southwest and received the waters from the canals that drained the de Laronde, Lacoste, and Villere plantations. On the left bank of Bayou Bienvenue, about a mile and a half from its entrance into Lake Borgne, was a small Spanish and Portuguese fishing village inhabited by about 30 men.

The fishermen and trappers there used the bayou to bring their catch to New Orleans. Whether or not they were participants in other less legal activities is a matter for conjecture. While in New Orleans selling their wares in late 1814, they gathered intelligence for their British sponsors about conditions, defenses, and feelings in the city.[266]

Although always concerned about treachery, General Jackson had no idea what was occurring beneath his nose while organizing his defenses of the city at his primary headquarters on Royal Street. Little did he know that several fishermen known as Maringuier, Old Luiz, Francisco, Graviella, Antonio el Italiano, El Campechano, Mannellilo, and Garcia, served the British invaders as pilots and guides to the back of the city.[267]

General Jackson gave the order days before that all land and water approaches to the city were to be blocked. The early British contacts with Lafitte proved their intent to use such waterways. There was every reason to believe that Bayou Bienvenue had accordingly been sealed. He was convinced that this problem had been solved. After all, direct orders had been issued to locals who knew the waterways.

The important mission to close Bienvenue had been initially given to a detachment from the 7th regiment, then later to Colonel de la Ronde of the Louisiana Militia, and finally to Major-General Villere. Villere commanded the district between the river and the lakes and owned a plantation adjacent to the bayou. He was presumed to be best acquainted with all of those waterways and most capable of securing them. [268]

Jackson was wrong. No obstructions had been positioned at Bayou Bienvenue as ordered despite the fact that that waterway approached the plantation belonging to the Major-General Jacques Villere who was given a direct order to close it. General Jacques Villere delegated duties to his son Gabriel. In defiance of Jackson's orders, the bayou remained opened for invasion.

The fishermen living there were known to the Villeres. They may even have prevailed on the Villere family to keep the bayou open in order for them to continue their business uninterrupted with promises of keeping a careful watch for the British. There are no records embracing this notion, but it is reasonable to at least consider this interpretation. There is also no information indicating that Major-General Jacques Villere was aware that his son, Major Gabriel Villere, had refused to follow Jackson's direct orders and left the bayou open.

On December 21st, General Jackson ordered a detachment of the 3rd Regiment of the militia to travel downriver and scout out the waterways below the city. These men were placed under the command of Major Gabriel Villere. Jackson held deep concerns about the British arriving suddenly near the city by one of the many waterways. That is why he had ordered them closed when he first arrived.

After arriving in St. Bernard Parish, Major Villere took leave in his home and sent a detachment down the open Bayou Bienvenue to check on the situation near Lake Borgne.

This small force consisted of eight men under command of a sergeant who some identify as Bernard Ducros. These nine men took small boats down the bayou to the Fisherman's Village where they were to give notice should they witness anything worth reporting. As for Villere, he made himself comfortable at home believing that his posted sentries would inform him if they had any indication that the British had appeared.

The fishing village consisted of twelve very large cabins capable of containing several hundred men. They were constructed with stakes, thatched roofs, and enclosed with Palmetto leaves and placed along the left bank of Bayou Bienvenue. About 40 or 50 fisherman, almost all Spaniards and Portuguese lived there. [269]

These fishermen worked the local waterways around Lake Borgne and the Mississippi Sound. From these waters, they gathered their catch and transported it by pirogue through Bayou Bienvenue and the Villere Plantation to River Road. They then conveyed their seafood by wagon to New Orleans' markets.

According to LaTour: *"It was their practice, when they came to town to sell their fish, to get all the information they could, for the purpose of carrying it to the English when they went out to fish in Lake Borgne."* [270]

When Villere's men arrived, only one fisherman was there, claiming illness. The others, he said, were off setting their nets. In reality, they were acting as pilots for the coming British invasion force. Villere's men posted a guard then went to sleep.[271]

As for the British, their moment had come. Although some expressed mixed feelings, optimism flowed for most. Colonel Malcolm located at Cumberland Island wrote his brother, an Admiral under Cochran, that the wealth in New Orleans will: *". . . repay the troops for all of their trouble and fatigue."* Others expressed apprehension. Mr. Glover, a British subject whose private letter had been intercepted expressed his concerns: *"My forebodings will not allow me to anticipate either honor or profit to the expedition."*[272]

Success would provide Pakenham with the governorship of Louisiana and the likelihood of an Earldom with the accompanying social and financial rewards associated with that position. Optimism reigned supreme among most of the British. They had no reason to suspect anything but success.

The British disembarked with confidence. Pakenham had written prior to leaving on the expedition that *". . . the troops he had seen embark for America from Bordeaux . . . must be very badly handled if they did not prove victors in any contest in which they might be engaged"*[273]

Despite the fact that the expedition was under his command, Major-General Sir Edward Pakenham would not arrive until Christmas Day. Admiral Cochrane could not wait. He ordered the troops to take to the boats. The process began on December 16th, but because of the shortage of barges and the distance to the staging area at Pine Island (Pea Island), it took until the 21st before all troops had been transferred from the fleet to the island . . . *"It is scarcely possible to imagine any place more completely wretched."*[274]

For five days, the British troops lay exposed to the cold winter elements as the army assembled. This took a toll on the soldiers, especially those Black troops from Jamaica who were not accustomed to such harsh winter conditions. Because they lacked the necessary winter equipment, many of them died of exposure. Lieutenant Robert Glieg of the 85th Light Infantry described the advancing army's misery: "... *confinement [to the boats] was but a trifling misery when compared with that which arose from the change of the weather. Instead of a constant bracing frost, heavy rains such as an inhabitant of England cannot dream of began. And against which no cloak could furnish protection, began.*"[275]

To make matters worse, following the driving rain generated by an approaching cold front, the temperature dropped and severe frost set in. The island lacked any resources for making fires, so the men were forced to endure the penetrating chill in their wet clothes. Some, so fatigued by the travails of the preceding day, fell fast asleep, not to awaken the next morning. Hypothermia haunted the British.

Because of the shortage of transport craft required to move the troops in one operation, the British commander divided his forces into several battalions. There were no means of moving all troops to the front simultaneously. General Keane gave the first command to Colonel William Thornton, "*an officer of talent and enterprise.*" These preparations took until December 22nd.[276]

By dividing their troops, the British became vulnerable to be "*attacked in detail*" which would allow the battalions to be cut down before support could arrive. Dividing one's forces places them at substantial peril and is considered an extremely dangerous operation. It defies traditional tactics. But the lack of boats required that the risk be taken.

As for the sailors, they were driven beyond exhaustion pulling at the oars in horrid conditions having to continuously ferry men, cannons, and supplies back and forth from the fleet to the front with little sleep, food, or rest. They labored twenty-four hours a day maintaining this eighty mile supply line. This herculean task took a tremendous toll on these sailors.

The first battalion of 1,600 men and two light cannons disembarked from Pea Island at 9:00 A.M. on the morning of December 22rd under the command of Lieutenant Colonel William Thornton. The morning was dark, chilly, and cloudy. But nothing could dampen the ardor of the excited and enthusiastic Britons. They were intent on the design of conquering the rich city of New Orleans.[277]

This first division was accompanied by General Keane and his staff along with several of the "Traitors" from the fisherman's village. The boats headed toward the mouth of Bayou Bienvenue, the canal their spies had directed them to take which would eventually bring them to within nine miles below New Orleans.

G.R. Gleig, a British junior officer, best described the circumstances visited upon the advancing troops: *"When we set sail, the sky was dark and lowering, and before long a heavy rain began to fall. Continuing without intermission during the whole of the day, towards night, it, as usual, ceased, and was succeeded by a sharp frost; which taking effect upon the men thoroughly exposed, and already cramped by remaining so long in one position, rendered our limbs completely powerless. Nor was there any means of dispelling the benumbing sensation, or effectually resisting the cold. Fires of charcoal, indeed, being lighted in the sterns of the boats, were permitted to burn as long as daylight lasted, but as soon as it turned dark, they were of necessity extinguished, lest the flame should be seen by row-boats from the shore."*[278]

As they approached the fishing village at the junction of Lake Borgne and Bayou Bienvenue, the invaders halted, anchored, hoisted awnings, and rested while an advance assault party in swift boats approached the shacks.

The British invading party reported that they advanced undetected: *"Nothing, as it appeared, was less dreamt of by the Americans than an attack from this quarter, consequently no persons could be less on their guard than the party stationed."* The British surrounded the camps, and found Villere's sentries all asleep *"not so much as a single sentinel posted"* and took them *". . . without noise or resistance."* The rest of the command then took to their oars and approached the fishing village establishing it as a staging area. [279]

American accounts differ. Just as the moon dropped below the horizon, Villere's men noticed something approaching in the darkness. *"By the last gleams of the setting moon they perceived five barges full of men, with some pieces of artillery, ascending the bayou; on which, thinking it imprudent to fire . . . they retired for concealment . . . a party determined to escape by the lake and give information of the arrival of the enemy."* Villere's men sought to escape by boat. Before they realized their danger, five barges of British soldiers quickly rowed up . . . bayonets glistening in the setting moonlight and captured them. [280]

One man, Mr. A. Rey, did slip away. But he was forced to walk the marshes for three days before finding help at Chef Menteur. By that time, it was too late for his information to be of any service.[281]

The British account seems credible because the British had no reason to distort events that the American sentries were completely surprised and taken without resistance. The Americans, on the other hand, had every reason to fashion their story so as to protect their reputations.

Having arrived at the mouth of Bayou Bienvenue [Bayou Catalan] the British were taken aback at what they saw: *"The place where we landed was as wild as it is possible to imagine. Gaze where we might nothing could be seen but one huge marsh covered with tall reeds, not a house nor a vestige of human industry could be discovered; and even of trees there were but a few growing upon the banks of the creek."* [282]

In the late hours of December 22nd, General Keane sent British Captain Pebbie (Piddle) along with Old Luiz and two other fishermen on a scouting mission. Disguised as one of the conspiring fishermen, he accompanied three of them up Bayou Bienvenue through the Villere Canal to the back of the Villere Plantation. From there it was a short hop to the bank of the Mississippi River. They sneaked around Villere's home and approached the river ". . . *whose water he boasted of tasting with impunity"* [283]

Upon his return, he notified his superiors that the way was easy right up to within nine miles of the back door of the city of New Orleans. The potential for a complete surprise was at hand!

In the meantime, the captives taken at the fishing village were questioned by British officers. Mr. Ducros was transported to General Keane and Admiral Cochrane for interrogation. Ducros informed his captors that the Americans had nearly 12,000 men at arms prepared to fight. This bit of intelligence, coupled with confirmation of the numbers when several of the other prisoners were questioned, undoubtedly led the British to exercise greater care about a attacking without their full complement of troops. Jackson had nowhere near that number of defenders.

Despite all of General Jackson's efforts, the British had, through treachery, bribery, and incompetence found the means of secreting themselves right below the city of New Orleans undetected.

For their part the British returned their boats to the fleet to complete the deployment of the second battalion. In the meantime, those at the fishing village began the arduous task of working themselves along the bank of Bayou Bienvenue through the marshes toward the Mississippi River.

They began to march along the bayou's bank. The British landing party had a difficult task ahead of them: *"Other ditches, similar to those whose course we pursued, frequently stopped us by running in a cross direction, and falling into it as right angles. These were too wide to be leaped, and too deep to be forded; consequently, on all such occasions, the troops were obliged to halt, till bridges were hastily constructed of such materials as could be procured and thrown across.* [284]

Having struggled through the marsh for several hours, they soon found themselves approaching firmer soil. The terrain transitions from marsh to wood finally to enclosed fields the closer you approach the river.

By 4 o'clock on the morning of December 23rd, the first division of troops under command of General Keane and Colonel Thornton had arrived at the mouth of the Villere canal. Their ordeal traveling along the bayous rendered them cold, tired, hungry, and filthy. He ordered his troops to rest for several hours. Keane wanted them fresh for his planned assault. [285]

Keane's men were less than a mile from the back woods of Villere's plantation and near their goal . . . the Mississippi River. They had achieved their position undetected.

After resting a few hours, they advanced again. At about 10 o'clock in the morning, they began their march towards the banks of the Mississippi, cutting cane as they went along. [286]

Although the first detachment had been able to bring along a few guns *"with the greatest effort"*, it soon became obvious that it would prove to be nearly impossible to keep the needed artillery supplied with ball and powder. The invaders were astounded by the time it had taken to move a few nine-pounders to the front. [287]

The supply line had been stretched so far that even at this early stage it had broken down. Responsibility fell to Admiral Cochrane. Many officers soon realized that the attacking force could not be supplied with artillery ammunition in large enough quantities to assure success. Critics after the fact attribute his negligence to greed. He persisted in using the British Army *". . . as a catspaw to obtain for him the prize money he so ardently desired."* [288]

Despite the obvious problems this invasion route generated, Cochrane and Keane persisted in driving their men forward.

Taking note of a plantation before them, they hurried at double-time to surround the buildings and capture the inhabitants living within. The British had achieved their goal. They had secretly worked their way from the fleet anchored at Ship Island, to Pea Island, across Lake Borgne, the length of Bayou Bienville, and through the marshes to arrive at a position just below New Orleans at the Villere Plantation. [289]

The Setting . . .

Conjure in your mind's eye the riverfront of St Bernard Parish as it appeared nearly 200 years ago.

St. Bernard Parish had become a Creole enclave of sugar plantations based upon the French long-lot land survey system. Each plantation frontage was measured in a number of arpents, one arpent being equivalent to 191.83 feet. The lot had a depth of forty arpents with a drainage canal to the rear running parallel to the river. Since the property frontage lay on the river, bends of the river shaped each lot.

That great body of water, the Mississippi River, flows tranquilly to the Gulf running with a current dependent on the seasonal volume of water. A levee runs along its banks to protect the plantations from high water. The old levee is not as high as today's, but it served its purpose . . . preventing the spring floods from inundating the farm lands. The levee then was a little more to the East than at present. Some of the lands along the river belonging to several of the plantations in 1814 would be reclaimed by the river in future years.

A batture provides dry land on the water side of the levee dotted with willow trees, underbrush, and driftwood during the river's low stages . . . which often occurs in December and January. The spring thaw was months away, so the river was low and land was exposed. But it still flowed to the gulf at about four knots.

Immediately behind the levee there was a dirt road built and maintained by the plantation owners. It traced the course of the river and connected each plantation to one other like pearls on a necklace. This "river road" also tied these rural plantations to the City of New Orleans.

Behind the plantation buildings the land sloped gently downward as it retreats further from the river. This area is drained for cultivation. The closer to the river, the higher the land. Gradually, the land falls to a cypress forest then finally to the marshes and bayous at the rear. The further one movers from the river, the property is lower and underwater.

Many of these French Creole planters owned homes in the Vieux Carre' where they enjoyed the city's rich social and cultural life. They left day to day plantation operations to overseers for supervision. These owners visited their rural estates periodically to check on the business at hand and to spend leisure time relaxing in their carefully crafted rural setting.

Others obviously relished the country life. They thrived in the pastoral scene enjoying man's timeless pleasure of gaining wealth from working the soil. These owners lived on their plantations full-time. They also appreciated that the city's vitality was only a carefree afternoon's carriage ride away.

"Sugar is King" in St. Bernard Parish. In fact, the first sugar was granulated in St Bernard by a Manuel Solis, who perfected the method. As the story goes, he invited several of his friends to a dinner party at his plantation in lower St. Bernard Parish. After a sumptuous repast, he served the traditional coffee at the meal's end, but placed dishes of refined sugar before each guest.

His guests were immediately shocked by this because up to that time no one in Louisiana had ever perfected the method of refining sugar. Word spread immediately throughout the region.

Solis had purchased a slave named Morin who was from Santo Domingo (Haiti), one of the many immigrants escaping the slave rebellion on that island. Morin brought with him the secret of refining sugar. Solis' dinner surprise was a result of Morin's knowledge.

Somehow, Etienne Bore' heard about this event and contacted Solis. The circumstances are not known, but it appears that he either purchased Solis's slave Morin or gained use of his talents. Whatever the case, through Morin Etienne Bore' gained knowledge of the granulation process.

Bore' then learned that Morin had brought with him Black Strap Sugar Cane, a special species rich in sugar content. This, added to the now special knowledge he had learned about refining, allowed Bore' to plow under his failing indigo crop and plant sugar instead, much to the shock of his neighbors.

When "grinding season" arrived, Bore's neighbors gathered to witness him attempt to granulate sugar. He succeeded and paid off his debts with the first harvest. Bore' gained fame from commercializing the granulating process which allowed "dry shipping" of sugar. This allowed sugar to arise as the chief cash crop in southeast Louisiana, and times were good by 1814.

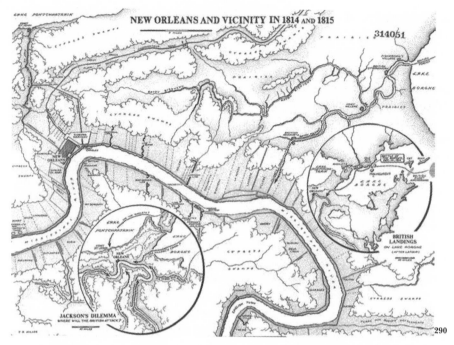

[All plantations were surveyed in accordance with the French "long lot" system where land was sold by the arpent along the river and ran to the rear of the plantation].

The plantations in St. Bernard profited from this sugar bonanza. Each plantation faced the river with gardens, orchards, and oak groves leading from the river road to the front of the plantation home providing a majestic approach to the magnificent mansions set further back. The houses were spacious, with large verandas and overhangs, an adjustment to the tropical climate. These architectural delights provide shade during the steamy summer days and a shield from the rain when driving tropical storms arrived. Most were stately, two story affairs with attractive gables and dormers. Each home made a statement attesting to the owners' wealth and station.

The kitchen was separate from the main house because of fear of fire when preparing food. In addition, barns and workshops were located close by. Slave quarters generally clustered not far distant, as seen at the Bienville Plantation schematic below.

Some of the plantations had become minor industries in addition to their primary agricultural function. In many ways, southern plantations resembled factories. Several manufactured bricks. Others maintained sugar milling operations. Most specialized in a variety of pursuits like blacksmithing and wood finishing. These were a community in every sense of the word. The owners all knew one another, socialized together, cared for one another, inter-married, and cooperated. Theirs' was a shared fate.

Behind the assortment of buildings and running into the marsh to the rear are the lands reclaimed for cultivation of sugar. This land provides the main income for the plantation. Vast acres of sugar cane grow verdant through the summer months . . . but it was late December now and the grinding season had nearly ended.

Sugar gets sweeter the longer it stays in the ground, but it must be harvested immediately before the first freeze, or it rots. Getting the most sugar per plant at the highest market price determines success or bankruptcy in the sugar business. That is the gamble, or some would say the skill, of sugar producers.

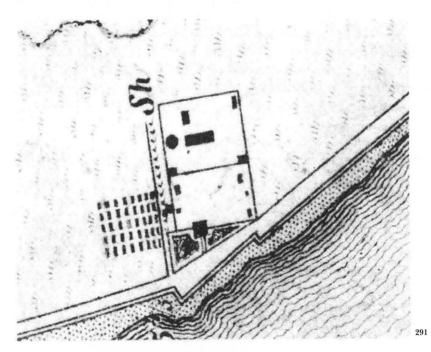

291

This is the typical plantation layout. The river, a levee, then the river road, then the main house and buildings . This is the Bienvenue Plantation in Chalmette

Each planter made his own decision about when to cut cane. Some cautiously cleared their fields; others gambled on the weather and left their crop in the ground to mature a bit longer. It seems that the Villeres left some sugar remaining in the fields, while Ignac de Chalmet harvested his crops totally. Sugar cane would cover the British advance to the back of the Villere home and provide the materials for the British fascines. An already cleared field, like that belonging to Chalmet, afforded the proper setting for battle.

Residents here lived a peaceful, calm, and unchanging life . . . until the late morning hours of December 23, 1814.

Scene of the Battle . . .

Of all the plantations that stood on the battlefield at the beginning of the campaign of 1814-1815, none has survived . . . with the exception of the remnants of the de la Ronde home that still occupys the median of St. Bernard Highway. It more resembles a red brick pile today than the stately mansion of yesteryear. Nevertheless, its presence provides a constant reminder of events in 1814 and establishes a certain appreciation for the extent of the battle lines.

The first plantation in the line south of the city that would become embroiled in the battle was the McCarty house. General Jackson took over this home as his headquarters on Christmas Day 1814. This two story structure had a second floor dormer that provided the general and his staff an advantageous view of the battlefield.[292]

The home survived the battle, but was significantly damaged by the artillery exchange of New Year's Day 1815 when the British sought to destroy Jackson's headquarters on the January 1st assault. In fact, family members would later gild some of the hundreds of British shot that had become embedded in the wood frames and columns as personal mementoes of the event.

293

McCarty House . . . Jackson's Headquarters

Immediately adjacent to the McCarty home was the abandoned home of Jean Rodriguez, merely 1/2 arpent wide (96.41 feet). It faced the river, but widened as it extended toward the swamp behind. This plantation resembled a pie wedge. The Rodriguez plantation was the smallest of those in the area and lacked a stately manor. It appears it may have fallen on hard times early.

Rodriguez Plantation [294]

The Rodriguez land provided one major advantage not shared by the others. The Rodriguez Canal, actually a mill race, formed the property boundary between itself and the Chalmet plantation immediately down river. The canal was designed to provide water power for the plantation. A gate in the levee allowed water to enter the canal and rush to the back of the plantation. In the process, the running water would be harnessed for power. Jackson would employ this natural feature as the foundation for his primary defense line.

The largest of the plantations to be affected by the battle belonged to Ignace de lino de Chalmet. It covered a frontage of over 22 arpents (4400 feet) and was a magnificent estate accumulated over time through several careful land transactions and inheritances.

Unfortunately for poor Ignace, his plantation also was the center of the conflict. On December 27th, after the first British assault, Jackson realized the dangers his buildings posed by allowing cover for British snipers, so the general ordered Colonel Mackrea the commander of the artillery to destroy all of the buildings on Chalmet's plantation which lay within 500 or 600 yards of their lines and set fire to the remains. [295]

Although Ignace would serve bravely on the American lines and owned a small home on Bourbon Street between Bienville and Conti streets in New Orleans, he never recovered from the destruction of his property. Immediately after the battle, he returned to the scene and poked through the ashes of his life.

His home endured the most damage. It broke his heart. Not only had the spacious home and accompanying buildings been destroyed, but the swollen bodies of shallowly buried British soldiers covered the grounds. Ignace went back to his French Quarter apartment and soon died at the age of 60 on February 10, 1815 . . . not even a month after the battle. (No picture of Chalmet's home exists).

296

The Chalmette Plantation destroyed by General Jackson. This sketch done in the 1860s shows the battlefield itself

Below Chalmette's property was the Bienvenue plantation. General Gibbs used this for his headquarters on December 28th, and established some artillery batteries on its western perimeter. Since the houses and associated buildings were set further back from the river than those of Chalmet, they were not in the line of battle. His plantation survived for some time after the battle only to fall victim to progress.

Some of the slave quarters were destroyed during the artillery exchange of January 4, 1815, when they came under fire from Jackson's west bank batteries. But this was a small price to pay when one considers what could have occurred.

Next in line downriver is the stately home of Colonel Pierre Denis de la Ronde, undoubtedly the finest of the plantation houses on the field of the Battle of New Orleans. His was a grand home of three stories. [297]

This home occupied a vast tract of land that has since been subdivided into the Versailles subdivision. De la Ronde planted a fine grove of oak trees from the river road to the front of his home. These trees remain in place today, a remnant of days past. They are called "The Pakenham Oaks".

The de la Ronde home is the only house that stood on the battlefield of 1815 of which some remnants survive today. Most of the damage sustained during the battle and immediately after was not from the conflict itself, but from looting and pillage. Sadly, the damage was not the doings of the disciplined, occupying British troops, but was committed by the Americans who possessed it for several days after the British retreat on January 19th. [298]

299

Denis De la Ronde House

An angry De le Ronde later presented an itemized bill to the government for the damages he received at American hands. This document (see appendix) is interesting for a number of reasons, not the least of which is because it provides some insights into the costs of furnishings in the early 19th century and allows a peek into plantation life during that time.

Moving further down river we come to the Lacoste Plantation. It stood until 1950. The British took over this property on the night of December 23, 1814 during the preparations for the first *assault* on Jackson's lines. Colonel Coffee's Tennesseans attacked the British at Lacoste, and the slave quarters for years bore witness to the violence of the exchange.

300

Lacoste Plantation

"... *The Negro huts of Mr. Lacoste's Plantation still exhibit evident proof of the unerring aim of the valiant Tennesseans of Coffee's division. In one spot particularly are seen one half of a dozen marks of their balls in a diameter of four inches.*"[301]

Lacoste's plantation would become an advance headquarters for the British under Lt. Colonel William Thornton. General Pakenham slept there on the night of January 1st. Being close to the front, it was also used as a repair yard for gun carriages and other pieces of equipment. When the British withdrew, the house was left intact.

302

Jacques Villere's Plantation "Counsel" (British arrived here first)

The Villere Plantation gained notoriety as the location where the British first penetrated American defenses. There is some controversy here. According to some sources, when the British barges attempted to follow the canal to the de la Ronde Plantation on the night of the 22rd, low water prevented them from moving west. They turned east instead toward the Villere Plantation. However, Gleig's account has the British approaching by foot, not barge. In which case, the decision to take the Villere site was not accidental.

Whatever the circumstances, it was the first plantation the British captured. Jacques Philippe Villere and his son Gabriel, both officers in the Louisiana militia, owned this pastoral delight.

"Counsel", the name Villere gave to his plantation, played a central role throughout the invasion. It immediately became General Keane's headquarters. Then on Christmas Day 1814 when General Pakenham arrived to take command of the forces in the field, he made it his own nerve center for operational planning.

The last Plantation to play a part in the events of 1814-15 belonged to Charles Coulon Jumonville de Villiers. The Jumonville Plantation was the scene of a brief encounter between British troops and Americans advancing up river from English Turn on the night of December 23. This action proved to be uneventful, merely a brief exchange of gunfire before the Americans withdrew downriver. [303]

The British converted Jumonville's home into a hospital after the December 23rd engagement. It is believed that Pakenham's body was brought here following his fall and his internal organs were buried under a stand of Pecan trees on that plantation prior to his being embalmed in a cask of rum for preservation and return home. As one writer sarcastically stated: Pakenham was ". . . *sent home to England in good spirits.*"[304]

In all, eight plantations were affected by the Battle of New Orleans to a greater or lesser degree. The scene of the campaign extended over a far larger area than most imagine. The eight plantations discussed were either in British hands and used as headquarters or hospitals; were under control of Jackson and employed by his staff; or were directly involved in the battles and endured damage accordingly.

Jackson had established two defensive lines between his position on the Rodriguez Canal and the city itself. If one defensive line was breached, Jackson's intention was to retreat to the next until forced to fight in the suburbs of the city itself. The second was "Line Dupre" two miles upriver from Jackson's headquarters. The Third line the General called "Line Montreuil" located about four miles upriver near the present site of the Industrial Canal.

This last line, if breached, would leave the British in the Fauburg Marigny just on the eastern outskirts of the city. Taking all this land into consideration, the area of engagement extended along the river nearly 10 miles south of New Orleans. This leaves little doubt as to the dimensions of this major campaign.

Chapter 7

THE BATTLES BEGIN . . .

For a variety of reasons, the British found their plan to approach the Fisherman's Village at Bayou Bienvenue delayed. They did not arrive until after midnight of December 22nd. The first British deployment consisted of: ". . . *760 rank and file of the 4*[th], *402 rank and file of the 85*[th], *396 rank and file of the 85*[th] *regiments, also 100 sappers, miners, and artillerymen, with two 3-pounders and 30 racketeers, in all 1688 men under the command of Colonel William Thornton.*"[305]

During the night of December 22nd and morning of the 23rd these British soldiers were ordered to push themselves up the unobstructed Bayou Bienvenue. The going was tough because the temperature had dropped to near freezing. Dampness and frost encrusted their uniforms. Extreme fatigue plagued these men who had spent the day loading supplies and preparing for the invasion. Adding to their woes, their commanders had ordered them to establish a base camp by morning near the river just below New Orleans.

"*Hurrying on at double-quick time*" they pushed their way through to the cane fields and by 4:00 am had arrived at the extremity of the Villere Canal at the rear of the Villere Plantation. They took their position about a mile from a cypress wood of nearly a mile and a half in depth, running parallel to the Mississippi River. According to participants they approached the border of the woods, near "*. . . a slip *of land from 15 to 1700 yards wide, intersected by strong horizontal railings, and several wet ditches, or canals, and principally planted with sugar canes.*[306]

There they rested for a few hours; then rapidly approached the main house. Colonel Thornton formed his forces into a wide front to surround the plantation and allow no escape. He took possession of the Villere Plantation and its occupants, including Major Gabriel Villere at about 10:30 in the morning of the 23rd.[307]

Their appearance came as a total surprise. Major Gabriel Villere was captured while sitting on the front gallery of his home *". . . looking toward the river and quietly enjoying a cigar, whilst his brother Celestine was engaged in cleaning a fowling-piece.*"[308]

According to Villere's account, he suddenly *". . . observed some men in red coats running toward the river.*" He leapt to his feet, ran into the house hoping to make his escape through the back door when he ran into Thornton and his advance guard coming through that same door. With sword drawn, Colonel Thornton demanded the crestfallen Gabriel's surrender.[309]

The British occupied the house, turned it into a headquarters, and secured the surrounding grounds. British soldiers ushered the Villere brothers into an adjoining room under guard to await the arrival of General Keane.

As soon as Keane arrived, Colonel Thornton urged him to immediately embark upon an assault on the city. They were only a two hours march from New Orleans. They possessed the element of total surprise, which would not last long. Had they done so, they may have carried New Orleans that very day. Jackson had no idea where they were, his limited forces had been dispersed throughout the region in search of them, and the surprised citizens of the city would have likely panicked instead of organizing a defense. [310]

Keane rejected Thornton's suggestion. Why is not a matter of record. One might suppose that he feared the boldness of advancing with so few soldiers, given that only a small portion of his attack force had landed. He also might have considered the prospects of the dangers inherent in taking such action without General Pakenham present to make the decision.

According to British Colonel Dickson's diary, Thornton was likely correct: *"Keane no doubt deserves the criticism that has been heaped on him for not immediately advancing on New Orleans. There can be little doubt that had he done so he would have carried the town by a coup de main, but his reasons were clear enough. The whole force had been chilled in the passage across the lakes and they had no opportunity of eating hot food for many hours. Neither the*

West Indians, who had been sent off without great coats, nor the British, would normally expect the weather to be so cold in Christmas week. [311]

The British had orders to secure a firm beachhead, make camp, establish defensive lines, and await the arrival of reinforcements and their Commander-in-Chief, General Pakenham. They did not have permission to start a battle. General Keane followed his orders, and the first opportunity for a quick victory slipped away.

Having made their headquarters, the British marched to the River Road that ran parallel to the levee. They turned right and proceeded upstream to the adjoining Lacoste plantation. They secured it and the surrounding territory.

The British described their newly conquered land in the most positive terms. They occupied a mile wide strip of land bordered by the river to their left and a cypress swamp to their right. Gleig's description of the swamp is telling: *"Towards the open ground this marsh was covered with dwarf wood, having the semblance of a forest rather than a swamp; but on trying the bottom, it was found that both characters were united, and that it was impossible for a man to make his way among the trees, so boggy was the soil upon which they grew"* [312].

At about noon, the British were ordered to halt and make camp. Search parties reported no enemy in sight so the troops took the occasion to: *". . . light fires and make themselves comfortable . . . water was brought from the river, and provisions were cooked."* Some were not satisfied with their fare, and they scoured the countryside entering every house seeking provisions: *". . . hams, fowls, and wines of various descriptions."* [313]

The troops enjoyed their meal. While some stretched out by the fires, others took advantage of a break in the weather giving a slightly warmer climate to bathe in the river. While the British were so occupied, Gabriel Villere began to consider some means of escape. He had to get word to Jackson that the British were encamped just south of the city.

Villere watched carefully for an opportunity to flee. When the chance arose, the Major broke from his captors, ran to the window, and leapt through the glass chased by a volley of pistol shots. He then hurtled the picket fence that surrounded the house and dashed into the woods. About fifty guards witnessed this escape and some fired their weapons but failed to stop him.

An infuriated Colonel Thornton immediately ordered his soldiers in hot pursuit, and ordered his men to *"Capture or kill him."* Thornton recognized the danger Gabriel's escape posed. At present the Americans had no idea about where the British forces were. Gabriel Villere would sound the alarm ruining any opportunity for surprise. [314]

Villere was forced to take cover in the foliage of one of the Live Oaks to the rear of his plantation. He was nearly betrayed by his favorite hunting dog who, having followed him, threatened to reveal his hiding place by settling beneath the tree. Villere regretfully took hold of a large limb and killed his dog. [315]

The British continued their search to no avail. After a suitable time had passed, Villere felt secure enough to lower himself from his hiding place and traverse across the rear of his plantation through the cypress marsh. He worked his way to his neighbor's home, the plantation of Colonel de la Ronde. He and a neighbor took a pirogue across the Mississippi River to M. de la Croix's plantation. There they saddled a brace of horses and sped to New Orleans using the ferry near Canal Street to cross over the river.

In the meantime, Jackson had become suspicious about British whereabouts. He sent his engineer Arsene de la Tour down river below New Orleans to check out the situation. Once la Tour approached the Chalmet Plantation he discovered numerous people, some slaves, fleeing upriver. They informed him that the British had suddenly appeared at the Villere Plantation earlier that morning.

La Tour ordered some of his men to report this finding to Jackson, while he advanced with the remainder of his force to reconnoiter the area. It didn't take long for them to discover the British camp and determine that nearly 1,400 soldiers had settled there.

Jackson learned of the British deployment south of the city from la Tour's men as well as information gathered by General Plauanche. Plauanche was stationed at Fort St. John on the bank of Lake Pontchartrain. He captured two men he suspected as spies, questioned them, and learned about the British advance through Bayou Bienvenue.

At about 1:30 p.m. General Jackson was disturbed while in discussions with his aides by the sound of horses galloping rapidly up Royal Street at a speed that violated Martial Law. The sounds ceased and the sentinel at the door announced the arrival of three *gentlemen* "... *stained with mud and nearly breathless with the rapidity of their ride.*"[316]

Major Gabriel Villere, Mr. Dussau de la Crois, and Colonel de la Ronde arrived at General Jackson's Royal Street headquarters with their important news. In rapid French an excited Major Villere sought to tell his story, but Jackson needed an interpreter to translate. This information confirmed what he had learned from la Tour and Plauanche about an hour before.

Villere's story provided needed confirmation and intelligence about the lands the British occupied. They were camped just nine miles downriver from the city itself. Jackson's immediate response was *"By the eternal, they shall not sleep on our soil!"* With that he invited his aides to join him in a glass of wine then remarked: *"Gentlemen, the British are below; we must fight them tonight!"*[317]

Although Jackson welcomed Gabriel Villere's intelligence, he expressed his fury over the fact that Villere had defied a direct order by not closing Bayou Bienvenue as ordered. Jackson had Major Gabriel Villere placed under arrest with the intention of court martial. (See appendix #13) [318]

After issuing his orders, Jackson sat down to dinner and ate a little rice, *". . . which is all his system could endure. He then lay down upon a sofa in his office and dozed for a short time. Before three o'clock he mounted his horse and rode to the lower part of the city, where then stood Fort St. Charles."*[319]

How many of the enemy were there? How well equipped were they? Did they have the means of moving immediately against the city? If not, when might they be prepared for an attack? The waiting game was over. The time for action had arrived.

December 23rd . . .

The stage was set. The commanders of both armies knew that a battle was only a short time away. But who would take the initiative? The British still labored under the misconception that their presence remained a secret. Jackson had to muster his forces immediately to effect either a strong defense or mount a surprise attack.

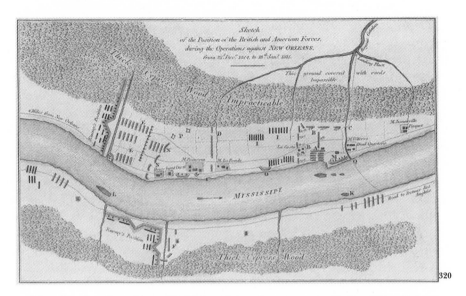

Map showing disposition of British and American troops at Battle of New Orleans

The map above illustrates the position of the British army. Within a short time the bank of Bayou Bienvenue had become a boggy mess impassible by foot soldiers. The British resorted to using their limited number of barges to bring their troops to the front. In the meantime, the British had fully established their encampment extending now from the Jumonville Plantation upriver to the Lacoste Plantation.

The first indication that their position had been compromised occurred at 3:00 P.M. Bugles from the advanced posts sounded the alarm. The Americans had appeared. British soldiers immediately *"stood to arms"* and prepared for battle. The sound of shots echoed through the camp . . . then silence. Notice was soon given to *"stand down."* The alarm had been triggered by the approach of several horsemen who immediately retreated when confronted.[321]

The British camp then returned to its personal routine of relaxing, eating, cleaning weapons, and sleeping. English officers believed they held the initiative and the course of events would be determined according to their plans. After all, Americans had never attacked a British army before, and there was no reason to assume they would now. But they failed to realize that the American general before them on this day was a type of man they had never confronted before. Jackson and his men were from the west. They represented a different breed of opponent than the New Englanders the British were used to fighting.

Jackson instantly seized the initiative. Within thirty minutes, the general had formulated a battle plan. Immediately, Jackson set the tone for all the actions that would later occur, and he proved once again that the best defense is a strong offense. This decision did more to secure the fate of New Orleans than any other. [322]

He ordered all troops protecting outlying areas to hurry to New Orleans. The only exception was those he had stationed near Chef Menteur. He was fully aware of the possibility that the forces along the river might be just one prong of a two front attack. Did the British have sufficient troops to hit him from two directions simultaneously?

Promptly, Jackson had the Volunteer Dragoons of Mississippi under Colonel Hinds, a company of New Orleans rifleman under Captain Beale, and General Coffee's mounted Tennessee riflemen heading down river to meet the enemy. He ordered the U.S. Marines commanded by Major Carmick to man their two guns and meet him along river road. He notified Commodore Patterson that he was to order his ship *Carolina* under command of Captain Henley downstream immediately across from the British camp, arm his guns, drop anchor, and wait until 7:00 P.M. At the appointed time Henley was ordered to open fire on the British camp with canister and grapeshot. [323]

By 4:00 o'clock in the evening, these troops had taken defensive positions on the Rodriguez Canal. Jackson recognized its strategic importance and made this the foundation of his defense line. His men were reinforced one hour later by a company of free men of color under command of Major Daquin. Plauche's French company literally ran from their position on Bayou St. John, through the city to the front, amid the cries and cheers of their Creole relatives lining the streets and balconies. As the hours passed, more troops arrived and took up their positions. [324]

The Louisiana Gazette of June 10, 1815 would number Jackson's forces that advanced against the British on the night of December 23rd as being 2,325.[325]

While all this activity was going on in the American sector, the British were leisurely setting up camp and securing their perimeter. They were tired from the preceding days' events and needed food and rest. Besides, General Pakenham had yet to arrive with the balance of their forces. They felt secure that their presence remained a secret.

At 3:00 P.M., a scouting party approached the British lines. Five mounted riflemen from the dragoons of Feliciana had advanced down river to reconnoiter the situation. This triggered the aforementioned alarm in the British camp. They stumbled upon a British advance guard. In the exchange, they suffered one horse killed and two men wounded. Thomas Scott was the first man to shed blood in Chalmette. [326]

Colonel Haynes of the Mississippi dragoons then advanced with 107 men. He too met strong opposition but was unable to accurately determine the size of the enemy forces. He did, however, arrest a slave in the service of the British who carried a proclamation from the British to the French and Spanish citizens of the city. Copies of this printed document had been nailed on fences along the British area of control. It promised security for surrender and read:

"Louisianians remain quietly in your homes; your slaves shall be preserved to you and your property respected. We make war only against Americans"

This was signed by Major-General Keane and Admiral Cochrane. Apparently, they were still under the illusion that the New Orleans population could be divided along ethnic lines.

The rest of the day passed without cause for alarm. Darkness fell and the British troops started their fires and began to prepare their meals with thoughts of settling in for a long awaited night's sleep. *"The night was now dark as pitch, the moon being but young, and totally obscured with clouds."*[327]

At about 7:00 P.M., the British noticed strange activity on the Mississippi River. Some sort of commercial boat had quietly drifted downstream and had anchored across from their position on the opposite bank. The British hailed the vessel, but no response was heard. They curiously watched. Some thought it might even be one of their own ships.

The American ship *Carolina*, commanded by Captain Henley, had drifted down stream in an apparently unthreatening manner. He noted that the British soldiers began to collect on the levee to view the strange apparition. Henley had taken up his offensive position and waited as ordered for the appointed time before firing. All was silent. The Americans refused to respond to prompts coming from the British soldiers calling from the river's bank and firing several musket shots at the ship.[328]

The British remained perplexed until they heard a command from the ship's stern: *"Now, boys, give it to them for the honor of America!"* With that said, the *Carolina* opened fire with canister and grape shot into the British camp. According to Gleig: *"The words were instantly followed by the flashes of her guns, and a deadly shower of grape swept down numbers in the camp."*[329]

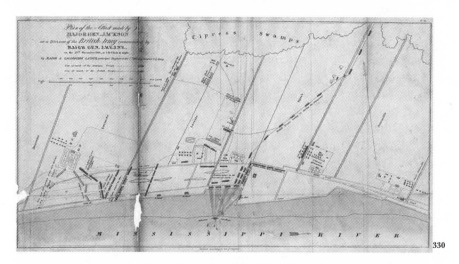

330

Map of December 23rd "Night Battle"

The British returned fire with their entire force for about 40 minutes. *"A few rockets were discharged, which made a beautiful appearance in the air; but the rocket is at best an uncertain weapon, and these deviated too far from their object to produce even terror . . ."* Finally, the British retreated behind the protection of the levee while the *Carolina* continued its barrages throughout the night. The ship's crew received no injuries while the British endured about 100 causalities.[331]

332

Colonel Denis de la Ronde

While the *Carolina* hammered the British camp, General Jackson organized his land offensive. He needed to delay any planned British assault. He realized that his only hope lie in harassing the British as much as possible until such time as the remainder of his army could assemble. That would take days. With 1,500 men, leaving the rest at Rodriguez Canal, and two 6 lb cannons he began his attack upon hearing the guns of the *Carolina* . . . as prearranged.

His plan was to have General Coffee attack the British right flank by the swamp while he attacked the left along the river levee. Colonel de la Ronde, on whose plantation the initial engagement would take place, accompanied Coffee. De la Ronde obviously knew the terrain well. Working around the perimeter of his plantation, de la Ronde led Coffee's men to the rear of the Lacoste plantation and began the maneuver to encircle the British camped at Villere's Plantation.

A spirited battle took place that night which mistakenly convinced General Keane that the intelligence he had gathered about Jackson having over 12,000 troops at his disposal might be correct.[333]

334

Major Jean Baptiste Plaunche

General Coffee's command of mounted firemen and other volunteers were joined by the local Orleans Rifle Company under command of Captain Thomas Beal. Meanwhile, the militia composed of the Free Men of Color under control of Major Louis Daquin joined with the soldiers under Major Jean Baptiste Plauche and marched to the front. Jackson himself commanded the troops positioned along River Road including a company of marines where he deployed the two pieces of artillery.

The first indication of a coordinated land attack working in conjunction with the *Carolina's* broadsides occurred when the British, while sheltering behind the levee, discovered a number of American skirmishers who had crept into the camp on their hands and knees, Indian fashion, to engage them.[335]

The battle became heated as both sides engaged in hand to hand combat. The British fixed bayonets and attempted to mount a charge. Confusion reigned throughout the battlefield.

British accounts reflect the essence of the entire affair: *"Rushing from under the bank, the 85th and the 95th flew to support the piquets, whilst the 4th, stealing to the rear of the encampment, formed a close column and remained in reserve. And now began a battle of which no language were competent to convey or any distinct idea: because it was one to which the annals of modern warfare furnish no parallel. All order, all discipline was lost. Each officer, as he succeeded in collecting twenty or thirty men about him plunged into the midst of the enemy's ranks, where it was fought hand to hand, bayonet to bayonet, and sabre to sabre."*[336]

Distinction between friend and foe was lost. Some troops were fired upon, but refused to return fire fearing that it might be their own men. Several accounts relate British and American forces so mingled that they made attempts to capture one another. Beale's Rifles actually captured a number of British soldiers, then moved to what they believed were "*friendlies*" only discover that they had walked into British reinforcements and were themselves captured.[337].

As for the actions on the River Road, the British made several attempts to seize the American guns on the road only to be driven back by heavy fire and the commanding presence of General Jackson himself. As la Tour recounted: *". . . no man could possibly have shown more personal valour, more firmness and composure, than was exhibited by him through the whole of this engagement, on which depended, perhaps, the fate of Louisiana."*[338]

Major Daquin's division composed of Free Men of Color conducted themselves with distinction. They heeded the call of General Jackson—*". . . at the cry of honour and of war against Britain, those brave men instantly united and joined our forces. In that memorable night they showed that they had not forgotten the exercise of arms."*[339]

The darkness, fog, and thick smoke hindered any effective coordinated moves on either side. The only light was provided by the flashes of musket and cannon. One can only imagine combat in such deplorable circumstances.

As the fight continued, a second wave of British soldiers approached from the Fisherman's Village. Admirals Cochrane and Malcolm were hastening the troops forward while they persisted in advising the American prisoners captured the night before that the British had no arguments with the French or Spanish citizens of Louisiana. At about 7:30 P.M. they heard the sound of gunfire and immediately ordered an advance to the front. These troops arrived within an hour and were instantly engaged in the battle. The arrival of these reinforcements blunted Jackson's offense.[340]

Amid the confusion of fighting in darkness, some soldiers fell to friendly fire. The British would later gain the numerical advantage, especially after the arrival of their second division from Bayou Bienvenue. However, fearing that their lines of communications and supply could be cut, they decided against a more aggressive posture and sought instead to secure their base at Villere. [341]

By 9:30 P.M., the main engagement had ended. By 11:00 P.M., most of the musketry had stopped. By 12:00 P.M. the firing had totally ceased on both sides. A thick fog had set in. That, coupled with the smoke of black powder, made it impossible to determine friend from foe. The additional British forces that arrived from Bayou Bienvenue hurried to the scene of battle upon hearing the unmistakable sounds of gunfire. These reinforcements caused Jackson to call off his offensive.[342] Nevertheless, he had achieved his goal.[343]

However, lingering doubts arose over the behavior of General Morgan stationed below the British camp at English Turn. He had command of over 350 militia and had received intelligence about the British occupation of Villere Plantation about 1:00 P.M. Although lacking contact with Jackson's headquarters, his men heard the cannon shot of the *Carolina* along with the sounds of ground battle and urged him to engage. He kept them in camp until their opposition grew too strong to control. He then led them to the southern edge of the Jumonville Plantation where they met some opposition.

Rather than engage fully, Morgan took a stationary position in the field until about 3:00 am, then ordered a return to camp. No one knows what impact an aggressive attack from the rear would have done to the confused British lines. It has been argued that an aggressive surprise attack by Morgan's command in the British rear, at any moment before 9:00P.M., would likely have routed the entire British division and forced them to lay down their arms or retreat to their boats. Unfortunately, Morgan failed to seize the opportunity.[344]

Further evidence about Morgan's unfortunate neglect comes from Magliore Guichard, President of the House of Representatives in his testimony before the Committee of Inquiry on the military measures employed by Jackson against the legislature. During questioning he stated: *"I expressed my surprise at his [Morgan's] not having attacked the British from the lower side on the night of the twenty-third; that he had done so with the men under his command, at the same time with the troops coming from the city, all would have been terminated on that evening . . ."* Morgan would have had to act on his own initiative, because there is no record of any orders originating from General Jackson's headquarters to him. Morgan lacked the necessary leadership qualities. This would become even more apparent in an engagement to come.

The Americans expressed great pleasure with their performance. They had attacked the British and inflicted harm on their enemy. Some argue that the result of the affair of the 23rd was that Jackson saved Louisiana. It cannot be doubted that the enemy, had he not been attacked, might have marched against the city that very night or early next morning. The city was not covered by any fortification, and was defended by hardly a few thousand men, mostly militia, who could not have withstood a coordinated attack by disciplined troops.[345]

In fact, had Jackson merely delayed his assault by several hours he would have been forced to engage a combined British army after it had been reinforced by the second wave. The implications of that are too disconcerting to imagine. He may have been soundly defeated on that night.

The British, likewise, considered the battle a victory. After reporting the actions of the night's battle in some detail, Gleig then described the battle as a *"contest of man to man . . . till a panic arising among the Americans, they dispersed in all directions and left us masters of the field."*[346]

The carnage proved shocking to British subaltern Gleig on the following morning: *"While thus wandering over the arena of last night's contest, the most shocking and most disgusting spectacles everywhere met my eyes. I have frequently beheld a greater number of dead bodies within as narrow a compass, though these, to speak the truth, were numerous enough, but wounds more disfiguring or more horrible I certainly never witnessed."*[347]

The horrors were a result of the brutal hand to hand combat. *"Many met their deaths from bayonet wounds, sabre cuts, or heavy blows from the butt ends of muskets . . . not only were the wounds themselves exceedingly frightful, but the very countenances of the dead exhibited the most savage and ghastly expressions."* Undoubtedly, many were victims of tomahawk blows delivered by Tennesseans, trained Indian-fighters. Something the British had never encountered before. [348]

The American dead revealed to Gleig much the same horror: *"These poor fellows presented a strange appearance; their hair, eye brows, and lashes, were thickly covered with hoar-frost, or rime, their bloodless cheeks vying with its whiteness. Few were dressed in military uniforms, and most of them bore the appearance of farmers or husbandman . . . they had most nobly died in defending their country."* [349]

Although organized fighting had ceased, the Americans would continue to harass the British through sniping and cannon fire. The Tennesseans in particular enjoyed going on "hunts" where they would sneak through the marsh close to the British lines and, using their highly accurate Tennessee long rifles, pick-off sentries at will. This, along with the continued hammering by the *Carolina* guns, throughout the night denied them much needed sleep and created alarm and fear among the enemy.

The British retreated to the protection of the Villere plantation as greater numbers of reinforcements arrived. But they left this battle with several thoughts in mind.

First, after hearing the commands in French and Spanish, as they had in Europe, orders yelled in back country slang, and seeing Black militia fighting on the front lines they realized that efforts to divide Jackson's army along national and ethnic lines had failed. The Americans had united in the defense of their country.

Second, Jackson's army fought tenaciously and would be a formidable foe. Little trust could be placed in the proposition that they would cut and run at first signs of battle as Admiral Cochrane had been advising. Jackson's army demonstrated determination and spirit by taking the offensive.

As for the Americans, the "affair of December 23rd" raised them from hopelessness. They had forced a British retreat through the press of their arms which instilled much needed confidence. They had bested an army that had distinguished itself on battlefields throughout Europe . . . especially in the Peninsular Campaign of Spain which witnessed some of the harshest fighting in the Napoleonic Wars.

In addition, they witnessed the personal bravery of General Andrew Jackson, who fiercely led his men while exposing himself to imminent peril. That instilled in them a pride and confidence in this recently arrived leader. There was no question about following this gallant man anywhere.

Arsene Latour, Jackson's engineer, had this to say in his memoirs about the December 23th engagement:

"But I cannot decline paying tribute of justice to General Jackson, so say that no man could possibly have shown more personal valour, more firmness and composure, then was exhibited by him through the whole of this engagement, on which depended, perhaps the Fate of Louisiana. I say, without fearing to be taxed with adulation that on the night of the 23rd General Jackson exposed himself rather too much. I saw him within . . . pistol shot!"[350]

The causalities on both sides were considerable and some the unfortunate result of friendly fire. Nevertheless, the skirmish had accomplished much to instill confidence in the Americans and provide Jackson with the much needed time to construct a proper defense line.

Jackson accomplished all that he desired. He successfully led his raw troops against famed veterans and forged his undisciplined and new-fledged soldiers in the baptism of fire. They now had confidence in him and themselves. He had stunned the enemy. He delivered a sudden and unexpected blow which made the British reel back. More important, he gained critical time which he needed to fortify and receive reinforcements. Furthermore, he made the enemy believe that he was stronger than he was.[351]

Despite the fact that this battle can only be considered a draw because both forces retreated to the original lines, the fact remains this bold attack on the part of the Americans took the British by surprise and seriously upset their original plans for taking New Orleans.

Reports indicate this "Affair" to have been bloody indeed. There is some dispute over the casualties on each side. Best estimates indicate that the British lost 46 Killed, 167 wounded, 62 missing for a total of 276. On the American side: 24 Killed, 115 wounded, and 74 missing for a total of 213.[352] Jackson estimated his losses at just over one hundred killed, wounded and missing. The *"Butcher's Bill"*, a contemporary term for accounting for those lost in action, is notoriously inaccurate.

The British report lists their losses specifically as: 4 captains, 1 lieutenant, 7 sergeants, 1 drummer, 33 rank and file killed in action. 1 lieutenant-colonel, 1 major, 2 captains, 8 lieutenants, 10 sergeants, 4 drummers, 141 rank and file wounded. 1 major, 1 lieutenant, 1 ensign, 3 argents (?), 58 rank and file missing. The action cost the British 276 men killed, missing and wounded. These numbers would appear to reinforce Jackson's claim of victory.[353]

So ended the events of the night of December 23rd. The morale of the Americans soared. Although they may have lacked the tactical training of the highly polished British Army, they had met the enemy and, in their minds, bested him. Some would later argue that this marked the end of the traditional European method of fighting because a rough collection of frontiersmen and Indian fighters had proven the advantage of the *"loose and irregular order in which the Americans traditionally fought."* [354]

As for the British, they were confused, angry, disappointed, hungry, wet, cold, and shocked about being attacked, enduring the loses of so many friends, and finding themselves still under the relentless guns of the *Carolina*. This is NOT what they anticipated.

General Jackson ordered several companies to occupy a temporary position on the de la Ronde plantation while he withdrew two miles toward the city and sought a location to establish a defensive line. The Rodriguez Canal, which at that time was merely a grass covered overgrown ditch afforded the best location. *"Here we will plant our stakes and not abandon them until we drive these red-coat rascals into the river or the swamp."* [355]

An interesting footnote to this choice of land, records indicate that Edward Livingston, serving as Jackson's Chief of Staff, had traveled over this piece of property in 1804 with the famous French General Moreau on his visit to the city. When Moreau passed this canal he stated that if New Orleans were ever to be attacked, there was the spot where the enemy could be most effectively resisted. Livingston shared this comment with Jackson, who accordingly selected the Rodriguez Canal as his main line of defense.[356]

Latour began constructing the earthworks. Jackson collected volunteers to extend, deepen, and widen the Rodriguez Canal. Slaves, businessmen, people of every sort responded to his call. He had the mud thrust up on the western bank of the canal and there began the construction of his defensive breast works.

There has always been a controversy about the use of cotton bales in Jackson's breastwork. Some have argued that the entire line was made of cotton bales. There is little evidence to support this other than the claims for the seizure of cotton by several merchants after the battle. Some evidence indicates that when first employed they were knocked about and set on fire by incoming shells. Others caught fire from the embers of Jackson's own guns causing a debilitating smoke to fill the air. Cotton bales failed to be effective.

It appears that they were removed, brought to the rear, and broken up for bedding. Some nevertheless persist in arguing that a few heavy cotton bales were employed as a stable base for mounting the American cannons. Even that is disputed.

Whatever the case with cotton bales, the volunteers and slaves brought to Chalmette worked diligently constructing a formidable breastwork. The canal was widened and deepened and the mud berm behind it elevated to considerable height. The Americans all knew that this was their only chance of stopping a full out frontal attack by a seasoned British army.

While these men were busily digging out the canal, negotiators in Ghent, Belgium, were affixing their names to a final draft of a treaty of peace. It was agreed upon on December 24th, the day after the night battle. Communications being what they were, news of the peace agreement would not reach New Orleans until mid-January. This information arrived after much blood had been shed and the outcome of the campaign decided.

The Rodriguez breastwork presented a formidable defense. Approaching soldiers would have to cross an open field, forge the canal, then climb a tall mud berm before penetrating Jackson's lines . . . all the while enduring the blazing guns of defenders.

In the meantime, Jackson realized that the British might decide to launch an attack across the river with an intended advance on New Orleans from that side. In anticipation of such an action he ordered General Morgan to remove himself from the Eastbank to the Westbank of the river.

Jackson's engineer Latour ordered the Mississippi River levee cut. His hope was that the river would flood the plain of the Chalmette Plantation and the British camp thus rendering it difficult to mount an offensive. He also ordered Morgan to cut the levee below the British position at Jumonville Plantation prior to leaving. This, he hoped, would place the British troops on an island surrounded by water thus isolating them.

This action initially alarmed the British. Dickerson expressed British feelings best: *"He [Jackson] was unaware of the consternation that swept over the British camp at the sight of the water pouring through the dyke, and feeling well marked by Pakenham's order for the arrest of the officer in charge of the picquet duty there. Continued breaches of the river wall would undoubtedly have turned back the British advance."*[357]

Although initially perceived as a success, this plan would eventually backfire!

The river's first surge wet the grounds. However, being December the level was too low to maintain a flood. Unfortunately, it was high enough to inundate both the Villere Canal and Bayou Bienvenue sufficiently enough to make it easier for the British to better float their boats and to bring up troops and supplies by water.

Little action occurred in the course of the following three days. The Americans continued reinforcing their position on the Rodriguez Canal while the British continued to bring up the remainder of their troops and laboriously work their cannons from the decks of the men-of-war onto barges then row them to the front.

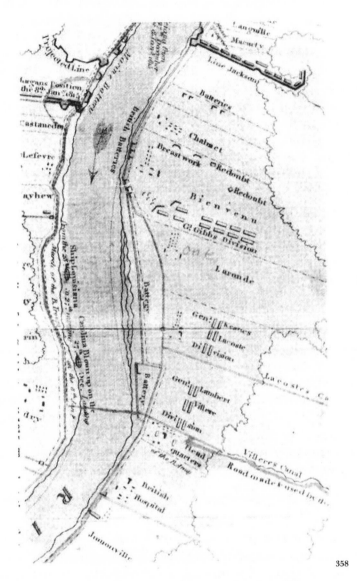

358

Position of General Jacksons defensive line
and the location of British troops.

In the meantime, Major Hinds of Jackson's forces sent his cavalry forward to monitor British activities and to fire some well-placed shots from their long rifles. The British, for their part, cut an opening in the river's levee and began to establish a battery aimed at the annoying *Carolina*. The ship that persistently poured shot into their position.

During this interim, Jackson learned of British activities along Chef Menteur. Mostly reports about British sailors setting fire to the dry marsh grass. Jackson always believed that his opponents would mount a second front. With that in mind, he sent a detachment over to observe activities occurring there.

Major Lacoste, fearing an attack, withdrew his forces to beyond the Lafon Plantation near Chef Menteur. He left a small detachment to report on British activities. Jackson then ordered Latour with two hundred of Coffee's men to reconnoiter the area to determine the potential for a threat. [359]

Latour expressed excitement about the potential of an engagement with British forces at Chef Menteur having at his disposal a detachment of Tennessee riflemen. He learned, however, that the reports of an enemy advance were mistaken. The British were in fact burning the marsh to allow them a clear view of any American advance. Their concern centered about having their lines of supply cut. Theirs was a defensive move not preparations for an attack.

Christmas Day, December 25th

On Christmas Day, Commander-in-chief Pakenham, the brother-in-law to the Duke of Wellington, the hero of the Peninsula Campaign, appeared at the Villere Plantation. He soon realized he had been mistaken about arriving too late to enjoy a victory. The British invasion force had not advanced an inch in two days. He arrived with General Lambert, a substantial company of reinforcements, and additional equipment. This brought the British complement to near full strength with even more soon to be arriving. Pakenham, being a very popular commander, rallied the British soldiers' spirits with his arrival.

The common British soldier had lost some confidence in their commanders over the past few days. In particular, they perceived General Keane as lacking confidence. The newly arrived officers and men had great fun in needling their comrades. Captain Cooke seeing his friend, Colonel Wilkinson, asked; "Why *Wilky, how is it that you have not provided us with good quarters in New Orleans as we expected?*" [360]

The response proved telling: *"Oh! Say no more about it. Bullets stopped us . . . bullets . . . that's all!"* Then after further discussions with his friend he volunteered a torrent of anger concerning *". . . the hesitation shown for the previous days, as to make the very military blood curdle in one's veins."*[361]

Morale among the British had eroded. Cold, wet, fatigue, hunger and lack of sleep had taken its toll. That, coupled with the endless disappointments and miscalculations, had created doubts in their minds about the ability of their commanders to achieve victory.

They had been attacked by Americans who they were told would run in flight at the mere sight of their bayonets. As for the general population, they were told they would welcome the British with open arms. British subaltern Gleig reflected: *". . . instead of finding inhabitants ready and eager to join us, we found houses deserted, the cattle and horses driven away, and every appearance of hostility . . . In a word, all things had turned out diametrically opposite to what had been anticipated; and it appeared that, instead of a trifling affair more likely to fill our pockets than to add to our renown, we had embarked in an undertaking which presented difficulties not to be surmounted without patience and determination"*[362]

Considering the sudden and unexpected turn of events, it should come as no surprise that these disenchanted and weary men welcomed the change in command. Lieutenant Gleig summed up the attitude among the rank and file: *"Hoping everything from a change, they greeted their new leader with a hearty cheer; whilst the confidence which past events had tended in some degree to dispel, returned once more to the bosoms of all."*[363]

Their melancholy arose chiefly because of the modest Christmas dinner they shared in a crude barn. Their holiday repast was so different from the boastful promise of Admiral Cochrane who had on more than one occasion stated *"I shall eat my Christmas dinner in New Orleans."* (When told of this boast, Jackson reportedly told a British prisoner: *"Perhaps so, but I shall have the honor of presiding over that dinner!"*)[364]

Foremost on their minds were the dead comrades whose faces were dearly missed during this humble holiday repast. Such thoughts gave them pain as one veteran reflected; *"nor were any other subjects discussed besides the amiable qualities of those who no longer formed a part of our mess and never would again form a part of it."* A few attempted to break the morbid mood with thoughts of victory, only to have such notions suppressed by the firing of the *Carolina's* cannon.[365]

While the British were sitting at table dining, a loud shriek was heard after one of the explosions and on running out they found that a shot had taken effect on the body of an unfortunate soldier. *"I mention this incident because I never beheld in any human being so great a tenacity of life. Though fairly cut in two at the lower part of the belly, the poor wretch lived for nearly an hour, gasping for breath and giving signs even of pain."*[366]

After being briefed about preceding events, especially the December 23rd attack and the continued *Carolina* bombardments, Pakenham took immediate action. The next day he ordered a proper battery to be constructed on the levee. He had a good fire built and ordered hot-shot prepared. Pakenham was not a man to put up with the harassing fire from shipping on the river without a fight. He intended to destroy the schooner *Carolina* in short order which had now been joined by the schooner *Louisiana*. These two vessels are all that remained of Jackson's meager navy.

Pakenham recognized the inherent danger these vessels posed. If allowed free reign of the Mississippi River they could terrorize his troops where they camped and possibly even break an offensive by virtue of their mobility. They had the advantage of firing canister and grape-shot obliquely through his lines wherever they might be stationed. The thoughts of being subjected to a cross-fire haunted him.

As long as these vessels occupied this position, any attempt at an advance would be met with untold bloodshed. They had to be removed! Nine field pieces, two howitzers, and one mortar were immediately brought to the levee.

December 27th . . .

Upon seeing the smoke and fire near the newly constructed battery, Captain Henley, commander of the *Carolina,* saw the danger to his ship. He recognized the evidence of a hot-shot furnace. Henley bent every effort to move his ship upstream to within the protection of Jackson's lines. But the wind was adverse and Henley's sailors had to resort to launching longboats. Employing warps, they attempted to tow the ship upstream out of harm's way. Their rescue attempt failed!

Pakenham's men had completed their assigned task, and the battery opened fire with five guns. The *Carolina* returned fire. However, through the accurate use of "hot shot," the British turned the tide. Within five minutes, hot shot had penetrated the main storeroom of the *Carolina*. With considerable luck, the second hot shot landed in the schooner's main hold, under her cables. Since these ropes were made of flammable hemp, it presently set her on fire. The fire raged out of control and soon threaten the powder magazine. The captain ordered the crew to abandon ship, with the loss of one killed and six wounded, they took to the boats and reached shore."[367]

Captain Henley confirmed the terror visited upon his crew in his own recount of the action. In reporting the attack on his ship, he described the battery's effectiveness: "*. . . hot shot were passing through her cabin and filling-room, which contained a considerable quantity of powder, her bulwarks were all knocked down by the enemy's shot, the vessel was in a sinking condition, and the fire increasing, and expecting every moment that she would blow up.*"[368]

Flames engulfed the ship so rapidly that the officers were unable to retrieve their uniforms or personal belongings. Only one artifact survives to this day. The ship's sextant was retrieved by Lt. Beverly Roy Scott. The seventeen year old officer tied the sextant along with some important papers in a silk handkerchief, leapt overboard, and swam to shore.

No sooner had the crew escaped than a resounding explosion announced the demise of the *Carolina*. The resonating sound rebounded through the streets of New Orleans startling local residents. [369]

Schooner Carolina's Sextant.

The British next directed their fire on the *Louisiana*, Jackson's sole remaining armed vessel on the river. Members of the British contingent criticized their own artillerymen for negligence during this affair. Instead of directly turning their fire upon the *Louisiana*, they continued to bombard the *Carolina*, perhaps out of rage. However, this mismanagement of firepower resulted in the Americans skipper having the time to tow the *Louisiana* out of range which preserved her for future use.[371]

The criticism among the British rank and file, who believed that Wilkinson expended too much energy and ammunition on the *Carolina* and not enough on the *Louisiana*, proved correct. In their view, both could have been sunk. That would have been decisive because the guns from the *Louisiana* would play havoc as a floating battery during later operations and by January 8th would provide some of the cannons used to arm Patterson's Battery across the river.

This round went to the British. No longer would Pakenham's men be terrorized from the river. They could slumber in peace. They could build fires to warm themselves and cook with the exception of the occasional sniping from the swamp to the rear. Already their commander-in-chief had made his presence known. Despite all of the hardships they had endured over the past days, they now had confidence that victory was soon at hand. In their slumber, they dreamed of the "*beauty and booty*" promised them upon taking the rich city of New Orleans.[372]

Despite losing the support of the *Carolina*, the Americans continued to probe the British lines along the de la Ronde Plantation. Suddenly, the British pressed forward with what appeared to be preparations for a major assault. The Americans fell back as the Redcoats occupied first the Bienvenue Plantation then the outskirts of Chalmet's Plantation.

[373]

British map showing deployment of troops.

They were closing in on Jackson's lines. Nervous energy activated Jackson's camp as it appeared the British intended major offensive the next day.

Jackson made his headquarters at the McCarty Plantation. From the gallery and dormer windows, he had full view of the battlefield. The general then set his soldiers to work reinforcing the defenses on the Rodriguez Canal from the river on his right to the cypress swamp to his left.[374]

Jackson was as ready as circumstances allowed for the coming attack. He had ordered men and slaves from the city to dig out the Rodriguez Canal and line it with fencing to prevent the mud from falling into the canal. The irregular work details made for an inconsistent breastwork. As one witness expressed: *"This circumstance, added to the cold and to the incessant rain, rendered it impossible to observe any regularity as to the thickness and height of the parapet; which in some places was as much as 20 feet thick at the top, and hardly 5 feet high; while in other places, the enemies balls went through it at the base . . ."*[375]

By sunset, Jackson's men had constructed a breastwork of varying height that ran the entire line before Jackson's army. Although not formidable yet, it would suffice for the short term and would become more imposing as the weeks wore on.[376]

In looking over the field before him, Jackson recognized the dangers Ignac de Chalmet's plantation might pose to his troops. Jackson would later order the magnificent Creole home and its surrounding buildings blown up then burned. He would do this to clear his line of fire and prevent the British from using these obstructions for cover. For the moment, that had to wait. As a first priority he ordered up his reserve units from the rear and distributed additional artillery along his now reinforced breastworks.[377]

To further secure his position, Jackson reinforced his two additional lines of defense: Line Dupre' at a distance of a mile and a half to the rear of Line Jackson and Line Montreuil at a distance of two and a quarter miles from his main line. Jackson had prepared "defense in depth" . . . a series of defensive positions to which he could retreat should the need arise.

General Pakenham made proper use of the time as well. Having removed the threat of the *Carolina*, the British General divided his army into two divisions: his right under command of Gibbs, his left under Keane. The left division consisted of the 95th, 85th, 93rd, and one Black corps. To his right he placed the 4th, 21st, 44th, and a second West Indian Black corps.

He possessed only ten pieces of artillery at the time, so he had them advanced with the left column but allowed the guns to be deployed as the geography allowed. The soft ground made erecting batteries a matter of deep concern.

The remainder of his forces he ordered to bring up supplies, ammunition, and what heavy guns from the ships as were available.[378]

Pakenham ordered his troops to advance in order toward the American lines. The sentries and occupants of the American outposts fired a few shots then began a general retreat towards Line Jackson at the Rodriguez Canal. Both sides secured their positions.

As for Jackson, he vindicated his promise that the *"British would not sleep one night while on American soil."* His Tennesseans brought truth to this statement by harassing the British all night long imparting psychological terror on their enemy through persistent sniping from the surrounding swamp. The continual harassment was designed to prevent rest and succor to the British invaders. He succeeded. According to British soldier named Glee: *"Thus was the entire night spent in watching, or at best in broken and disturbed slumbers, than which nothing is more trying, both to the health and spirits of an army."*[379]

Americans and British alike prepared themselves for the arrival of dawn.

What neither side could have known about were events unfolding half a world away. On December 24th, Todd, the son-in-law of President Madison and one of the commissioners representing the Americans at treaty negotiations in Ghent, invited several gentlemen to have refreshments with him. *"At noon after having spent some time in pleasant conversation, the refreshments entered, and Mr. Todd said: 'It is twelve o'clock. Well gentlemen, I announce to you that peace has been made and signed between America and England'"*. Soon thereafter the remaining members of the delegation (Gallatin, Carroll, Clay, and Hughes) entered and confirmed Todd's acclamation.[380]

Perhaps, had there been some quicker means of communication to the front, much bloodshed could have been avoided. However, it must be kept in mind that the treaty in question firmly stated that it did not go into effect until fully "ratified." That would not be proclaimed until February 18, 1815, after approval of the Senate and signature of the President on February 17th.

Nevertheless, one is left to wonder what impact this might have had on events about to unfold in Chalmette. Since at this point so much blood had already been spilled, it is possible that the British officers would have met with Jackson; they would have toasted one another while celebrating the declaration of peace; then they may have quietly sailed away. Interesting to note that the war began after the Orders in Council had been rescinded and the last battles were fought after peace had been agreed upon.

A lack of timely communications played such a critical role in the War of 1812.

December 28 . . .

Jackson had taken his position at the McCarty House about two hundred yards behind Line Jackson. From the roof dormer, he observed the British operations through a telescope borrowed from his French aide. He was surprised, puzzled, and troubled by the enemy's inactivity. What could they be planning down river at the Lacoste Plantation headquarters? Why would they allow him to strengthen his position day after day without the slightest attempt at interference? Pakenham was no fool, there had to be a reason for this seeming idleness."[381]

December 27th proved to be a busy day in the American lines. Several pieces of artillery were brought forward, they dug the Rodriguez Canal deeper and wider, and they built up their protective berm. Two companies of Louisiana Militia reinforcements were placed in the line while making room for the detachment of Baratarians soon to arrive. Jackson would even place the crew of the now destroyed *Carolina* in his lines to man the cannons newly emplaced.[382]

Jackson again took careful note of the Chalmet Plantation. Hinds Dragoons had been using it as a headquarters. Now it posed a problem in that it could act as cover during a British advance. Jackson no longer hesitated. He ordered it to be destroyed when the opening guns were fired.

In the midst of all of this military activity, word came to Jackson that some members of the legislature had been secretly meeting at night and considered sending a delegation to the British offering to surrender the city. Abner L. Duncan, a member of the legislature, had been privately informed by Colonel Alexander Declouet that such an effort was seriously afoot.[383]

They had communicated on horseback when Declouet, at a fast gallop, caught up with Duncan near the battle lines in Chalmette on the night of December 27th. He urged Duncan to contact Jackson while he contacted Governor Claiborne.

He cited discussions he had with Guichard, Speaker of the House who reportedly stated that: *"General Jackson was carrying on a Russian*

War, and that is was better to save private property, by timely surrender, and he, colonel Declouet, had been invited to join in the measure." Declouet told Duncan that it was his duty to report the same to Jackson. [384]

Interestingly, according to Declouet the French members of the legislature promoted this conspiracy, with leadership provided by Blanque, the man who Lafitte had informed about Captain Lockyer's letters, and the Speaker of the House Mr. Guichard.

An interesting conversation occurred between Guichard and Colonel Declouet just prior to the December 28th battle. While in Chalmette, Declouet confronted Representative Guichard about the secret meetings and wanted to know why the legislature had not adjourned. To which Guichard, after an extended discussion ended the matter by saying: *"You will always be the same, your suspicions never abandon you; and I added, that the legislature ought to be the centinel of the people, ready in a crisis like the present, to take such measures as the calamities of war and the circumstances might render necessary; I concluded by requesting him to discontinue the subject."* [385]

A possible key bit of testimony came from Guichard himself when testifying later about this event. He stated that during a prolonged conversation with Declouet that started one night, then continued again at breakfast, Declouet questioned him about: *"Why these nightly meetings? Why those secret meetings? What does it signify?"* To which in response Guichard: *"Made no answer, and I contented myself with shrugging my shoulders."* [386]

One would think that if NOTHING was afoot, Mr. Guichard would have been more aggressive in denials. Less we forget, at this point in time, the British presented a formidable force.

According to witnesses, Jackson's immediate response was typically Jacksonian: *"Tell Governor Claiborne to prevent this, and blow them up if they attempt it!"* [387]

Jackson issued a Military Order dated December 28th in which he sought to adjourn the legislature though the application of Martial Law which was in effect. A legislative committee convened after the battles on January 11, 1815, and investigated the issue. But being led by one of the principle accused conspirators, one wonders if the committee's work was more cover-up than striving for the truth.

Another interesting note is that the investigation reserved special condemnation for Colonel Declouet. All other witnesses were sworn on a Bible. In contrast, the legislative committee required Colonel Declouet to swear upon a *"consecrated cross"* provided by Father Antoine Sedella . . . why?

One is left to believe that this controversy sprang from either the imagined suspicions of Colonel Declouet, or from a real attempt to surrender the city to the British. The investigation sought evidence of written "*proposals*" which seldom exist when people privately meet to discuss potentially treasonable matters. So this subject remains a matter of some controversy although Jackson's response has become the stuff of legend.

With all that was taking place, General Jackson certainly did not need a political distraction of this magnitude. His abrupt response would later be used against him. His first order of business was the enemy before him; he had no time for conspiracies to his rear.

The weather in New Orleans is notorious for is variability. The last two weeks were filled with driving rains and bone chilling cold. December 28th opened differently. The sun shone bright and as the mist evaporated, only chilled droplets remained glistening on the grass. A beautiful day welcomed the combatants.

The British had been harassed all night by the Tennessee "Hunters" who sniped at their outposts. "*Having continued this detestable system of warfare till towards morning, the enemy retired and left us to rest. But soon as day began to break, our piquets were called in, and the troops formed in order of attack.*"[388]

As the sun rose, the calming songs of birds were soon replaced by the peel of bugles and the beat of drums. The British had called their thousands of men to arms. Pakenham planned a "*Reconnaissance in Force*" to probe the American defenses and: ". . . *if fortune favors and the prospect pleases, he will leap over them [the Americans] into New Orleans and into the House of Lords.*"[389]

At dawn on the 28th, the British opened hostilities. General Gibbs, on Pakenham's right, took his station near the edge of the swamp while General Keane, on the left, positioned his forces along the river road. Both advanced skirmishers to clear the area of American snipers and scouts. "*It was a clear frosty morning, the mists had dispersed and the sun shone brightly upon our arms as we marched*".[390]

Hostilities started with Congreve rockets, but these served only to startle the horses once the Americans realized their ineffectiveness. The British then advanced along both fronts. They were in high spirits, fully expecting the Americans to fire a few shots then run away. They savored the taste of a quick and decisive victory as the columns formed ready for attack.

From the American lines, the British advance appeared more like a formal parade than an assault. They moved in solid columns, compact and orderly. Their approach was preceded with a shower of rockets and a persistent fire from their artillery batteries along the front and other artillery emplacements on the levee. They presented a bold and imposing demonstration.[391]

As for the British, they had little fear as they advanced in close formation. *"Our spirits, in spite of the troubles of the night, were good and our expectations were bandied about and many careless words spoken; for soldiers are, of all classes of men, the freest from care and on that account perhaps the most happy. By being continuously exposed to it, danger with them ceases to be frightful."*[392]

The British advanced without incident until within sight of Jackson's line. Only then did they first perceive the danger. A heavily armed defensive line lie to their front, an armed ship anchored to their left in the river offering flanking fire (the *Louisiana*), and an impassable swamp situated to their right. They were boxed in.

To his relief, Jackson saw: *". . . a band of rough looking armed men coming down the road from the direction of the city."* The Baratarians had arrived. Dominique Youx and Beluche had run all of the way from Fort St. John and were immediately placed in charge of several batteries. Soon to follow were the gun crews of the *Carolina* who had escaped the destruction of the ship. They too took command of batteries. Jackson suddenly had effective gun crews.[393]

The captain of the *Louisiana* patiently waited until the advancing troops had come well within the range of his guns. The ship then opened a blistering fire as did the batteries all along Jackson's line.

According to a British soldier engaged in the operation: *"During the advance of the British, the ship which had been so unfortunately spared, opened a heavy enfilading fire upon them; and continued it during the whole of the afternoon. Her fire, and that from the enemy's heavy pieces at his works, did considerable execution."*[394]

"Captain Humphreys' battery had incessantly played upon and severely galled him [the American ship] *from an early hour in the morning, but the guns of the Louisiana, from her position, were better calculated than any other to annoy him, as her broadside as in an oblique direction to his line of march. One single ball from her killed fifteen of his men."*[395]

The American defenses had a profound impact on the British assault. They were trapped in a withering cross fire from Jackson's infantry and artillery to the front as well as the *Louisiana* to their left. Again, in the words of Lieutenant Gleig: *"That the Americans are excellent marksmen, as well with artillery as with rifles; we have frequent cause to acknowledge; but, perhaps on no occasion did they assert their claim to the title of good artillery-men more effectually than on the present. Scarce a ball passed over or fell short of its mark, but all striking full in the midst of our*

*ranks, occasioned by terrible havoc . . . a tremendous cannonade mowed down
our ranks and deafened us with its roar.* "[396]

Within thirty minutes, two British field pieces and a field mortar
had been disabled. Gun crews were killed, and the survivors began to
leave the field. The artillery duel had been lost!

The British infantry, having formed lines, advanced under a heavy
discharge of round and grape shot. They stopped when they took
note of the canal in front of Jackson's line. This was an obstacle they
had not anticipated. A halt was ordered and the exposed men were
commanded to shelter themselves as well as they could from the
American fire. For this purpose they were hurried into a wet ditch in
advance of Jackson's line. It was of sufficient depth to cover the knees.
Here, they lay down to conceal themselves behind some high weeds
which grew along the ditch's bank. They remained prone until dark
thus escaping the many bullets which passed over their heads from all
directions. [397]

The fire power was so fierce that the British lines broke and fell
back to Bienvenue's Plantation. Pakenham, seeing that the American
position was stronger than anticipated and well defended, ordered
a retreat. First, the cannons were removed by sailors. Then, the
troops began to withdraw by regiment in a most organized manner.
It is estimated that they lost nearly 56 men in the attempted assault.
Jackson's loses were seven killed and ten wounded. As for the
Louisiana, she suffered one sailor wounded and the ship sustained one
minor hit with hot-shot.[398]

Despite the anticipation of spending a comfortable night bedded
down in New Orleans, the British officers found themselves unrolling
their bedrolls in the slave quarters adjoining the Villere Plantation for
another bad night's sleep. The Americans had witnessed: "*. . . the most
splendid and imposing army they had ever seen sink, as it were, into the earth
and vanish from their sight.*"[399] Once again their spirits soared. They had
forced the retreat of the massive invading British army.

As for the British, they encountered frustration again. The heroes
of the Peninsula War and the conquerors of Napoleon, the stately
Ninety-Third Highlanders, found themselves lying low in wet ditches,
some for as long as seven hours, under the relentless cannonade and
sniper fire. Finally, they ignobly slipped away behind fences, huts, and
burning houses. Some even crawled along on the bottom of ditches,
happy to get beyond the reach of the murderous American guns. [400]

From this opening engagement a problem revealed itself for the
British: "*As communications between the store ships and the frontline began
to be sucked under by the mud, difficulties began to manifest themselves for*

the gunners." The decision to employ deck guns on a muddy wet field proved a mistake. Gun crews could not properly manage their weapons in these conditions. [401]

When Pakenham's chief artillery officer, Colonel Dickson, arrived on Christmas Day only 12 guns had been brought to shore, and the 9-pounders had only a day's supply of ammunition. One of his gunners, Munro, had sought to have over 200 rounds apiece for his guns, but none had as yet arrived. In fact, the conditions on the ground were so bad, that only the 3-pounders could be moved at all. Attacking a strong defensive line requires large siege guns, 18-pounders. Although Admiral Cochrane would order them brought from the fleet, managing these large weapons would prove an even more daunting task.

The lack of powder and shot proved a persistent problem as well, partially aggravated by the differences in naval and land strategies. Naval vessels fire less often than land batteries. Cochrane applied naval calculations for usage.

What made matters the worse for the British was a chronic lack of support. A great many of the stores necessary for servicing and supplying the guns were not sent by the naval officers in charge of forwarding supplies. This occurred despite the fact that they had been urgently demanded by Dickson. Having never conducted land operations, the navy had little understanding of the equipment needed to manage land batteries. [402]

Dickson had only 68 rounds a gun for the 18-pounders, instead of the required 350 and only 40 rounds were sent forward for the carronades. His supply was nowhere near what was needed to overwhelm Jackson's defense line and smash his fortifications prior to an infantry assault. This problem persisted throughout the engagement.[403]

Crippling a ship at sea required far less fire-power then demolishing gun emplacements on land. It took massive amounts of ordinance to destroy a heavily protected and well constructed breastwork. The navy never quite understood the difference and Admiral Cochrane apparently was not aware of this fact

Was the action on December 28th an actual attempt to begin an offensive, or merely a probe of Jackson's lines? Perhaps Pakenham had listened too closely to the advice of Admiral Cochrane who persisted in believing that the Americans would *"cut and run"* at the first signs of a sustained attack. Cochrane had even chided Pakenham about his hesitation in ordering an attack, stating that he would use his 3,500 sailors to overrun the American position if British soldiers lacked courage.

Meekly and disheartened, the British troops sulked back to their base camp. Once again their assault had been turned. Once again they had been defeated by this strange assembly of enemy combatants. Their confidence was shaken. Their physical and mental condition deteriorated.

It was only after debriefing his officers that Pakenham realized that the potential for victory had slipped through his hands. On the British left, Gibbs and Colonel Rennie had sorely pressed Coffee's men in the swamp and were driving in his pickets. They were within one hundred yards of turning Jackson's flank. Fearing disaster, Coffee ordered Colonel Henderson and two hundred Tennesseans to advance to Rennie's rear.

The Americans overran their position and came under fire from Gibbs's major force. Henderson and five of his men were killed. As the British pressed the offensive, suddenly orders were given to pull back . . . much to Rennie's anger. He reluctantly obeyed. Orders were orders! [404]

Had Pakenham realized the penetration achieved by his forces on his right, he would have employed his reserves to reinforce this action and quite possibly have turned Jacksons left, gotten behind his defensive line, and carried the day. Unfortunately, with a lack of communication, there was no way he could have known about Gibb's successful advance.

From the American perspective, the engagement proved to be another victory for Jackson's strange little army. Once again, it had bested a highly trained, motivated, and experienced European fighting force.

Following this, a period of light skirmishes ensued interrupted by several artillery duels and the persistent "hunts" that the Tennesseans so enjoyed, firing from the swamp into the British right. The British considered such tactics as unmanly and tantamount to assassinations. Despite their extensive relations with Indians, they obviously never appreciated the Indian way of making war.

The British were unaccustomed to such savage behavior. There were rules to war after all, and these crude Americans proved themselves to be uncultured. They knew nothing about the code of chivalry and the customary rules of conducting war according to the accepted standards of European custom. Their conduct was uncommonly crude. [405]

During the interval, the British organized their forces and planned new tactics for a major assault. They also gained further reinforcements bringing their assault force to nearly 10,000 strong. Eventually it would number nearly 14,000. Meanwhile, their sailors were bringing forward heavier naval guns and establishing forward batteries.

Jackson's troops kept busy as well. The Louisianans frantically raised the height of their mud berm, lined its exposed front with timbers, and dug out the canal in front. Having recognized the near disaster Coffee experienced on the left, Jackson extended his lines deeper into the swamp and established a dog-leg which would make turning his flank harder. He, despite his misgivings, also began construction of an elevated artillery battery a little forward of his right line near the river.

Although his officers embraced the advantage of this battery, Jackson held deep concerns about this *"forward redoubt."* Granted, he could see its advantages. Such a battery could sweep the front of his lines with grapeshot should the British advance to this line. However, Jackson also believed it a threat. Being located forward of his lines, he could not defend it. Should the British take this redoubt they could easily turn its guns against his own men and affect a successful penetration on his right by the river. As events would prove, Jackson's concerns were well founded!

The Americans took advantage of the break in hostilities to strengthen their position. In six mere days, Lafever completed the parapet which ran the whole length of the canal. He also leveled the earth to form glacis on the opposite side to provide a stable base for artillery operations.[406]

These guns would give Jackson command of the levee and the Rodriguez canal. With the arrival of Jean Lafitte's gunners, in particular Dominic Youx and Beluche'; Jackson gained additional artillery, much needed supplies, and some hearty men. He now only had to impatiently await the arrival of his long expected Kentucky reinforcements of frontiersmen from upriver.

In addition, after witnessing the effectiveness of the *Louisiana's* barrages, Jackson ordered Patterson to establish an effective battery across the river just forward of Line Jackson to command the front of his lines. Patterson established his position on the site of a Westbank brick kiln. By taking guns off of the ship, this would allow all of the *Louisiana's* guns to come into play instead of having one side remain silent.

This was done because a lucky shot on the *Louisiana* would have cost Jackson all of its guns. He remembered well of the *Carolina*. A fixed battery on the Westbank was less vulnerable and just as effective.

The British immediately recognized the problems this created for them. With a cross-fire established, they could not hope to arrange their forces in columns ". . . *along lanes between the American cannon balls.*" This development changed things considerably for them.

As Jackson reviewed his defensive situation, he ordered Morgan's men, who had moved from below Jumonville Plantation to the Westbank of the river, to establish a defensive line in advance of the Westbank battery commanded by Patterson. Should the British cross the river and attempt to take the Westbank battery, it would cost them dearly to get there.[407]

Jackson appreciated his Westbank battery's importance and vulnerability. That battery would prove to be of critical importance in the days to come. Because of its position, it was able to rain a continuous fire of canister and grape-shot across the British advancing army, wreaking havoc in their lines. However, should it fall into hostile hands, that same battery could be turned against Jackson's line giving that same advantage to the enemy.

The Westbank battery had to be protected at all costs!

Pakenham made adjustments as well. He held a council of war and ordered heavy siege guns from the navy. He also established a hospital at the Jumonville Plantation. He realized that he was not facing the ineffective defenders that the British confronted at Washington, D.C., but a different breed of determined fighter and he adjusted his plans accordingly.

He also appreciated that the longer his troops froze in the open air and were deprived of the basic human needs like proper food and sleep, the less effective they would become. He needed to get this over with as soon as possible. Pakenham's officer corps knew: *"The longer an attack was delayed the less likely it was to succeed.*"[408]

Pakenham had learned that he could not take the Americans by frontal assault without tremendous loss of life and no guarantee of success. He could not turn their flanks because of the geography of the battlefield. No competent field commander would ever have chosen this as a place to plan an offensive. Furthermore, he held no hope of drawing the Americans from behind their defensive position into an open fight. This left only one alternative. He had to break their lines with a powerful artillery duel.

Accordingly, the British sailors labored all night creating several forward redoubts to house their guns. Throughout that time, the

American artillerists continually hammered them. Nevertheless, the British succeeded in setting their cannons and, on December 31st, opened fire on the American artillery. This duel was the prelude to yet another attempt by the British to force the American lines.

New Year's Day, January 1st . . .

General Pakenham had learned something from his advance on December 28th. Although repulsed, he did gain some insights about Jackson's defenses. It would not be as easy as first thought; however the obstacles were not insurmountable. He decided that he must employ textbook approaches much as one would against a European walled city if he hoped to take Line Jackson. This would require a major increase in artillery. If he could dislodge Jackson's guns, the door was open for an infantry assault.

On the evening of December 31st, Pakenham ordered Cochrane to bring him thirty additional cannons. Ten ship 18-pounders and four 24-pound carronades were brought forward from the fleet at considerable labor. Four of the 18-pounders, protected by hogsheads of sugar, were placed on the main road to fire upon the *Louisiana*.[409]

Even now Pakenham experienced problems. The dirty work required to haul the heavy cannons to the front and place them into position in the soft soil exhausted his men. None wanted the duty. The working party whose job it was to prepare the batteries melted away into the darkness. Pakenham was roused from his slumber by artilleryman Harry Smith who informed him of the problem. The Commander-in-Chief himself had to go forward to supervise the effort. Although he achieved some measure of success, the end results were wholly inadequate to the need. Morale had become an issue. [410]

New Year's Day 1815 opened like any other January day in bayou country. The cold damp climate often lends itself to heavy fogs . . . especially near its waterways. A thick fog left only about twenty yards visibility. It persisted beyond 9:00 o'clock. Many in the American lines began to believe that this would be another day of rest. They began to celebrate News Years Day with music and general gaiety. Jackson even ordered a grand review of his army. All was gaiety among the Americans.

Lieutenant Greig describes the scene: *". . . we could perceive all that was going forward with great exactness. The different regiments were upon parade, and, being dressed in holiday suits, presented really a fine appearance. Mounted officers were riding backward and forward through the ranks, bands were playing, and colors floated in the air . . . in a word, all seemed jollity and Gala."*[411]

Towards 10 o'clock the fog began to lift *". . . with a rapidity perfectly surprising."* The British took note of the American distractions and revelry. They seized the opportunity.[412]

Pakenham's plan resembled that of December 28th. The only differences being a much greater flanking force to be advanced through the swamp and the additional heavy guns in three redoubts designed to crush the American artillery and breach the lines for the frontal assault.

Indeed, one could not even apply the term "battery" to what had been erected. The emplacements consisted of a single line of sugar barrels, some filled with dirt. *"A single shot would shatter the half inch staves of the barrel. So shallow were the defenses that there was nothing to stop gunners from being hit at any time above the waist."*[413]

The Americans, on the other hand, had overcome their problems. Their cannons were well mounted making for a stable platform. They also had an unlimited supply of labor from the city. They impressed hundreds of slaves into crews who worked alongside the many willing citizens.[414]

As for the "Line Jackson's" breastworks, there is little agreement among the British. Some argue that the Rodriguez Canal was just a slight depression with some water. British Colonel Dickson, who examined it with his telescope from a nearby tree, described it differently.

He reported a formidable fortification with a deep trench cut in front nearly twelve feet wide and filled with water from an opening in the river. The front was constructed *". . . with an imposing backward slanting stockade of heavy timbers, reinforced behind with earth backing. The sloping ditch of the American line would roll any shells that fell short into the ditch, which would extinguish them. At the same time it would completely protect the American gunners from musketry while they worked."*[415]

This battle would open with an artillery barrage designed to destroy the opponent's batteries. Despite the professional training of the British officers and men, their tactical and logistical disadvantages would decide the outcome.

"The first of January was ushered in with a very thick fog, which did not begin to disperse till towards eight 'clock."[416] When the fog entirely lifted at about 10:00 o'clock, a heavy artillery barrage from the three British batteries began.

The Americans were taken by surprise. *"How changed the scene! At a signal from the central battery of the enemy, the whole of their thirty pieces of cannon opened fire full upon the American lines, and the air was filled with the red glare and hideous scream of hundreds of Congreve rockets!"*[417]

Their main target was the McCarty Plantation house, Jackson's headquarters. Within minutes, nearly one hundred cannon balls had found their mark on the house forcing the occupants out. Despite the incoming shells and flying splinters and debris, surprisingly, no one was even injured.

After the initial attack on Jackson's headquarters, the British employed their cannons against Jackson's lines along with a barrage of Congreve rockets . . . noisy little things, but quite ineffective. The enemy's goal was to destroy the American artillery and to breach the breastworks.

The immediate effect of this sudden and powerful barrage caused confusion in the American lines. The view from the British camp proves revealing: *"The different regiments were upon parade; being dressed in holiday suits, presented in really fine appearance . . . all seemed jolly and gala . . . when suddenly our batteries opened, and the face of affairs instantly changed. The ranks were broken; the different corps dispersing, fled in all directions whilst the utmost terror and disorder appeared to prevail."*[418]

Jackson returned fire with his ten pieces of artillery. *"Jackson's first glance when he reached the line, was in the direction of Humphrey's Battery. There stood this right arm of the artillery, dressed in his usual plain attire, smoking that eternal cigar, coolly leveling his guns and directing his men."*[419] The general then continued down his lines encouraging his men: *"Don't mind those rockets; they are mere toys to amuse children."*[420]

Behind the British lines could be seen the columns of troops ready to advance. This was a classic artillery duel in preparation for a major land assault. Some British soldiers felt General Pakenham had lost an opportunity by not advancing immediately.[421]

The cannonade lasted for ninety minutes. Imagine the overwhelming sound of fifty large bore cannons *". . . fired once to three times every minute, an average of two discharges every second."* The battle lines were engulfed in so much smoke that gunners resorted to aiming from memory being unable to sight their targets. The resounding noise must have occasioned some anxiety in the City of New Orleans as citizens pondered the outcome. Would Jackson prevail, or would the British soon be charging up the streets of New Orleans? [422]

Soon it appeared the British effort was faltering. Though the exchange persisted, the Americans were getting the better of it. According to Jackson's engineer Latour: *"Our batteries were the principal objects against which the enemies fire was directed; but we were not less intent in demolishing his, for in about an hour's time, our balls dismounted several of his guns, when the firing ceased, the greater part of his artillery was unfit for service.* "[423]

Lafitte's privateers Dominique Youx and Beluche', deported themselves well. Their trained eyes and experience of firing accurately from a heaving deck resulted in the destruction of numerous British artillery batteries.

For their part, the British soon realized that they lacked the necessary ammunition to continue the barrage. Their problem stemmed from the nearly eighty mile barge trip it took to bring cannon, ball, and powder to the front. Even worse, the damp and soft conditions of the soil made firing guns designed for hardwood decks troublesome. When fired, the recoil simply sunk the guns into the mud. British gunners continually struggled to reset their cannon and attempt to find effective aim in the most trying conditions.

Even more frustrating came the realization that most of the balls fired by the British had little effect. They buried themselves harmlessly in the soft mud of the thick embankment. Others flew over its summit and caused casualties on those who were bringing up ammunition, as well as on some who were retiring from their posts, but little else. Although the Americans endured some casualties in the rear, the intent of the bombardment failed. The American defensive line held and the British effort failed. [424]

At one point, when two American caissons with 100 rounds in each exploded, the British thought they had won the day. The English troops arranged in the ditches gave three cheers of *"huzzhas"* and prepared to advance. But an immediate return barrage from Jackson's line dispelled any illusions of a quick victory. His artillery had not been silenced.

An attempt by Pakenham to test the American left near the swamp resulted in his troops coming under the withering fire of the Tennessee "hunters" who practically lived in the waist deep swamp camouflaged among the trees in their worn deerskins. They stood in knee deep water during the day and slept on floating logs tied together at night. These hearty frontiersmen provided an impenetrable defense.

As for the Tennesseans, their well-known skill with their long rifles caused terror among British sentinels and advanced-posts. Their uniform, consisting of a brown hunting dress, camouflaged them and made it nearly impossible to locate them. The cover of woods and dry grass through which they approached hid them and allowed them to shoot down the British sentinels, whom they never missed, with impunity." [425]

Toward noon the fire of the British forces had diminished. As for the Americans, they continued showering shot and shell at a furious rate. The sugar barrels employed by the British to protect their position had been crushed and the contents had turned their batteries into a sticky mess of "simple syrup" mingled with mud. They had afforded absolutely no protection.

By 3:00 o'clock in the afternoon, the cannon fire ceased. The Americans took this opportunity for the smoke to clear and their guns to cool. The British sailors who manned the guns were running to the rear while many in the army once again *"took to the ditch"*. They watched as the remaining Redcoats could be seen dejectedly withdrawing toward their base camp. Obviously their attempt to intimidate the American troops had failed. Once again, they had been bested. Dejection and confusion reigned among the officers and men alike.

By late afternoon it was over. British casualties were reported to be thirty killed and forty wounded. Jackson's troops endured a total of 34 dead and wounded. The eleven killed died on the road behind Jackson's lines. They were felled by British shells fired over the breastwork.[426]

The Americans conducted themselves well. They achieved this despite the fact that their guns were served by their largely civilian crews, *"who still wore the red woolen sailor's caps, or floury miller's hats of their peaceful employment."*[427]

Recalling the immediate, shocking impact of the opening fire of the British artillery on the American lines, Lieutenant Gleig sadly commented: *"Oh, that we had charged at that instant!"* He recognized the value of the initial surprise and felt that insistence on winning an artillery duel cost them success. Yet another opportunity for victory had slipped through their fingers.

From the perspective of some British officers, this was just one more occasion where failure to take the initiative had cost them victory. Because of a lack of ammunition, they had to move quickly taking advantage of the initial confusion in the American lines. By waiting for their batteries to destroy the American artillery, which never happened, an opportunity was lost.

Pakenham's second attempt had failed. Others recognized the problem as well. Another soldier reported: *"The haste that had been shown in equipping the batteries, and the lack of ammunition to supply them, had their inevitable effect. The failure of our batteries upon the enemy's lines was a severe and unexpected blow to our hopes of success."*[428]

The British officers and soldiers experienced a profound emotional impact of yet another defeat. *"For a two whole nights and days not a man had closed an eye, except such as were cool enough to sleep amidst showers of cannon-ball and during the day scarcely a moment had been allowed in which we were able to so much as to break our fast."* Hunger and fatigue haunted the men, proving once again Jackson's initial promise that they would not sleep a night on American soil. [429]

Gleig recounted the attitude of the men: *"We retired, therefore, not only baffled and disappointed, but in some degree disheartened and discontented. All our plans had as yet proved abortive . . . It must be confessed that something like murmuring began to be heard through the camp."* [430]

The British soldiers' living conditions deteriorated with every passing day. The cold damp December weather had taken a toll. The brutal climate coupled with the lack of supplies because of the distance from the fleet made the men feel abandoned. In landing, the army had borne great hardships, not only without expressing discontent, but with actual cheerfulness. They believed the false promises of quick victory and all that comes with it. They now found themselves entangled amidst difficulties from which there appeared to be no escape, except by victory. Their provisions, being derived wholly from the fleet, were both scanty and course . . . hard tack and salt meat. Their sleep was continually broken by snipping and cannon balls. Morale in the British camp rapidly collapsed. [431]

When the battle closed, the British faced an additional problem. It was an unusually severe winter in Louisiana with nearly constant rain and unseasonable cold. It had cleared for a short while, and then a sudden change in the weather occurred. A cold front came through which brought more rain and turned the battlefield into a quagmire. It took the entire night of heavy exertion on the part of the whole army with assistance of the available sailors to move the undamaged guns to the rear.

In the meantime, Commodore Patterson continued his bombardment of the British camp and the battlefield. From January 2nd to the 5th, he persisted in tormenting his enemies employing the eighteen guns on the opposite bank to sweep their lines. The British casualties, including the action of January 1st, were 32 killed, 44 wounded, and two missing for a total of 78 combatants. The Americans lost 11 killed, 23 wounded for a total of 34 casualties.

Things were not developing as anticipated. New Orleans was no closer than on their arrival ten days before. Major-General Sir Edward Pakenham had to step back and devise a new plan. He had to divine some means of flanking the Americans and breaking their lines. But how???

As for General Jackson, what thoughts tormented his mind? Certainly, if the British had tried and failed to broach his line on two occasions, could he expect them to repeat such a vain attempt again? Jackson had taken the opportunity during the lull in fighting to further reinforce his line. General Pakenham must know this. Certainly, Pakenham would attempt something new. But what?

Other matters of significant gravity weighed heavily on General Jackson's mind as well. On January 3, 1815, a mere five days before the decisive battle that would determine the fate of the United States, General Jackson sent a letter from his headquarters four miles below New Orleans to the Headquarters of the 7th Military District. He raised two critical points, one totally shocking.

In this dispatch he focuses first upon a missing shipment of much needed arms: *"Again I must apprise you that the arms I have been so long expecting, have not arrived. All we hear of them is that the man who has been entrusted with their transportation, has letters on the way for purpose of private speculation—depend upon it . . . this criminality let me call it . . . if it is not corrected [will lead] to the defeat of our armies and to the disgrace of those who superintend them.* "[432]

Jackson goes on to state that without the needed arms it will be nearly impossible to defend New Orleans: *"Every reliance can be placed on the bravery of my men, but without arms it is impossible they can affect much."*

As the General comes to the close of the January 3rd report, Jackson proposes a shocking suggestion. Remember, this is just five days before the decisive battle in Chalmette. Throughout his long ordeal from the Indian wars, defense of Mobile, capture of Pensacola, and protecting New Orleans, the General has endured extreme pain. His agony is attributable to his shoulder wound suffered in the duel with the Benton boys and the intestinal ravages from his still lingering dysentery. Jackson's physical condition has deteriorated significantly over the past few months.

As his report comes to a close Jackson adds: *"Permit me again to suggest to you the propriety of turning your attention, in time, to some proper officer to take command of the army here, when my want of health, which I find to be greatly impaired shall oblige me to retire from it."* [433]

Imagine the impact Jackson's exit from command would have had on the morale of his troops and the outcome of the decisive January 8th battle? His courage, determination, and optimism motivated his men to achieve great victories. Losing him would have caused incalculable damage to the American cause and likely would have instilled confidence among his British adversaries. Thankfully, by the time his letter arrived and could have been acted upon, the city of New Orleans had already been saved. [434]

Despite his dire physical condition, General Jackson steeled himself and persisted in maintaining the defenses in Chalmette anticipating another assault. It would come soon enough.

January 4th . . .

Rumors persisted that the British might be opening a second front. This increased Jackson's anxiety about Chef Menteur. He lacked the troops to defend against such a threat. He might prevail over one attack at one time on one front. But should the British open a second front . . . defense was impossible. They had the men . . . he did not!

A scouting mission, led by Colonel Kemper, determined that the British had fortified a position at the junction of Bayou Mazant and the Villere Canal. Their purpose once again was to secure their lines of communication with the fleet.

Relieved on hearing this news, Jackson focused his attention on improving his defensive position at Chalmette. He would receive help when his long awaited Kentuckians entered camp. Thankfully, General John Adair arrived at Jackson's headquarters to announce the arrival of the Kentucky militia. Jackson could breathe a little easier with this news. But to his shock, of the nearly 2,250 reinforcements that arrived, only 550 were properly armed.

"Hardly, one third of the Kentucky troops, so long expected, are armed, and the arms they have are not fit for use." Jackson expressed exasperation: *". . . the defeat of our armies, and the dishonor not only of our officers commanding them, but of the nation, must inevitably be the consequence of so defective an administration."*[435]

Jackson could not believe that Kentuckians would arrive without their notorious long rifles. He immediately appealed to the Louisiana legislature for money to purchase the needed weapons. [436]

Louis Louaillier, a member of the state House of Representatives secured from the legislature $6,000 to purchase clothes and arms for these pitifully equipped warriors. Subscriptions arranged in New Orleans raised an additional $6,000. Other fund-raising ventures contributed as well providing a total sum of $16,000. [437]

They needed food, clothes, bedding, and arms. For clothes, the women of New Orleans, almost without exception dedicated their energies for days sewing jackets and pants out of available blankets for these desperate men. In one week local ladies stitched 1,200 blanket coats, 275 waistcoats, 1,127 pairs of Pantaloons, 800 shirts, 410 pairs of shoes, and a large number of mattresses from blankets. The entire city bent its energies to providing for their basic needs.[438]

Arms were a different matter. The Quartermaster in Pittsburg sought to save money by not sending the promised arms downriver by steamboat as requested, but by slow moving flatboat. They arrived after the campaign ended.

As for the remaining 1,700 members of the Kentucky militia, Jackson instantly pressed them into action near the center of his line where up to this point there was weakness. This move would prove fortuitous.

Here is where a major problem ensued that nearly caused the loss of the city. Upon bringing his troops to Chalmette, General Adair placed them with the Tennessee militia along 1,300 yards, nearly 2/3rds of the front, unprotected by artillery. They reinforced what had been the weak portion of Jackson's line. They needed guns. On January 7th, Adair approached the Mayor and Committee of Safety requesting he be given several hundred stand of arms held in reserve in the city. He argued they did no good in a warehouse.[439]

Since the arms were held for fear of an uprising in the city, the fact that the city fathers had allowed them to be given to Adair had to be kept secret. The city delivered them to the front in concealed boxes.

Unfortunately, General Jackson was not made aware of General Adair's requisition for these arms. When Jackson would later send a portion of Adair's unarmed Kentuckians to defend the Westbank, he believed they had access to these reserve arms. They did not!

Jackson also took the opportunity of a lull in action to strengthen his position. He demanded every able bodied man, free or slave, to come to Chalmette and bend his back to turn his still modest breastworks into an effective defensive barrier. He knew that the British would soon throw everything they had against his lines. If they were breached, the city of New Orleans would fall and the United States might well lose the war.

The fate of a nation depended upon this narrow Rodriquez Canal supported by a mound of mud. It had to be as strong as possible to repel a determined, attacking enemy.

American defenses on the 1st of January were weak, there being only a very small proportion of the line able to withstand the cannonballs. However, by the 8th of January, the whole extent of Jackson's line, as far as the woods, had been hardened against the enemy's artillery.

Not surprising, actions on the lakes had not ceased. On January 6th, sailing-master Johnson surprised a British supply vessel bringing food to the front. They burned it and took ten British sailors prisoner. From these captives they learned that the British were: ". . . *digging out Villere's canal, and extending it, in order to get his boats into the river.*"[440]

Next, through his other spies, General Jackson learned that soldiers and sailors were laboriously struggling to drag barges through the now widened channel to the river. All of this activity indicated an impending attack, but what form was it to take?

Jackson sent out his scouts and his officers, including his engineer Latour, to the Westbank to examine the British lines through their telescopes. It soon became apparent what the English were up to. They were preparing to send an amphibious force across the Mississippi River to assault General Morgan's position on the west bank.

But this, too, raised a question. On which side would the major assault be made? Would the main assault be delivered on Jackson's or Morgan's side of the river? General Jackson's line was defended by 3,200 men. With another 800 troops distributed about watching for other British activity. Morgan had only several hundred.

When Jackson's men discovered that the British were busily fabricating scaling-ladders and fascines (tied bundles of sugar cane 11 inches in diameter and four feet long) he knew the answer. The main attack would be at Chalmette. The fascines would be tossed into the Rodriguez Canal to act as a foundation for the scaling-ladders that would be employed to top the American breastworks allowing the British infantry to overtop his defenses.

Jackson ordered his men to scour the countryside in search of wooden planks with which to support the enemy side of his berm. The incessant rain had softened the soil. He did not want mud sliding into the canal making a British advance easier.

Jackson's line was now over a mile long and ran completely from the river to inside of the cypress swamp. In the swamp, the defenders stood in knee deep water. Jackson distributed eight artillery batteries along this line.[441]

As further security, Jackson also mounted guards about four hundred yards behind his lines to prevent any of his men from abandoning their positions. Over the past year, he had experienced soldiers attempting to leave his command. He even had several shot during the Creek Indian War! Jackson left nothing to chance.

Up to this point in time every effort of Pakenham's had failed. As his planned "easy victory" in Louisiana eluded him, his frustration and that of his army grew. New plans had to be devised. There had to be some means of undermining Jackson's defenses. His reputation and that of Great Britain could not be blemished on a sugarcane field in St. Bernard Parish, Louisiana. That was beyond comprehension.

One wonders if Pakenham ever considered his peculiar situation. Granted, Admiral Cochrane's men secretly had placed him just below New Orleans, but where? Pakenham faced a strongly defended, well engineered obstacle to his front with a river to his left and a swamp to his right. The good admiral had left him little room for land maneuver. No army commander would have permitted such a circumstance. [442]

To his advantage, on January 6th, Pakenham's forces were augmented with reinforcements for the 7th and 43rd regiments numbering 1,700 men under the command of General John Lambert. His compliment of fighting men had reached their maximum. If nothing else, Pakenham had the needed men and these reinforcements brightened the spirits of his troops.[443]

Pakenham was tired of playing games in Louisiana. He was about to take decisive action. He designed a simple and deadly plan. His new plan was worthy of the school in which Sir Edward had studied his profession. It was bold. Pakenham decided to divide his army. He planned to send part across the river. This detachment should seize the enemy's guns which had tormented him so much, and turn them against the American line itself. The remainder of the army would await the sound of gun fire on the Westbank as their signal to make a general assault along the whole of Jackson's front on the Eastbank. Pakenham planned to focus the brunt of the Eastbank attack on that portion of Jackson's line unprotected by artillery as was revealed by earlier actions. He did not know that Jackson had reinforced his part of his line with the newly arrived Tennessee and Kentucky troops. [444]

To achieve this coordinated attack, he would send a force of 1,600 men across the river to the Westbank under the ever aggressive Colonel Thornton during the early morning hours. These men would take up their positions and advance upriver toward the troubling American battery on the Westbank. At the appointed hour just before daybreak, they would launch their attack on General Morgan and Patterson's position.

When that occurred, Morgan's position could be overrun and Patterson would be forced to turn his guns away from defending the Chalmette battlefield across the river to protect his own position. This would remove the deadly cross-fire that had so hampered Pakenham's first attempted assaults.

If all worked well, Thornton might even be able to turn the Westbank battery against Jackson's own forces, thus destroying his position near the river. Having achieved that goal, Thornton was ordered to leave a small force at Patterson's Battery and advance upriver with the rest of his troops. The fact that he carried rockets with him indicates the intention to create panic by firing into the city. Less we forget, New Orleans was in many respects still made of wood! The ensuing panic in the city would create an infectious terror among the civilians manning Jackson's lines.[445]

Once these guns were taken, this would take the pressure off of Pakenham and allow him to advance Gibbs' forces to circle the American left while General Keane would threaten the American right. Gibbs would drive in with a spirited bayonet charge while the advancing 44th, furnished with the fabricated fascines, would fill the Rodriguez Canal and then place the scaling-ladders that would allow Gibbs to top the embankments.

At the same time, Colonel Rennie would advance his corps along the river batture. They would be protected between the river and the levee without fear of being decimated by a Westbank battery that now would be in British hands. Nor would they suffer fire from the Americans on Jackson's line in Chalmette. The levee would serve to protect him from this quarter. Rennie was to take Jackson's forward redoubt and turn it's guns.

The signal for attack? The main assault in Chalmette would be at the ready, positioned for attack before daybreak. When Pakenham heard the gun fire coming from Thornton's assault on Morgan, it would signal him to advance on Jackson's lines in Chalmette. It was a good plan that had every hope for success.

In summary, the British at Chalmette would coordinate their attack in two directions, along the river and near the swamp. The center would be less involved. At the same time, Thornton would fight Morgan on the Westbank. Pakenham planned for all elements to be attacking simultaneously.

Major-General Pakenham had lived up to his reputation and had devised an excellent plan, but it required careful adherence to a predetermined timetable. Every element had to work in coordinated unison . . . like a delicate timepiece . . . for victory to be achieved. But certainly, victory was attainable.

The plan might have worked . . .

But for a Piece of Wood!

Chapter 8

BUT FOR A PIECE OF WOOD . . .

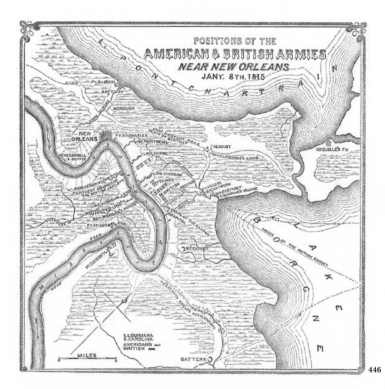

446

Large Area Map show disposition of American & British Troops

The moment had arrived. A decisive battle awaited. American and British forces had faced one another across a sugarcane field since December 23rd. For seventeen days, they fought skirmishes and traded artillery barrages. The British had probed American defenses. Americans had learned British tactics. The courtship dance had now ended . . . time for the ultimate engagement had arrived.

Both sides prepared for a battle that would determine the fate of the city of New Orleans, its port, access to the Mississippi River Basin, control over the western territories, and possession over the vast wealth trapped in the city's warehouses since the British naval blockade began. Even the legitimacy of the Louisiana Purchase lay at stake. It might well be argued that the fate of a nation hung in the balance.

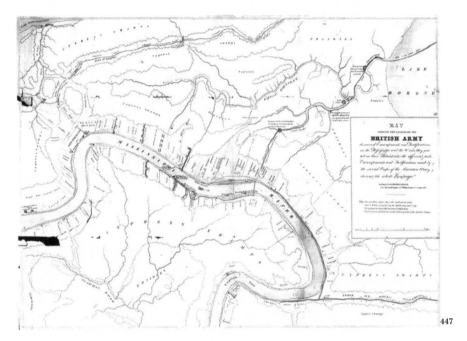

447

Map showing track of British entering and leaving campaign area and Jackson's defense lines.

The opposing camps spent the final days and hours preparing for a decisive action. His frontal attacks and artillery barrages had failed to dislodge the Americans. Now General Pakenham re-designed his battle plan. He was especially pleased with the appearance of General John Lambert who arrived on January 6th with considerable reinforcements. This gave the British a total attacking force of over 14,000 men. Fresh troops were welcomed.[448]

Pakenham had grown confident he had found the key to victory. As mentioned in the last chapter, his revised plan called for a coordinated attack on both sides of the river at the same time. To achieve this, he ordered Colonel William Thornton to flank Jackson's forces by crossing the Mississippi River at night and taking those pesky Westbank batteries before dawn. But to succeed, he had to disembark immediately after dark. The colonel's goal was to capture Patterson's battery then turn those guns against Jackson's own line closest to the river. The sound of Thornton's guns would signify that the troubling American Westbank battery was under attack, had to defend itself, and could not help Jackson.

That would signal General Pakenham to launch a forceful two pronged main assault on Jackson's main line coupled with an attack on the forward redoubt on Jackson's extreme right. This combined assault would rout the Americans and award his troops their long delayed victory.[449]

The general arranged his battle formations on the Chalmet Plantation by dividing them into three columns. However, they had to cover over 2,000 yards of a cleared sugarcane field before reaching Line Jackson. Throughout this entire time, the soldiers would be exposed to cannons firing round balls and grape-shot along with the steady fusillade of Kentucky long rifles. [450]

General Keane would make a demonstration or sham attack upon Jackson's right with the 93rd and 5th West India regiments. His was a "follow-up force" ready to take advantage of any situation that might arise by shifting to the advantage. General Gibbs, with the main attack, would force the American left, on what he believed was a weak point in Jackson's line, employing the 4th, 44th, and 21st Regiments. Meanwhile, Colonel Rennie, taking advantage of Patterson's now silenced battery across the river achieved by Thornton, would use the cover of the levee to attack Jackson on his extreme right along the river using the 21st Royal Fusiliers, the 43rd, 93rd. and 1st West Indian Regiment. General Lambert would keep the rest of the forces in reserve awaiting a call to come to assistance when and where needed. [451]

All told British records disclose a total of 4893 rank and file British soldiers in the initial assault supported by 200 seamen and 400 marines for a total effective force of 5,493 men, excluding reserves. This number also excludes executive officers and non-commissioned officers. The American count of British forces is significantly higher.[452]

Next, Pakenham ordered Colonel Mullins of the 44th to make the ultimate sacrifice. His division would move to the forward redoubt before dawn where the recently made ladders and fascines had been stashed. After taking them up, they would assume a position in advance of Gibbs' attacking force running ahead with their bundles to fill the ditch in front of Jackson's breastworks. The purpose here was that the fascines would be thrown into the canal then the boarding ladders placed on top to allow Gibbs's men to charge up and over Jackson's breastworks in quick order.

Pakenham had given Colonel Mullins a critical mission. Failure to succeed would doom Gibb's assault. Mullins, son of a lord, would behave most dishonorably. He hoped to join his wife after the battle. She was an elegant woman presently waiting in the fleet. They planned to avail themselves of the pleasures waiting in New Orleans.

Mullins, accustomed to a privileged life, recognized the "*hopelessness of the enterprise.*" To be ordered to lead the attack carrying only bundles of sugarcane and ladders in place of arms was sure suicide. In clear hearing of his men and other officers, he declared his regiment had been "*. . . ordered to execution.*"[453]

Sergeant Cooper did not think this decision wise and counseled Pakenham accordingly. The 44th had never distinguished itself as a storming party, which requires a special degree of spirit de corps. Pakenham agreed and expressed the same to Harry Smith stating that these two regiments had never been employed in this manner before. Despite reservations . . . Pakenham issued the orders to the 44th under Colonel Mullins to lead Gibbs' charge carrying only fascines and ladders.[454]

The Americans spent the evenings before January 8th making final defensive preparations. On the 6th, some of Jackson's officers suggested that he create a forward redoubt on his right, near the river and forward of his lines. Jackson doubted the advantage of this advanced position, fearing that it might fall into British hands where they could turn his own guns against his lines. Jackson's fears would prove to be justified because the British would target this position seeing its advantage.

Despite his misgivings, his officers prevailed, and Jackson allowed it to be erected. It was constructed with three artillery embrasures which commanded the road, the river-bank, and flanked the front of the lines. The redoubt lay forward of the original defense lines with a wooden plank walkway connecting the two. It more resembled an island than an integral part of the breastwork. [455]

456

Americans Digging out Rodriguez Canal

Spies, deserters, and direct observations had revealed that the British were hard at work bringing up barges and digging out the Villere Canal. At the same time they were constructing boarding ladders and fashioning fascines. This meant that Pakenham intended to strike on two fronts. Jackson, however, did not know which was the main point of attack?

That is why Jackson was overjoyed by the timely arrival of the long awaited Kentucky reinforcements who arrived on January 4th. General John Adair announced the approach of over 2,250 back woodsmen under the command of Major General John Thomas. [457]

Although shocked when he inspected the new arrivals: *"Hardly one third of the Kentucky troops, so long expected, are armed, and they arms they have are not fit for use."* He pushed them to the front on both sides of the river:[458]

Jackson sent 700 to the Westbank and distributed the remaining along his own lines, particularly in that area to the left of his centerline where his ranks had been thin. Their timely arrival would prove critical because they occupied that part of Jackson's line determined by the British as being weak and subject to their main attack.

Had these men been able to take possession of the weapons held in New Orleans that might have altered the outcome of what was about to unfold. However, as mentioned, those weapons had already been distributed to Adair's men in Chalmette. These men would cross the river and enter the line unarmed! This miscommunication would contribute to the coming Westbank debacle.

Meanwhile, on January 6th, sailing-master Johnson departed Chef-Menteur with three small boats. He succeeded in burning a British brig ferrying supplies of biscuit and rum on her way to Bayou Bienvenue. His action deprived the British of needed supplies and provided General Jackson with ten prisoners.[459]

The General strengthened his position in Chalmette. His line now extended a mile and a half from the river into the swamp as far as possible. His main breastworks had been increased in height and the Rodriguez Canal dug deeper. But despite these efforts, his breastworks were only five feet high. Reports that Jackson had constructed an impenetrable obstacle are exaggerated.[460]

Jackson positioned his forces along Line Jackson. Eight batteries of various sizes were distributed along his front. He possessed one 32-pounder, three 24-pounders, one 18-pounder, three 12-pounders, two 6-pounder long guns, one 9½ and one 6" howitzer for a total of twelve pieces of artillery. However, because of the soft terrain, about 1,300 yards lacked artillery. That is where Jackson deployed the Tennesseans and Kentuckians.

Jackson's whole force in Chalmette numbered about 4,000 men, but only 3,200 were actually manning the front lines. The Adjutant-General's Office would later report that Jackson possessed nearly 5,200 men at arms. Much of the confusion stems from published British estimates designed to make their defeat less humiliating. The British, on the other hand, argue that Jackson had significantly more combatants than stated and they had far less than reported by the Americans.[461]

Jackson divided his troops into two divisions along his front. To the right Daquin, Lacoste, Plauche, and Beale's Rifles commanded the line. He placed Generals Carroll and Coffee to his left. He positioned his reserves in the rear under General Adair. The reserves, as mentioned earlier, had just received delivery of their arms on the night of January 7th. [462]

Recognizing the threat to the Westbank, Jackson had sent those unfortunate reinforcements across the river to General Morgan and Commodore Patterson. Although he remained uncertain where the main attack might come, he had to be prepared to defend both fronts.

In a dispatch dated January 7th, Jackson contacted General Morgan about the defense of the Westbank. In it he stated: *"I beg that you will continue your usual diligence in inspecting the movements of the enemy and keep me constantly advised of them."* He also agrees with Morgan that Fort Leon downriver should be further strengthened and raises concern about the slow movement to achieve the same: *". . . you will therefore attend to that matter . . ."*[463]

Additionally, Colonel Bartholomew Shambaugh communicated to the camp on the Westbank that they should be held in every readiness and have two days provisions available for every man in order to meet any attack. [464]

Commodore Patterson had spent all the time available constructing an effective battery using the cannons and gun crews from the *Louisiana*. He knew his position would play a critical role defending Jackson's line across the river. He was not expecting to defend his own position on the Westbank.

Morgan, on the other hand, had the duty to protect both Patterson and the Westbank. Concern about Morgan's position caused Jackson to dispatched his trusted engineer Arsene' de Latour to the Westbank to help plan the defenses. Latour examined the landscape and sought to locate the most effective position for Morgan to establish his defense.

Morgan had set his line at Raquet's Canal, about 300 yards in advance of Patterson's battery. Morgan had only about 420 men: 260 militiamen who were later joined by Col. Z. Cavelliers' 160 men from the Louisiana Militia. On January 6th, Colonel Dejean's regiment completed his line. With this weak force, Morgan sought to defend only 200 yards of entrenchment near the river while leaving over 2,000 yards to his right undefended. The Westbank defensive line was protected with about four yards per man.

Latour carefully examined the Westbank terrain then determined that Morgan's lines should be moved back to a position that left far less open land, leaving only a total of 900 yards, to be defended. He then returned to Jackson's headquarters. Unaccountably, Morgan refused to follow Latour's suggestion. He returned to his original position. This would create problems.[465]

Confusion reigned among Jackson's officers. Where would the British strike first and hardest. It was not until the afternoon of January 7th that Jackson knew for certain that his lines would bear the main assault.[466]

Half the troops passed the night behind the breastwork dutifully scanning the battlefield. The rest would try to catch up on sleep. These men alternated with one another on watch. Everyone waited for the coming day with anxiety and impatience. Yet they bravely held their positions expecting to be vigorously attacked in the morning and knowing that the enemy had from 12,000 to 15,000 bayonets to bring into action, supported by over 3,000 sailors, marines and artillery. [467]

After a very active day, Jackson finally laid down to relax on a sofa in the damaged McCarty Plantation. This would be his only moments of rest.

Commodore Patterson began hearing significant noise from the British camp across the river. This concerned him, so he traveled down river on the Westbank to a point directly opposite the British headquarters at the Villere Plantation. What he discovered shocked him.

He heard British soldiers laboring through the night widening and deepening the Villere Canal so it could accommodate the boats and soldiers for the planned invasion of his side of the river: Patterson could hear almost everything that passed on the Eastbank. Furthermore, by the light of the camp fires he could see British soldiers drawn up along the levee. He heard the cries of the sailors as they struggled to bring the boats along the shallow, caving canal, and their shouts of joy as each boat was launched with a loud splash into the Mississippi. From the great commotion, and the sound of so many voices, it was obvious that a main body of the enemy was about to cross. [468]

Patterson first thought about sending down his ship *Louisiana* to impede this attack, but soon remembered that he had stripped her of her guns for his battery and the ship itself was now being employed as a powder magazine. He had no means of stopping this aggressive action. Jackson had no control over the Mississippi River. Once the British launched their boats . . . the river became theirs. [469]

The Commodore immediately sent Shepherd across the river to Jackson's headquarters to inform him of his discovery and seek reinforcements. Patterson was now convinced that the main attack would be directed against the Westbank.

About 1:00 A.M., Shepherd arrived, entered the command post, and urgently requested to see Jackson. Commodore Patterson had sent him to awaken the general with the news that Morgan's position would likely be the first to come under attack. Morgan requested additional reinforcements. [470]

Jackson ordered Morgan to calm down. *"Tell General Morgan that he is mistaken. The main attack will be on this side and I have no men to spare. He must maintain his position at all hazards."* Jackson knew his lines, not Morgan's, would be the main point of attack. But he was aware that Morgan would have to defend his position at all costs. [471]

Jackson did not wholly neglect Morgan, however. He informed him that help was on the way. After all, he had ordered General Adair to send an additional 500 men from his reserves to support the Westbank. Unfortunately, this detachment, under the command of Colonel Davis, composed that unarmed force of Kentuckian referenced before. Making matters worse, they were delayed in crossing the river. He was not aware he was sending unarmed men to the front!

They did received all available weapons from the naval arsenal on the Westbank, but that amounted to little more than vintage muskets, some with common pebbles in place of flints in their locks. Only 260 of Davis's 500 men were even armed. Furthermore, they arrived tired and hungry after having finally crossed the river and been hurried forward marching five miles to their positions. They arrived only moments before the enemy's landing. [472]

As the coming day unfolded, Jackson learned to his chagrin that he had not paid sufficient attention to his Westbank defense.

Now fully awake, Jackson then turned to his officers: *"Gentlemen, we have slept enough. Arise, for the enemy will be upon us in a few minutes"*

Jackson walked his line inspecting his troops and reassuring his men. Upon reaching the battery manned by Dominique Youx, the Baratarian, Jackson observed them making coffee. They offered him some, which he took: *"That smells like better coffee than we can get. Where did you get such fine coffee? Maybe you smuggled it?"*[473]

To which Youx responded in this thick accent: *"Mebbe so, Zehnerale!"* The coffee was described as being as black as tar and its aroma could be relished twenty yards away.

As he walked the line reassuring his men, many were surprised how many he knew by name. He knew fully one half of the Kentuckians and every Tennessean. This should come as no surprise because he had spent so many months in the saddle with them fighting the Creek Wars.

Pakenham had devised a sound plan with every reason for success. Unfortunately, impatience, incompetence, arrogance, hesitation, cowardice, and finally indecisiveness rendered his carefully scripted design for victory a failure of historic proportions.

His problems arose almost immediately.

474

Admiral Sir Alexander Cochrane

A stubborn Admiral Cochrane insisted upon widening and deepening the Villere Canal to bring his boats forward. The army suggested rolling the barges on logs just as they had brought up the heavy artillery. But Cochrane remained unmoved. Since the maneuver involved unloading ships, moving boats, and crossing water it became a Royal Navy operation. It would be done the navy way under his command.

To achieve this arduous task, British commanders divided their already exhausted and dispirited men into four companies working in rotation. The British army became a digging machine. With pick and shovel, these men slaved to dig out the canal in time for the attack: *"The fatigue undergone during the prosecution of this attempt no words can sufficiently describe, yet it was pursued without repining, and at length, by unremitting exertions, they succeeded in effecting their purpose by the 6th of January."*[475]

Pakenham's scheme should have worked. But Cochrane's stubbornness doomed it. Once the canal had been completed the plan called for the barges to be brought forward. When they were in place, the soldiers were to construct a dam at the back of their new structure. Then diggers would cut the river's levee and allow the entering water to float the barges. The trapped water would raise the boats. Then the troops, composed of Thornton's 85th, some marines, and sailors would effortlessly row with muffled oars across the river and surprise the Americans. Pakenham designed the assault on the Westbank for 1,400 men.

This simple plan too soon began to fail. The high water that had initially washed in when Jackson cut the levee in late December had subsided. The river was lower now and so was the canal. They had to dig deeper. This made the work of bringing up the barges nearly impossible.

The soil was soft. As the British struggled to bring up their barges the canal sides caved in trapping some of the larger vessels making it impossible for the smaller ones behind to gain position.

The time and effort it took to complete the task "Cochrane's way" cost the British valuable time and prevented the needed number of barges from arriving. As time ticked away Thornton became anxious. The appointed hour for departure came and passed with Thornton and his forces still on the Eastbank.

When Pakenham awakened in the early morning hours, he was shocked to discover that a critical component of his plan had not been completed. Success required that Thronton's forces would depart near midnight, leaving them sufficient time to cross the river, form ranks, advance, and take Patterson's battery. A stunned Pakenham met with an impatient Thornton still on the Eastbank. Thornton was forced to proceed with only 600 men instead of the 1,400 troops Pakenham's plan required because too few barges had arrived at the levee.

The reduced forces took to the boats. Then, when the British cut the levee, the water did indeed rush in and float the manned barges. However, the dam to the rear collapsed, as Pakenham had feared, allowing the water to run out into the marsh at the rear of the plantation. The boats then settled back down into the muck.

British soldiers manhandled the barges through the mud into the river where finally Thornton and his now reduced command of 600 men instead of 1,400 began to paddle to the other side. Even here an unanticipated problem arose.

Cochrane compounded his errors. He failed to gauge the current of the Mississippi River. "But for a Piece of Wood", the British may have carried New Orleans. Had he merely tossed a piece of driftwood into the current he could have calculated the drift, which was about five miles per hour. He then would have realized it was virtually impossible for Thornton's men to row against such a current in a timely manner. By failing to perform this simple task, Cochrane condemned Pakenham's last hope of a successful campaign to utter failure.

Thornton's men would have had to leave much earlier if they harbored any hope of success. This bold soldier now faced a major problem. Already delayed, Thornton pushed off with less than half of his planned force to begin his journey to the other side of the river. His small flotilla, under the command of Captain Roberts of the Royal Navy, immediately found themselves in trouble. Despite their frantic rowing, "Old Big Strong" (the Indian name for the Mississippi River) was carrying them rapidly downstream. They were headed in the wrong direction![476]

General Pakenham waited a while on the riverbank as Thornton's flotilla paddled off soon to be lost in the thick fog that blanketed the river. He listened for any indication of their arrival on the West Bank. Unfortunately, he failed to realize that the river's current had taken this flanking force rapidly downstream.

By the time Thornton made landfall on the Westbank, he was one and a half miles downriver from his appointed destination. Worse, before even disembarking, they heard the reports of gunfire and the glare of a Congreve rocket signaling the commencement of hostilities on the Chalmette plain. Action on the Eastbank was designed to be triggered by the sound of HIS guns! Not the other way around.

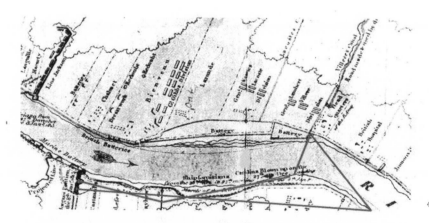

477

This map illustrates the problem faced by Colonel Thornton and his forces on the night of January 7th. The green line, which is the course he actually took is not to scale. He ended up nearly 1.5 miles below his intended landing.

Thornton's men were exhausted from paddling. But despite their fatigue, the colonel pressed to rally his troops and force marched them as quickly as possible to make up for lost time. They advanced along the river's bank flanked by their boats each mounting a carronade in the bow. What then occurred on the Westbank is a tale all its own (see Chapter 9).

As Thornton disappeared into the fog, General Keane approached Pakenham and suggested that the omens were not right. Victory hung on the success of Thornton's flanking maneuver. Should that fail, Patterson's effective cross-fire would not be silenced. Only an unsupported frontal assault remained. That would likely be doomed to failure as had all the earlier similar attempts. Wait one day, Keane suggested, and all will be in place. The Americans lacked the assets to defend both sides of the river simultaneously. The situation called for patience.

Pakenham had reached his limit of patience. There would be no further delays. Everything on the Eastbank was ready. Recalling his forces once again might do irretrievable damage to the morale of his men. Besides, he still held out hope that Thornton might succeed. Turning away from the river he said: *"I will wait my plan no longer."*[478]

He now turned attention to the matters immediately at hand.

Pakenham had arranged his men in their assault positions. They wore their heavy haversacks in proper form with bayonets fixed. They were standing ready in the dark, cold, foggy early morning hours waiting for the signal to advance. The rifle fire of Thornton's attack would provide that signal. Minutes passed . . . hours passed . . . silence . . . only silence.

The British had held their position since 4:00 A.M. Here they waited. The young soldiers were excited with anticipation which perhaps also served to conceal the real nature of their feelings. The seasoned veterans augured ill of the coming attack. Their battle hardened experience and the events of the past days assured them that dawn would bring much bloodshed and suffering. [479]

Perhaps none were as anxious as the 44th Regiment under command of Colonel Mullins. His detachment had been ordered to secure the ladders and fascines. They were to approach the American lines in advance of Gibbs' attack. Mullen's himself questioned the efficacy of his orders: *"My regiment has been ordered to execution. Their dead bodies are to be used as a bridge for the rest of the army to march over."*[480]

Recognizing the dangers inherent in this entire operation, other officers likewise presumed doom. Colonel Dale of the 93rd Highlanders, ". . . *a brave and thoughtful officer,"* was asked his opinion about the success of the venture by the company surgeon. He turned to Dr. Dempster of his regiment, and giving him his watch and a letter said: *"Deliver this to my wife—I shall die at the head of my regiment."*[481]

A number of the younger officers expressed greater excitement and were less inclined to consider death. Their minds focused more on a grand victory with the "*booty and beauty*" to be had in New Orleans. The heroic dreams of youth eclipsed the horrific realities envisioned by seasoned veterans.[482]

As the British took their places, Jackson's advanced forces silently withdrew from their forward positions and returned to their own lines. They informed the general that they had perceived ". . . *the enemy moving forward in great force.*"[483]

The Americans sprang to action, the bold banner of their national flag unfurled in the center of their line. Some soldiers stood atop the breastwork struggling to peer through the mist. A frosty fog covered the field which made viewing their opponents impossible. Nevertheless, they manned their positions, loaded their muskets, charged their cannons, and quietly awaited the coming dawn. The sun's rays would eventually melt the mist revealing their enemy. They must be ready.

On the Eastbank of the river, Pakenham still waited . . . expecting at any moment to hear the sound of Thornton's guns on the opposite shore which would signal that Patterson's battery had been neutralized. Minutes turned to hours, and no sound of Thornton's attack reached the troops on the Eastbank. Time continued to pass, the sun ascended, the temperature rose, and the fog began to dissipate . . . melted away by the warming air. Still, no sounds from across the river.

As the mist cleared, Jackson's batteries began to make out the British formations nearly 500 yards away. A long red line appeared before them. American Lieutenant Spotts of battery #7 responded first. He opened fire with his heavy gun.[484]

The opening salvo had been fired. Suddenly, battle was joined! The noise, chaos and confusion that so marks a battlefield suddenly erupted.[485]

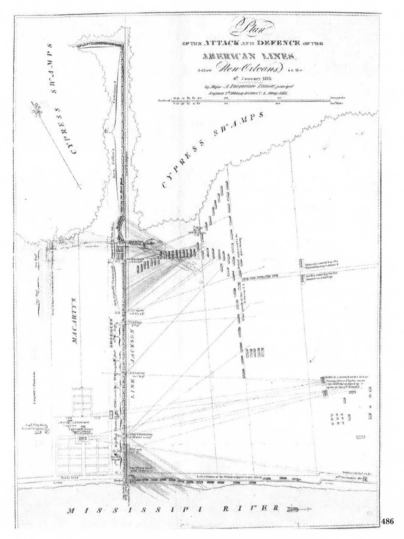

British attack of January 8ᵗʰ on American Lines

The British responded with a Congreve rocket fired from the swamp toward the river. This signaled the opening of the British offensive. The first rocket was soon followed by a second rocket ordering the attack on the right. Upon seeing these signals one of the surviving officers sadly referenced: *". . . that the fatal, ever-fatal rocket should be discharged as a signal to begin the assault on the left."*[487]

The long line of Redcoats divided into columns and began its advance. Unaccountably, Pakenham had required his men to advance at a slow march with full packs on their backs. Gibbs headed toward the swamp with the 44th in front followed by the 21st and 4[th.] But the 44th had failed to retrieve the ladders and fascines as ordered.

Gibbs could not stall any longer waiting for the 44th to perform its duty while he stood in an open field under a fusillade of lead. He ordered his men to advance anyway. They approached Jackson's left commanded by Generals Coffee and Carroll. Meanwhile, Jackson's batteries, including that of Morgan and Patterson on the Westbank, continued to hurl their fury across the river into the British lines.

The English continued their advance over the torn bodies of their wounded and dead comrades. Their formations were fixed and their pace carefully regulated . . . so very proper! *"Whole platoons were prostrated, when their places were instantly filled by others, and the column pressed on, without pause of recoil, toward the batteries on the left and the long and weaker line covered by the Tennesseans and Kentuckians."* The British lines near the swamp wavered. The storm of artillery hurled at them forced them to take cover behind a bulge in the woods to their left. (Some maps dispute this aspect of the terrain, British maps do not show it, Latour's map does)[488]

Gibbs' troops endured withering fire from canister and grape-shot, in addition to continuous fire from infantry. The carnage was dreadful as wide swaths were carved into Gibbs' lines. Confusion ensued because the 44th had neglected to bring up the fascines and scaling-ladders as ordered. These assets were the key elements of the attack. Gibb's assault force was forced to retreat.

Gibbs had forewarning of the potential for this problem. Major Sir John Tylden of the 43rd regiment stated:

"On the morning of the 8th of January, I was in the field as a senior officer on the adjutant-general's department. I accompanied Sir Edward Pakenham, shortly after four o'clock, to the house of Major-General Gibbs. Immediately upon his arrival, General Gibbs reported to Sir Edward Pakenham, in my presence, that Colonel Mullins had neglected to obey the order given to him the evening before, in not having his regiment at the head of the column, with the fascines and ladders, but that he had immediately, on finding it out, sent an officer to the regiment to hurry them on that the mistake might be rectified. General Pakenham then ordered me to find out the 44th regiment, and to know if they had got the fascines and ladders . . . I did so and found the 44th regiment moving off at the redoubt; just before day, in a most irregular and unsoldierlike manner with the fascines and ladders."[489]

Colonel Mullins failed to perform his duty. Whether this was a result of confusion or cowardice is a matter of conjecture. Whatever the case: *"Instead of perceiving everything in readiness for the assault, he*

[Pakenham] saw his troops in battle array, but not a ladder or fascine on the field."

The British court of inquiry held in London after the war ended reported:

"The 44th regiment, owing chiefly to the negligence of its commander, failed to be in readiness with the fascines and ladders. These had been placed in a redoubt, 1200 yards from the enemy's lines; by which redoubt the 44th, in its way to camp to its station, passed, till it arrived at the advanced battery about 500 yards nearer to the enemy's lines." It seems they simply walked past the proper redoubt in the dark and arrived at a more forward redoubt, one lacking the necessary ladders and fascines. [490]

The 44th either did not understand their orders or simply failed to obey them. Whatever the case, Mullin's soldiers had placed themselves in the fore of Gibb's attacking line armed and ready to attack, but without the required ladders and fascines. [491]

Furious, Pakenham galloped across the battlefield in search of Mullins. Upon finding him he ordered the 44th to retrieve their ladders and fascines and take their proper place in the advance of Gibb's men. Without these essential assets, there was no way to bridge the Rodriguez Canal or mount the breastworks. [492]

Once equipped with the necessary scaling equipment, the 44th returned to their position in Gibb's line. Gibbs now attempted a second attack.

According to the testimony of a British officer present:

"The misunderstanding, for such it was, being now, for the first time, cleared up, the commanding officer of the 44th, lieutenant-colonel Mullins sent back 300 men, under Lieutenant Debbeig, to bring up the fascines and ladders. Before the 44th returned, the firing commenced; and many of the men threw down their "heavy" loads; took up their muskets. There was not one ladder placed." [493]

Although Mullins did eventually obey his orders, it was too late. The ladders and fascines achieved little more than decorating a bloody battlefield. The moment had been lost. During the delay, *". . . a dreadful fire was accordingly opened upon them, and they were mowed down by the hundreds, while they stood waiting for orders."* Ultimately, some elements of the 44th would toss all equipment aside and join the general attack. The British assault stalled. [494]

Their courage and determination faltered. Panic took hold as men sought some means of saving their lives with little regard for the success of the attack. General Gibbs approached General Pakenham and reported: *"I am sorry to have to report to you, the troops will not obey me, they will not follow me."*

Pakenham, alarmed by the confusion caused by Mullin's cowardice, charged across the battlefield to *".. . rally his broken troops."* He *"pulled off his hat and rode to the head of the column and cheered the men on . . . ."*[495] While approaching the disordered 44th, which had returned to the battlefield, he called out for Mullins to step forward . . . Mullins had disappeared.

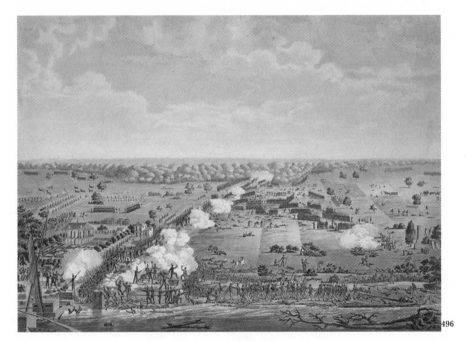

[496]

Painting depicting January 8th battle in Chalmette

General Gibbs, angry at what had occurred cried out: *"Let me live until tomorrow and I'll hang him to the highest tree in that swamp."* He then ordered his men forward without the 44[th]s scaling equipment. In tight order they approached the American lines cheering again while the American artillery cut *". . . great lanes through the column from front to rear and huge gaps in their flanks."* [497]

According to Colonel Dickson's diary: *"Gibb's column stopped advancing, stood still, and fired at the enemy's line, thus throwing away the foothold gained for them by their advance companies. This was the most fatal thing they could have done; Had they pushed on, their losses could hardly have been greater than they were, while a determined effort would have carried the enemy entrenchment and brought about the cessation of the fire that withered them."*[498]

The British troops advanced in the face of unspeakable carnage. Torn bodies were flung about by grapeshot and cannon balls. The dead and dying littered the battlefield. Yet they continued their advance toward the American lines, fully knowing what likely awaited them once they closed on Jackson's breastworks.

As they approached the American line, the well aimed cannon shot shattered the British lines: *". . . cutting great lanes in the column from front to rear, and tossing men and parts of men aloft, or hurling them far on one side."*[499]

Throughout the attack a young Free Man of Color, the drummer boy named Jordan Noble, maintained a constant beat to arms. Locals celebrated his heroism of that day, and he would later become a fixture in many later New Orleans parades. [500]

No one can question the bravery and discipline of the British army. Despite the unquestionable carnage they experienced, they bravely persisted in advancing . . . until, of course, it became obvious to all that the American lines were impregnable while hurling massive amounts of cannon balls, grape-shot, and rifle slugs into their ranks.

Nevertheless, they attempted to maintain their lines and push forward sustaining even more massive losses with each passing moment. Later some would criticize this mode of attack. They would argue that had Pakenham not encumbered his men with equipment and a slow march but had instead employed a strong bayonet charge, he would have prevailed. But *"the weight of the knapsacks prevented our springing up . . ."* over the breastworks.[501]

An author, writing under the pseudonym "Cold Steel", also refers to the advantages of the American rifles as having proven: . . . *a far more destructive force."* The British regulars certainly experienced that.

TThis picture portrays General Gibbs' attack. Not the
44ʰ with ladders and fascines before him

When they got within 200 yards of the American lines, the
Tennesseans and Kentuckians fully revealed themselves from behind
the breast works. What had previously been Jackson's weak link in his
line had become a strongly defended position. The British lacked this
critical intelligence.

Arranged in four ranks, they poured a murderous fire into the
advancing British. The first line fired then move to the back to
reload. They were followed in turn by the second rank, then the third,
and so on. These revolving ranks had the net effect of continuous,
unrelenting and accurate fire power. British survivors referred to this
experience as: "*rolling thunder.*"

There were nearly 1,986 rifles along the line. Initially, the smoke
from the cannons blocked the view of the approaching enemy.
Jackson ordered the cannons silenced. Once the air cleared of smoke,
General Carroll held his fire until the enemy came within close range
then the order "*Fire! Fire!*" rang out. Although adapted to artillery
fire, the British soldiers were not accustomed to being individually
targeted. The British line wavered. They could not take the intensity
of the incoming barrages. In five minutes, the whole front of their
formation was shaken as if by an earthquake. The officer corps had
been decimated. In less than ten minutes the first line of the enemy's
column had disappeared, exposing the second which was about a
hundred yards in its rear.[502]

The artillery once again began to hurl grape, canister, and shot into their ranks. Reports from the field indicate that the action did not last more than twenty-five minutes. By that time, half of the approaching British soldiers lay dead or wounded on the ground, and no mounted officers could be found. The survivors were rapidly retreating to the rear.[503]

Lieutenant Colonel Jones, commanding the 21st, provides a personal account of the opening salvos:

"We were ordered to proceed in the same manner and to the same place we had got to before. After pushing through the wood, with great difficulty, we approached that part of the enemy's line we formerly found unprotected. A tremendous fire of grape and musketry was opened on us which killed and wounded a great many men, and we found, with all our efforts, that on this part of the line it was impossible to make any impression. Jones was wounded towards the enemy's extreme left, when cheering on his men. We remained under fire a considerable time, and made several vain attempts to get over, when a staff officer came up and ordered us to retire into the wood."[504]

Gibbs' line was about to falter. As they approached the ditch some officers were heard to cry out: *"Where are the 44th! If we get to the ditch, we have no means of crossing and scaling the lines."* Then the cry went out that the 44th was finally advancing under direct command of Pakenham himself with the needed fascines and ladders to overcome the American breast works.

An angry Pakenham had taken charge of the attack, directing them to the front. Waving his hat and urging his men forward, Pakenham suffered his first wound; a musket ball shattered his right arm. Soon more officers fell until there were not enough left to command. [505]

Some questions swirl about Pakenham's first wound. According to a letter Jackson sent years later to then President James Monroe, he identified the shooter: *"I heard a single rifle shot from a group of country carts we had been using and a moment thereafter I saw Pakenham reel and pitch out of his saddle. I always believed he fell from a bullet of a Free Man of Color, who was a famous rifle shot."* However, Pakenham was shot on the left of the American line while the Free Men of Color were stationed to the center and right. [506]

The carnage continued. Unlike the gamesmanship of Europe, Americans were Indian fighters. They paid no respect to rank. In fact, they employed their highly accurate long rifles to target officers specifically. Gradually Pakenham's command structure began to evaporate. Columns dissolved into detachments. Some even sought the protection of an area of the wooded swamp that protruded into the battlefield. Others sought cover among the dead and wounded who riddled the battlefield.

There they were again rallied when General Gibbs cried out *"Here come the 44th! Here come the 44th!"* They threw down their knapsacks and charged Carroll's position on the American left. Keane, seeing the possibility of a breakthrough on the American left, dispensed with the planned order of battle and moved obliquely across the battlefield exposing his men to the full line of American fire. He sought to reinforce Gibbs attack.[507]

The British were encouraged to see the 93rd Highlanders marching to support their position. With Gibbs commanding the British right and the Highlanders in clear view, the column was ready. Gibbs ordered Major Whittaker of the regiment to advance. Almost immediately on giving this order, Gibbs was mortally wounded in the abdomen. He was removed from the battlefield in excruciating pain and suffered through the night. He died the following morning.

As the column advanced, they faced a 32 pounder *"loaded to the muzzle with musket balls"* that fired directly into their ranks at point-blank range right into the head of the assault force. It cut a swath through the lines killing nearly 200 men. *"The smoke was so great that we could not see our two companies, which had been sent in advance; but those brave men, under their gallant leader, passed on, into the ditch."* They cut steps in the parapet with the hopes of scaling it.[508]

Major Duncan McDougal of the 85th regiment was aid de camp to Pakenham. He accompanied him throughout the action of January 8th. *"The column of attack appeared to be moving in a regular manner . . . However, a firing commenced; and, presently afterwards, I saw many individuals of the 44th regiment, as well as a group of three or four, scattered over the field, some of them running to the rear with fascines on their shoulders"*[509]

Pakenham was shocked at this occurrence. He could not imagine British soldiers acting in such a dishonorable manner in the face of the enemy. He turned to the men and said: *"For shame, recollect you are British soldiers; this is the road you ought to take!"* But his plea availed him not. Even their commanding General could not rally these broken men.[510]

Pakenham turned to Sir John Tylden and ordered General Lambert to bring up his reinforcements. The order was never transmitted. When the bugler raised his arm to signal Lambert, he was struck by a rifle ball and the bugle tumbled from his wounded arm. Lambert remained in the rear having never heard the call.

Pakenham placed himself in front of his troops and was able to gain some control over the deteriorating situation despite his wound and began to move the column forward under his personal command.

When he had gone a mere thirty to forty yards, his white horse was shot out from under him. McDougall rode up to him and surrendered his own horse to the general, a small Creole pony, and helped him mount it

In the midst of the horror and confusion, Pakenham, unable to manage his own horse because of wounds, was being led through the maelstrom by his aide, McDougal. Suddenly, the frightful crash of grapeshot struck, as Pakenham shouted encouragement to his men.

"Suddenly, there came a terrible crashing of round and grape-shot through the ranks that scattered dead men all around him. One of the balls passed through his thigh, killed his horse, and brought both to the ground. Pakenham was caught in the arms of his faithful aide, Captain M'Dougall . . . mortally wounded."[511]

A ball of grapeshot had penetrated the General's thigh and killed a second horse. As he tumbled from his mount into his aid's arms *". . . another ball struck him in the groin, which produced an immediate paralysis."* A mortally wounded General Sir Edward Pakenham, bleeding profusely, was brought to the rear and placed under a live-oak tree. The surgeon arrived in time to examine him and declare his wounds mortal. He gasped a few breaths and never saying a word, soon died in Captain McDougall's arms.

[512]

This painting shows Major-General Pakenham sustaining his mortal wound. He is seen falling from his horse.

". . . the fall of their leader, deprived the column of its best chance of recovering success. On his fall, the firing recommenced with all its fury, and, beyond the spot where the General led them the head of the column did not advance . . . At no period in the field did I see any part of the 44th regiment in body . . . It is my opinion, that the whole confusion of the column proceeded from the original defective formation of the 44th."[513]

Major General Sir Edward Pakenham, brother-in-law of the Duke of Wellington, hero of the Battle of Salamaca, veteran of the Peninsula Campaign against Napoleon, and commander of the invasion force attacking New Orleans had met a cruel fate on a sugarcane field in St. Bernard Parish, Louisiana.

McDougal, Pakenham's aid, went even further in his condemnation of the 44th. *"Had it not been for the misbehavior of the 44th regiment, Sir Edward Pakenham's life might have been spared; and, with such an officer to command in chief, the day must have been ours.*"[514]

Further to Jackson's left, elements of Coffee's brigade came under attack by Lieutenant Colonel Jones of the 4th who penetrated the swamp seeking to turn Jackson's left flank as General Gibbs had nearly achieved on December 28th. They succeeded in gaining some ground before sinking in the soft mud and were eventually either captured or killed by the Tennesseans *"who astonished the Britons by the squirrel-like agility with which they jumped from log to log, and their alligator-like facility of moving through the water, bushes, and mud.*"[515]

Although Jackson occupied that portion of his line where the Free People of Color had been positioned, he makes no mention of their activities in his report. Nevertheless, Vincent Nolte of Plauches' battalion reported that the *". . . New Orleans colored regiment was so anxious for glory that they could not be prevented from advancing from our breastworks and exposing themselves.*" In the action, Sergeant Belton Savary was badly wounded and died two days later. One third of the wounded on January 8th were from the Black regiments as was one of the thirteen killed.[516]

General Keane pushed forward with the gallant 93rd Highlanders. These brave men stormed forward in support of Gibbs in the full force of Carroll's muskets. Colonel Dale fulfilled his prophecy when he was felled by grapeshot. General Keane suffered a serious shot through the neck. Though able to survive the wound, he would be taken from the battlefield soon after Pakenham, wholly incapable of offering any assistance or advice.

The 93rd, now under the command of Major Creagh, continued its slow march across the field of battle subjecting itself to continuous fire. Then they suddenly responded to an order to halt and stood within one hundred yards of the American lines. The Americans looked on dismayed as the Highlanders just stood there taking fire and not moving a muscle. They had been ordered to "halt", and they had halted. Then their commander was killed. Nearly five hundred of their numbers were felled before these brave soldiers broke and ran to the rear.

Command then fell to Major "Wilky" Wilkinson, the only ranking officer left in the field of battle. Under his command, the broken ranks attempted to scale the American breast works. As he climbed the American defenses and raised his head over the summit, ". . . *a dozen guns were brought to bear against him, and the exposed portions of his body were riddled with bullets.*"[517]

With what little strength he had remaining, he tumbled over the parapet into the American lines where the Kentuckians and Tennesseans ". . . *carried him to a place of shelter.*" His bearers gently laid him down saying: *"Bear up my dear fellow; you are too brave to die."* In response, Wilkinson responded: *"It is all over with me. You can render me a favor; it is to communicate to my commander that I fell on your parapet, and died like a soldier and a true Englishmen."* The assault failed and Wilkinson, too, sacrificed his life.[518]

Lieutenant Lavack advanced with Wilkinson. He too reached the summit of the breastworks and jumped over demanding the surrender of the Kentuckians before him. *"Oh no"*, replied one, *"you are alone, and therefore ought to consider yourself our prisoner."* Later, Lavack would report that he turned and: ". . . *conceived to my indignation, on looking around, to find that the two leading regiments had vanished as if the earth had opened and swallowed them up.*"[519]

Without officers or leadership, the once highly disciplined British heroes of the Continent broke ranks and began a general retreat to the protection of their own lines. In less than twenty-five minutes, the main attack of the British had been broken. British dead and wounded riddled the field.

This Sketch shows Colonel Rennie making his attack on Jackson's forward redoubt. He succeeded in taking it, lost it in a counter-attack that cost him his life.

While all of this transpired Colonel Rennie ordered the 21st Regiment to advance along the river's batture, despite being bombarded by Patterson's Westbank guns which Thornton was supposed to have silenced. He pushed rapidly onward with his two columns of men along the riverside of the levee unaware of events unfolding on the other side of the embankment. He surprised the Americans with the suddenness and boldness of his attack.

His men drove back the American pickets, turned the American right flank, drove out the defending soldiers, and seized the punishing artillery emplacement Jackson had constructed near the levee on the extreme right of his line. The Americans: *"astounded by the suddenness of the attack, fled across the plank and climbed over into the safety behind the lines."* Rennie charged the redoubt despite the failure of all else. Jackson's apprehensions about the forward redoubt proved correct.[521]

Rennie executed his orders with great bravery. He urged his men forward and arrived at the ditch. Although his advance was greatly hampered by Patterson's battery on the left bank and the cannon mounted on the redoubt, he still reached the American works. Passing over the ditch, Rennie, with sword in hand leaped upon the wall, and call to his troops, ordering them to follow his lead. [522]

Upon taking the redoubt, Rennie yelled to his men *"Hurrah, boys, the day is ours."* Here they remained for some time awaiting support . . . but none arrived. At that moment, Beale's Rifles turned their weapons in Rennie's direction and opened fire. Colonel Rennie, Captain Henry, and Major King, were immediately killed along with most of those who had followed him to the redoubt. The survivors crouched down in fear for their lives.

After the Battle, discussion ensued among the Americans over who actually killed Rennie. Withers, a New Orleans merchant and crack shot, settled the controversy: *"If he isn't shot above the eyebrows, it wasn't my shot!"* he quipped. When Rennie's body was examined he had indeed suffered a shot to the forehead. Withers was given the duty and honor of sending the valuables to the colonel's family. Which he did.[523]

British soldiers would later reflect on the accuracy of the rifle fire. *"Fire that would riddle a light infantryman's hat if he raised it above the parapet."*[524]

Seeing this and losing their commander as well, these soldiers, under cover of the protecting levee that allowed their advance, hurriedly retreated from the battlefield to join their fleeing comrades.

General Lambert, ordered by Pakenham to stay back in reserve, witnessed the unfolding catastrophe in horror. He rushed forward. But it was too late to save the day. The terror stricken retreat had become a rout. The seasoned veterans of many a major conflict could not be turned. They were fleeing for their lives leaving weapons and pride behind! Some lay down besides the wailing wounded and the shattered dead seeking cover.

Although the discharges of muskets and cannons would continue through most of the early afternoon hours, in reality the British offensive had been effectively broken within twenty-five minutes of the opening guns.

At eight o'clock, Jackson could see no sign of another assault. The enemy had withdrawn. He ordered a ceasefire for small arms. Jackson then walked his lines congratulating his men for their bravery and effective defense. When the smoke finally cleared Jackson took note that the imposing and gorgeous military array of the British assault force, the two columns of attack, the Highland phalanx, and the distant reserve, had all vanished from the battlefield. Off in the distance, his spy glass revealed a faint red line of the enemy still receding."[525]

Closer to the American lines witnesses saw: *". . . the British troops concealing themselves behind the shrubbery, or throwing themselves into ditches and gullies. In some of the latter, indeed, they lay so thick that they were only distinguishable in the distance by the white shoulder belts, which formed a line along the top of their hiding-place."*[526]

Descriptions of the battlefield are gruesome to the extreme. One British soldier, Henry Cooke, described the action. *"The first objects we saw, enclosed in this little world of mist, were cannon balls tearing up the ground and crossing one another and bounding along like so many cricket balls through the air, coming on our left flank from the American batteries on the right bank of the river. Suddenly, there was a regular lane cut from the front to the rear of the column."*

Grapeshot was an especially effective death-dealing weapon: *"There was a 32-pounder exactly in our front. This the enemy filled up to the very muzzle with musket balls, and laid it with the nicest accuracy. One single discharge served to sweep the centre of the attacking force into eternity."*[527]

One can only imagine what the scene was like for those trapped in the hail of musket balls, cannon balls, and grapeshot. Sergeant Cooper, who assaulted the American lines, describes the scene: *"Another man, about ten or twelve files to my right, was smashed to pieces by a cannon ball. I felt something strike my cap; I took it off and found a portion of his brains sticking to it about the size of a marble. A young man on my left got a wound on the top of his head, and ran to the surgeon behind us . . . close to him another man had his arm, near the shoulder, so badly fractured that is was taken out of the cup [shoulder joint]."*

Cooper continues his horrific description, most of which was the result of artillery: *"A few yards behind sat a black man, with all the lower part of his face shot away; his eyes were gone and the bones of his brow all damaged and dripping blood. Near him in a ditch lay one of the 43rd, trying to hold in his bowels."*[528]

The fire of the musketry stopped at 8:00 A.M. The artillery kept up its fire until about 2:00 P.M. The main British attack had been turned in just under thirty minutes after the start of hostilities. The gunfire that followed resulted from excitement or attempts to clear the field of those enemy soldiers who remained on the Chalmet Plantation.[529]

Jackson reflected on looking over the field of red: *"I never had so grand and awful an idea of the resurrection as on that day. After the smoke of the battle cleared off somewhat I saw in the distance more than five hundred Britons emerging from the heaps of their dead comrades all over the plain, rising up, an still more distinctly visible as the field became clearer, coming forward and surrendering as prisoners of war to our soldiers."*[530]

The Americans were overcome by what they saw. The writhing of the wounded, their shrieks and groans, their convulsive and sudden tossing of limbs, were horrible to see and hear. Seven hundred dead, fourteen hundred wounded, and five hundred captured were the result of twenty-five minutes work.[531]

From the moment the British army had come into view, the musicians of the Battalion D'Orleans picked up their musical instruments and began to play *"Yankee Doodle Dandy."* They continued these harmonious strains as the vanquished foe fled from the field.[532]

Perhaps of greater interest, not all of Jackson's line participated in the battle. Although his breastworks ran from the river to the swamp, most of the action took place either around the forward redoubt on his right or near the edge of the swamp to his left. The center of his line remained untouched. Less than one half of Jackson's men had reason to fire a weapon. Thus the damage inflicted occurred at the hands of even fewer men that one would suppose necessary, mostly the Tennessee and Kentucky militia.[533]

In less than an hour, a loose band of American citizens shattered a highly trained and battle hardened British army that had fought Napoleon in the Spanish Peninsula Campaign. A decorated officer corps lay horribly slaughtered. A panicked British army discarded their weapons with their pride and retreated to the safety of Jumonville Plantation to care for their wounded, all the while wondering what had happened to them.

By 8:00 A.M., about two hours since the opening salvo, the muskets had silenced. The order had been passed down to "*cease fire!*" Jackson, now appearing somewhat relaxed for the first time in nearly a month, took the opportunity to walk his lines offering compliments to his soldiers and urging them to hold their positions. As he passed through his troops, the musicians struck up "*Hail Columbia*" to the cheers of his men.

Back in New Orleans, the morning opened with the sound of cannons and muskets coming from down river. The fateful day had arrived. The doors of the Ursuline Convent were opened and devout Catholics began to gather in the chapel that Sunday morning praying for a miracle.[534]

The priest held a High Mass, his voice accompanied by the muffled roar of distant cannons. From the windows of the convent, the nuns could look east and see the smoke rising from the Chalmette Battlefield. All hoped for victory, but many feared the worst.

A Mrs. Henry (Emily) Clement lived in New Orleans during these trying times. She composed a letter to her friend, Jacob Woods, three days after the January 8th battle in which she describes the events as they unfolded:

"Our house in the Faubourg, owing to a bend in the river, brings us in a straight line but two miles from the battle ground, so that we can hear all the battle as it rages. The battle of January 8th commenced at the dawn of day and continued without cessation until 10. The cannon began firing first and it seemed like one continued peal of tremendous thunder, and the small arms roared like a distant thunder. The horror of that morning is beyond my abilities to describe, if I should attempt it, I shall only say we prepared to run as far as we

could, knowing that if that merciless foe get the upper hand that not only all our property, but even our lives would be destroyed."[535]

They all prayed before the statue of our Lady of Prompt Succor which the Mother Superior, Mother Francoise Victoire Olivier de Vezin, had placed on the main altar. At that moment they made a vow. Should the Americans be victorious, a solemn mass of thanksgiving would be sung every year thereafter.[536]

As the Reverend William DuBourg raised the host in performance of the sacrament of communion, horse's hooves were heard galloping on the street outside. A courier suddenly burst through the doors of the church proclaiming the great American victory in Chalmette. The British threat had been turned. Following mass, the Abbe' DuBourg offered up *Te Deum* accompanied by the joyous voices of all those present.

As for the British, solemnity marked the occasion. The bodies of about forty soldiers lay in the canal before Jackson's lines. Another hundred wounded or fear—stricken survivors lay among them. Hundreds more lie dead across the battlefield while the many wounded "*. . . rolled over the field in agony, or crawled and dragged their shattered limbs over the muddy plain, not a living foe could be seen by the naked eye.*" From the American position, one could walk one quarter of a mile over the bodies of dead or wounded British. [537]

Ignace de Chalmet's once pastoral plantation, his tranquil retreat, had become a scene of unspeakable carnage and waste. All of his fine buildings had been destroyed and his once verdant fields were now riddled with hundreds of bodies. Many were dead and more wounded. The pitiful moans of the wounded and that peculiar smell that belongs only to blood joined to fill the air with stench and horror.

The whole battlefield to Jackson's left and the contested portion of river road near the forward redoubt were covered with the bodies of British soldiers who had fallen. After a truce had been agreed upon, some Americans asked their British counterparts: "*. . . why did you march up so boldly in our lines, in face of such a fire?*" To which the Brits responded: "*. . . were we not obliged, with the officers behind, sticking and stabbing us with their swords!*" The bloodied clothes and flesh of the men bore testimony to the truth of these comments.[538]

The "*Butcher's List*" tells the tale. The bodies of dead and wounded British soldiers stretched for a quarter of a mile beginning at the base of Jackson's breast works onward toward the Bienvenue Plantation. 2,600 English soldiers were lost . . . . 700 killed outright, 1,400 wounded many of whom would eventually die, and 500 captured.

On the American side, only 8 were killed and 13 wounded . . . an incredibly disproportionate number.[539]

According to Arsene de Latour, Jackson's engineer, the total number of British killed, wounded and captured exceeded 3,000. The British dispute this number.

General Lambert could only look on in horror. He had lost control of the situation and had no means of forming his lines for another assault. Furthermore, he could not assume that a different outcome was even possible.

Lambert then appealed to General Jackson for a truce in order that he might recover the wounded and bodies of the dead. (Description of this event is in next chapter) Jackson readily agreed. After a declared ceasefire, a line would be established in the battlefield. Jackson's men would bring the dead and ambulatory wounded to this line to be handed off to the British. The severely wounded would be brought to New Orleans for care.

Lambert carried his dead to a spot on Bienvenue's Plantation which had been marked out as a cemetery for the "*Army of Louisiana*". Interesting to note that at this time, there is no evidence of where these soldiers were buried. This despite the fact that in 1860, one historian of the war named Lossing, would comment on the site:

"*There they were buried and to this day 'God's Acre' has never been disturbed. It is distinguished in the landscape by a grove of small cypress trees, and is a spot regarded with superstitious awe.*"[540]

The location of this resting place has been a matter of the greatest curiosity for local residents and historians. Despite numerous attempts to locate this site, no one has ever found evidence of where these brave soldiers were buried. Even recent efforts employing modern technology have failed. This is hard to imagine, given that nearly 1,000 men had been interned?

Some believe the graveyard could be at the site of the former Bienvenue Plantation. This is where the Kaiser Aluminum Plant would be constructed in the late 1940s and where the St. Bernard Port Authority is presently located. In which case, the gravesite today would be covered over by asphalt and industries. The remains of these brave men seem to have completely vanished . . . as if the earth swallowed them up and left no visilbe sign of their heroic sacrifice.

541

*Pecan Trees where Generals Pakenham and Gibbs, along with
other officers had their internal organs buried prior to being
packed in drums of rum for transport back to London.*

The wounded prisoners captured by Jackson's men were transported to New Orleans where local citizens carefully tended them. Some decided to stay after their recovery. The British took back with them those who were ambulatory.

The dead officers were brought to Villere's Plantation where, with a solemn torchlight ceremony, they were laid to rest in the garden. The corpses of the ranking officers (Pakenham, Gibbs, and Rennie) were disemboweled, placed in casks of rum for preservation, and shipped home to their families. They buried the viscera beneath a stately grove of Pecan trees . . . which some say never again bore fruit.

Pakenham's body was returned home and interned in the family vault in Killnean County, Westmeath. His statue and that of his friend General Gibbs share a pedestal in St. Paul's Cathedral. The inscription states simply that they fell in an assault on the enemy's works at New Orleans. [542]

A letter from the Duke of Wellington to Pakenham's brother expresses his sense of loss over the death of the Major-General. His strong feelings about Admiral Cochrane are transparent: *"We have one consolation that he fell as he lived in the honorable discharge of his duty; and distinguished as a soldier and a man. I cannot but regret however that he was ever employed on such a service, with such a colleague."* [543] The results of this battle resonated around the world as word of what happened became known.

One combatant from Massachusetts described the scene in a letter home dated January 9, 1815:

"Yesterday the British experienced the most bloody butchery ever recorded in American history in an attack which they made against the strong lines of General Jackson, where they were entirely slaughtered from the heavy fire of 18 or 20 pieces of artillery playing upon them with round balls and grape shot . . . The British attacked the lines with undaunted bravery, many were killed at the parapet, after having crossed the ditch over the bodies of their men they had filled it with. The field of battle is covered with dead and wounded."

He goes on to mention the British prisoners in custody of Americans:

"There is now in town, besides those which were sent to Natchez, 406 in number, in the gaole 168 prisoners, in the Barracks 26 wounded, 5/6ths of which cannot recover having five severe and more wounds. In the hospital at the camp a vast number are still, which are hourly sent to town in barges and carts . . . upwards of 200 prisoners are still at Camp Jackson." [544]

Other reflections follow. There is no substitute for reviewing the firsthand experiences of participants. Each American witness expressed excitement over the great victory tempered with horror when reflecting on the carnage that victory caused. British survivors provide the clearest details about the horrors they endured when charging the guns that damp Sunday morning and the loss of so many brave friends.

Private William Ford of the Tennessee Volunteer Cavalry wrote his father about the victory. He describes the December 23rd battle and mentions that it lasted only about one and a half hours before the smoke became so thick fighting had become impossible. As for the January 8th battle, he describes it thusly: *". . . there never was an army so shamefully beaten a whole field on the memorable 8th of January almost covered with Red Coats and the loss on our side in killed and wounded not to exceed fifteen men. The hand of providence was never more conspicuous."* [545]

On February 13th D.B. Lyles of Baltimore wrote to James Riddle in Alexandria, Virginia expressing the glee etched on the faces of the residents living in New Orleans: *"[I] . . . feel particularly joyful today at the mutual change of the times since you left here. I need not state to you the cause of the change as I suppose you well have heard . . . natural indeed is the change on every countenance you can see a smile."*[546]

Conversely, British writers composed letters expressing the horrors of the conflict and the angst of defeat. A much humbled Sir Fredrick Stovin, who wrote so optimistically to his mother in early December about the coming victory, now reflected bitterly in his letter to her penned January 24, 1815. Once he had returned from the battlefield to the safety of the *HMS Tonnant,* he had time to compose his thoughts and discuss his own wound and the loss of his fellow officer General Edward Pakenham.

Concerning his own injuries, Stovin appears very stoic: *"Since accounts of our disastrous [attack?]my dear mother will have reached you before this I will, I fear, have excited many alarms and forebodings which this letter will dissipate. I have nearly received a severe wound in my neck with the ball having entered behind one ear passing through and out behind the other . . . it has left me with a formal neck."*[547]

On the issue of the loss of his friend and comrade Pakenham, Stovin is less detached: *". . . nothing but time will fill the vacuum occasioned by the loss of my inestimable friend and patron Sir Edward Pakenham. It has almost unhinged me and gives me a distaste to the service on which we are employed. It is a subject not to be written on only to be felt."*

Indeed, he even protects his friend's reputation. He draws particular attention to the fact that his friend and general had nothing to do with choosing the scene of battle. He discusses the battle as such: *"I refer you to the dispatches for all military by which you will hear about difficulties we had to encounter when we had been told to expect none. But it was badly conceived and ill directed in the planning. Sir Edward had nothing however to do with that being unavailable on board ship . . ."*[548]

Sadly, another letter from the British side highlights the confusion of war. Catherine Sara Dorothea Wellesley, the Duke of Wellington's wife and sister to General Pakenham penned a letter dated January 30, 1815, to an unnamed friend where she extends her heartfelt thanks for informing her that her brother was alive and well. Obviously, this was incorrect. He nobly died on the field of battle. She would soon enough learn the truth.[549]

As word of the dimensions of the American victory reached Europe, many military men studied the battle and made assessments. General Pakenham would endure much criticism in some quarters, but he was not available to defend his actions.

Jackson's aide, Latour, took the occasion to reflect on the outcome of the battle. Having reviewed events he concluded that the attack was wanting on one obvious respect: *"It was in my opinion, that they did not on the onset sacrifice the regularity of their movements to promptitude and celerity. The column marched on with the ordinary step, animating their courage with huzzas, instead of pushing on with fixed bayonets, au pas de charge. But it is well known that agility is not the distinctive quality of British troops."*

In general, Latour felt that their: *". . . movement is in general sluggish and difficult, steady but too precise, or at least more suitable for a pitched battle, or behind entrenchments, than for an assault."* He further felt that the British soldiers themselves suffered from a particular disadvantage: *"The enormous load they had to carry contributed . . . to the difficulty of their movement. Besides knapsacks, usually weighing nearly thirty pounds, and their muskets, too heavy by at least a third, almost all of them had to carry fascines from nine to ten inches in diameter and four feet long . . . very heavy . . . or a ladder from ten to twelve feet long."*[550]

Latour believed that the weather conditions causing a muddy battlefield coupled with the difficulties of trying to scale the slippery American breastworks under heavy burden should have been anticipated by the British officers. They had sufficient experience in this arena since December 23rd and knew the conditions: *"But they were blinded by their pride."*[551]

The records hold an interesting letter to "Susan" dated January 26, 1815, from an unknown volunteer participant from Massachusetts. This man, who OPPOSED the war, found himself in the city when attacked and took up arms to defend it. He provides a glimpse of how it must have seemed: *". . . the event happened on the memorable morning of the 8th. About the break of day when the whole British army marched out of their camp, and attempted, with great bravery, to storm and drive us from our Intrenchments; situated between them and the City, and extending from the River in a direct line across to the impenetrable swamp & woods on our left, a distance of about three fourths of a mile."*[552]

Later in the letter he describes the battle's aftermath: *"Militia in general fight as well under Intrenchments, and in fact are better Marksmen, than British regulars; which accounts for our decisive success surely on the ever memorable 8th of January 1815 for that was a day of proud triumph to the American Arms. Upwards of three thousand of Lord Wellington's Troops killed, wounded, prisoners, and missing. The destruction of officers almost unparalleled in the history of other battles . . ."*[553]

What is particularly noteworthy about this gentleman is that he was from New England, the hotbed of opposition to the war. In fact, he states as much himself, but also tempers those feelings with his reflection about the politics of the war. In one short paragraph, he sums up the attitude of many: *"I have always considered this an unnecessary war, but have uniformly rejoiced in all the defeats of the British by sea and land. It makes the world respect America, & I trust will shortly induce the British to consent to an honorable peace. The conduct of some of the politicians of my native state I do not approve."*[554]

For a battle of this magnitude, the combatants engaged in actual combat for a surprisingly short period of time. Most accounts have the assault turned within less than an hour. Musketry could be heard until about noon and some cannon fire beyond that time.

However, British Colonel Dickson provides an actual timeline. He led his troops towards the Bienvenue Plantation, next to General Gibbs headquarters, intending to join with Pakenham. Suddenly, the sky was glowed red with a Congreve rocket. The one that signaled opening combat. Hearing the cannon's salvos, Dickson rushed his men forward. By the time he had advanced within 600 to 700 yards of the American lines, the British troops were in full retreat. *"The battle had been fought and lost in the time it took Dickson to ride 1,000 yards. Was that more than four minutes?"*

Further confirmation comes from his account of the British batteries firing only about five volleys before being silenced having their own panicked troops crossing their line of fire. *"How long would it take for a field gun to fire five rounds? Five minutes?"*[555] These insights indicate that despite the fact that violent carnage persisted for twenty-five minutes, actually the assault may have been broken in less than five minutes.

Dickson's appraisal provides an insight into the incredible violence and the surprisingly swift carnage visited on the advancing British soldiers. Can it be true that experienced veterans of the Peninsular Campaign who participated in many bloody battles where tens of thousands of men were slaughtered over days of combat, panicked and fled in terror within five minutes? The answer is "YES."

The Battle on the Eastbank of the Mississippi River had concluded. The sugar plantation belonging to Ignac de Chalmet bore the marks of a killing field. It was a decisive victory for the Americans. However, events about to unfold on the Westbank would cause General Jackson and his engineer, Arsene de Latour, anguish. Could all that had been gained on one side of the river, be lost on the other? Is it possible that New Orleans could still fall into British hands?

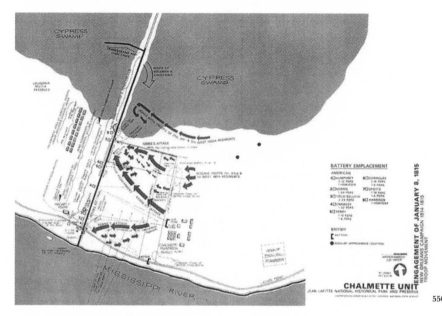

This map displays the movements of the British army during the attack on Line Jackson during the Battle of New Orleans on January 8, 1815.

Chapter 9

TROUBLE ON THE WESTBANK . . .

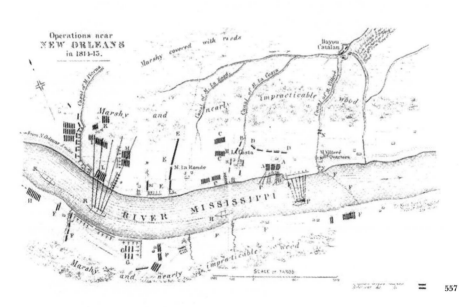

Map Showing Position of Troops in Area

Although General Jackson enjoyed a splendid victory on the Eastbank of the Mississippi River, the same cannot be said for events that unfolded on the Westbank. Here American lines crumbled before the attack of their British foe. The fate of New Orleans hung in the balance because American defenders failed to maintain their lines. It appeared that all gains on the Chalmet Battlefield had now been lost on the other side of the river. The battle on the Westbank of the Mississippi was nearly a catastrophe for the Americans! [558]

In his official report to the Secretary of War dated January 9, 1815, General Jackson expressed his shock and horror at the collapse of his lines across the river: *"The entire destruction of the enemy's army was now inevitable, had it not been for an unfortunate occurrence, which at this moment took place on the other side of the river . . . This unfortunate rout totally changed the aspect of affairs."*[559] Jackson believed that all that had been gained on the Chalmette Battlefield could be lost across the river.

Arsene de Latour, expressed similar concerns. *"After having perused, with pleasing sensations, the recital of the brilliant defense made by our troops on the left bank, every American, whose bosom glows with the love of his country, must learn with pain the contrast exhibited in what took place on the right, the consequences of which were likely to be so disastrous, that even now my mind shudders at the recollection of that moment, when, seeing our troops on the right bank fall back in disorder, while the enemy was rapidly advancing towards the city, all of us who were at Jackson's lines, were suddenly hurried from the transporting joy of victory to the fear of shortly seeing all its advantages wrested from our grasp."*[560]

Both men professed the gravity of the situation as reflected in their respective official reports. Eminent danger shocked both men. The British had successfully flanked their position, and the city of New Orleans faced peril. General Pakenham's plan appeared to be working despite his personal sacrifice

The campaign for New Orleans might yet be decided in Britain's favor despite the considerable losses endured at Chalmette. All was not lost for the British. Thus, the action on the Westbank deserves careful consideration.

From the beginning, General Pakenham had realized that limiting himself to a frontal attack on Jackson's well defended position would be fruitless and costly. He had already attempted to turn Jackson's left flank through the swamp on December 28th. That effort had nearly succeeded under command of General Gibbs, but it failed because Pakenham, not knowing about his subordinate's achievement, ordered a troop recall.

Other offensives over the weeks had resulted in similar disappointing outcomes at considerable cost of lives and munitions. The situation demanded a new approach. How can the American defensive lines be breached? What can be done to force victory? The

British commander gathered his officers at his headquarters to devise a new plan.

General Pakenham devised a brilliant strategy for turning Jackson's distant right flank on the Westbank of the Mississippi River. Both Jackson and Pakenham recognized the importance of controlling the Westbank. Pakenham's plan was simple. Send the aggressive Colonel William Thornton with 1,400 men across the Mississippi River at dusk and have this force ready to advance upon the American positions before dawn.

The details of this operation as it related to the delay it caused for the Eastbank assault have already been discussed. However, because of the importance this flanking maneuver had on the entire expedition, the entire story of the Westbank assault deserves discussion in its entirety, begging forbearance for any repetition. This is especially the case regarding Jackson's defensive efforts.

According to the plan, after taking Patterson's Westbank battery, Thornton was ordered to fire a Congreve rocket into the sky signaling his success. This signal would mark the moment for Pakenham to begin the assault on Jackson's Eastbank line. It would also signal Colonel Rennie to advance along the river batture without suffering casualties from cannons firing across from Patterson's battery. He would be protected by the levee from Jackson's men in Chalmette. Rennie's goal was to take Jackson's forward redoubt on his right near the river and turn the guns there against Jackson's own men. This would focus attention on the American right and open a breach for Keane, while simultaneously facilitating opportunities for Gibbs' attack on Jackson's left. [561]

The sound of Thornton's guns from across the river would protect Pakenham's troops from the troubling crossfire that had so plagued him over the past days.

Jackson respected Pakenham's ability and anticipated such a maneuver. He recognized the vulnerability and sought to reinforce the Westbank position with the limited reinforcements available.

Commodore Patterson had located his artillery battery in an abandoned lime kiln just downstream from Jackson's line and in a perfect position to enfilade the British with crossfire, which he had been doing for the past several days. This emplacement was reinforced with the cannons from the *Louisiana* and played a critical role in upsetting Pakenham's assault plans. The cross-fire punished his troops in every attempt to breach Jackson's line.

On December 24th, General Jackson ordered General Morgan of Massachusetts from his position below the Jumonville Plantation on the Eastbank to assume command of Westbank defenses. Jackson sent him to establish a defensive line downstream from Patterson's Battery to protect it and prevent any British advance up that side of the river. He was further advised to place 100 men at Fort Leon about twelve miles further down river near English Turn to hamper any attempt by Admiral Cochrane to advance up river by boat.

Morgan began to secure this position and advanced some of his force under command of Felix Arnaud to act as forward pickets at Mayhew's Plantation farther downriver. From this forward position, Arnaud was expected to keep a watchful eye out for any enemy activity and immediately engage any British forces attempting to come up the river on the Westbank.

Because of its vital importance, Morgan had to protect Patterson's battery at all costs. His effort to set up a primary defensive line down river from Patterson is where problems arose.

Unaccountably, Morgan would decide that the suggested location for his line across the river from Jackson's own in Chalmette was *"too narrow."*[562] Given that he had few and untested men under his command, one would believe a commander would welcome a short space to defend. Morgan, however, decided to place his forces farther down river at the Raguet Canal.

Uncertainty over how to defend the Westbank would plague the Americans. Several ideas arose, but Morgan's determination to stick with his original arrangement would contribute heavily to the Westbank disaster.

Morgan initially placed his forces near the saw-mill on Flood's plantation. After a few days, he relocated these troops forward to Jourdan's plantation next to Floods, a little farther down river. Here he established his line at the Raguet's old canal at the lower boundary of the plantation. They remained there until January 7th. His total contingent at this location at this time amounted to about 260 men.[563]

On January 4th, the Louisiana Militia under command of Zenon Cavelier crossed over to reinforce Morgan. They encamped at Cazelard's Plantation that Morgan had selected for his headquarters. These men later joined with the rest of Morgan's men at Raguet's canal adding 175 more men. This gave Morgan an effective fighting force of 435 defenders on the Westbank.[564]

565

TThe Cazelard Plantation house was Morgan's headquarters. It would be overrun by Thornton and the flag taken and is presently on display at Whitehall in London.

The Raguet Canal line was over 2,000 yards long from the river to the swamp. Morgan fortified only the 200 yards near the river and that with only a knee high mud embankment. The remaining 1,800 yards were completely open and defended by only 200 *"tired and poorly armed Kentuckians"* that Jackson had rushed over. 1,800 yards of the Raguet's canal lay undefended. [566]

On January 6th, the first regiment under Colonel Dejean left its position on the Piernas canal and joined with Morgan at Raguet's Canal. However, this reinforcement amounted to only about 110 men *". . . some ill armed, the rest without arms."* These soldiers were positioned to the extreme right of Morgan's line near the woods, leaving a wide undefended expanse between the defenders.[567]

While Morgan erected his defenses down river, Latour worked tirelessly establishing a breastwork at Bois Gervais Canal close to Algiers Point to serve as a final line of defense should it be needed. Jackson, concerned about Morgan's choices, sent Latour down river to review the situation carefully.

Latour met with Morgan, his staff, and Commodore Patterson. Afterwards, he toured the area to evaluate the position. Jackson had ordered Latour to design a defense works and re-deploy the Black workers that had been laboring on entrenchments at Bois Gravais and

Patterson's Battery to help build Morgan's line. It was essential that Morgan's line hold should the British attempt to force it by a Westbank assault.

After examining the area, Latour decided that the best terrain to construct defenses was not at Raguet's Canal which had 2,000 yards to defend, but at a position between Raguet's and Jourdan's canals: *". . . a place where the wood inclines towards the river, leaving only a space of about nine hundred yards or open ground. The adjoining wood being impassible, the works occupying this whole space could not be turned."*[568]

Latour discovered an ideal site. The distance between the wood and the river was small. Even more important, open ground lay in front which made any enemy attack exposed to American fire. This position would require only 1,000 to 1,200 men to defend.

Latour left Morgan with his advice assuming he would follow it. Latour could not order Morgan to obey because the General out ranked him. Nevertheless, he felt convinced that his reasonable suggestion had been accepted and returned to Jackson's headquarters to report the same.

Unbeknownst to Latour, Morgan redirected the Black laborers back to work on his original choice at Raguet's Canal.

On January 6th, captured prisoners had first revealed Pakenham's designs on the Westbank. By the Afternoon of January 7th *". . . there no longer remained any doubt of his intention. A little after sunset General Morgan was informed that the enemy was ready to cross the river and that he might hourly expect to be attacked."*[569]

This information caused General Jackson to order General Adair of the Kentucky militia, to send those unarmed, additional five hundred men to reinforce Morgan on the evening of January 7th. These men under command of Colonel Davis, arrived at four o'clock in the morning in deplorable condition. Crossing of the river coupled with fatigue from a five mile march through deep mud and a lack of food reduced Davis' detachment to only 250 effectives by the time they reached Morgan's line.[570]

Jackson likely assumed these men had been equipped with the reserve arms stored in New Orleans. He did not know he had ordered poorly armed men to be sent into battle. One wonders what could be expected from such demoralized, hungry, under-equipped, and exhausted soldiers.[571]

Davis deployed what remained of his men at Mayhew's canal about a mile in advance of Morgan's position as an advanced guard. He joined Major Arnaud and his 100 men of whom fifteen were without arms and the remainder equipped with only personal fowling pieces.

None possessed proper military weapons. Furthermore, they lacked any artillery. This force occupied the most forward American position and would be the first to face the enemy.

As it turned out, the American Westbank defenses were these: Heavily fortified Bois Grevais line established near Algiers Point by Latour; Patterson's Battery located just below Jackson's Line at Chalmet Plantation providing cross-fire on the British advance; Morgan's line at Raguet's canal below Patterson, 2000 yards to control of which only 200 yards was effectively defended; and an advanced defense line at Mayhew Canal near Andry Plantation under command of Arnaud protected with a few hundred untrained, unarmed, inexperienced citizens recently reinforced by some hungry and exhausted Kentucky militia.

Although the Westbank position was not as secure as the battle lines in Chalmette, Jackson nevertheless expected his troops to perform honorably and defend their position to the last man if necessary.

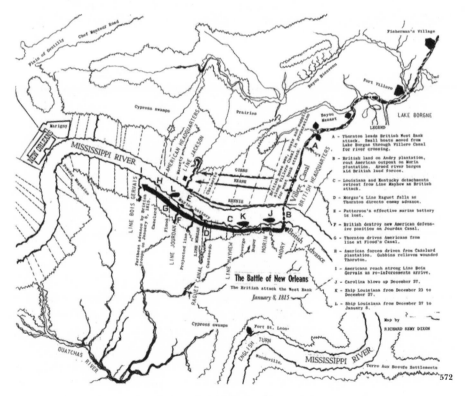

Map Tracing British Movements

As time passed, Jackson's apprehensions grew. He penned a letter to Morgan on January 7th, the day before the fateful attack. In it, he advised Morgan: *". . . to continue your usual vigilance in ascertaining the movements of the enemy and keep me constantly advised of them."* Jackson further advises that: *". . . Fort Leon ought to be further strengthened, that it may be safely done with a part of the force under your command. You will therefore be pleased to attend to the matter."*[573]

On the Westbank, Pakenham's plan would actually exceed his expectations, despite some initial serious setbacks. But for it to advance his operations on the Eastbank it had to be pulled off without a hitch. The essential element of precise timing could not be lost. That, however, was not to be!

Pakenham ordered Colonel Thornton to take 1,400 men across the river by barge.

The sequence of events that resulted in the late deployment of Thornton's mission has been discussed: Chocrane's use of a canal instead of hauling the boats, the collapse of the dam trapping the boats, and the resulting reduction in size of Thornton's assault force. The action is now picked up as Thornton starts across the river.

At about 5:00 A.M., Col. Thornton and only 460 soldiers and sailors with a sprinkling of marines (confusion over size of his force, some accounts say 600 men.) using muffled oars disembarked in their few boats to cross the river. They almost immediately disappeared in the thick fog. At this point, a much more serious problem arose.

No one had bothered to calculate the current of the Mississippi River, which ran at about 5 knots. By simply tossing a piece of driftwood into the stream, the strength of the current could have been measured and calculated. They could then have compensated for the time needed for Thornton to cross the river. But, no one performed that minor task. Failure to do this upset the timing of the coordinated plan. The coming disaster might have been avoided, but for a piece of wood!

Despite their determined efforts to paddle swiftly across the river, the current swept Thornton's troops downstream. One can only imagine the anger and frustration felt by Colonel Thornton. He was an aggressive campaigner and one anxious for success. Finding himself the victim of persistent incompetency and hesitation had to have nearly driven him to the breaking point. Once again, he was placed in a nearly impossible situation as a result of the actions of others.

After an exhausting and too long crossing, Thornton and his much reduced force finally touched the Westbank below the Andry Plantation . . . after dawn. He landed too late to achieve the main objective of his enterprise . . . turning Patterson's guns from targeting

Pakenham's attacking troops. Nevertheless, Colonel Thornton aggressively pushed his men forward determined to successfully secure the Westbank.

The detachment under command of Colonel William Thornton landed much later than planned, farther down river than anticipated, and in far fewer numbers than expected. This small force composed of soldiers, marines and sailors, reached the Westbank too late to achieve their primary goal. Rather than Pakenham initiating combat at the sound of Thornton's guns, Thornton arrived to the sounds of American cannons on the Eastbank. The Chalmette battle had begun!

Undaunted by the setbacks and failure to achieve his immediate goal of striking first and before dawn, Thornton aggressively preceded up-river. He had his orders and intended to accomplish his task. In the early morning hours of January 8th, Colonel Thornton's troops disembarked unmolested on the Westbank.

Thornton coordinated his land attack with his small naval force . . . the boats that carried him across. He employed these vessels to advance upriver along the river's bank beside his men firing bow carronades loaded with grapeshot as his troops advanced. Employing this tactic, Thornton drove his men forward and the Americans back.

Had the Americans remained vigilant and confronted the British when they first attempted to make their landing, the outcome might have been different. The coming disaster could have been prevented.

But the exhausted Kentuckians and Felix Arnaud's men, who were situated about one mile in advance of Morgan's main line at Mayhew's canal just above the Andry Plantation, all soon fell asleep after posting a small guard. Had they been more alert, they might have stalled the attack. They failed to do this.[574]

Thornton landed unmolested and attacked at full charge while firing grape-shot from his accompanying boats. Suddenly awakened, Thornton's surprise attack put this small detachment of Americans to flight after a brief fight. Arnaud's men fired a few rounds then immediately retreated to the Mayhew Plantation. As for Davis's unarmed Kentuckians, they fled in confusion. Some retreated with Arnaud. Others disappeared into the swamp not to be heard of for the rest of the day.

Continuing with his carefully laid plan, Thornton advanced again and routed the Kentuckians and others at the Mayhew Plantation house where they had taken up a position behind the mill race. The Americans stood and fired about two rounds, then fled without firing a shot after they commenced their retreat. The remaining Kentuckians headed for Morgan's Line at Ragout's Canal while Arnaud's men headed for the woods.[575]

As the remaining Americans ran back to Morgan's line in hopes of finding some safety, Morgan rode out to them. When Davis, in charge of the retreating Kentuckians arrived, Morgan ordered him to take a position to his far right . . . near the swamp. This position, however, left the center vacant. The entire front was over 2,000 yards long and 1,300 yards below Jackson's line on the Eastbank. These hapless men formed up within his lines to the right of the Louisiana militia.[576]

Davis took note of the dangerous situation. Instead of having over 500 men protecting this position, only about 170 men were available to defend nearly 400 yards of practically open ground. Making matters worse, these men were stationed far apart to cover the entire line which left considerable distance between them.

Morgan's position was hopeless. He had expected over 1,000 men and three pieces of artillery. Instead, he commanded a total of 600 men. 1,000 men might have sufficed to repel the British. Undermanned as he was, Morgan knew he had little hope of holding his line.[577]

As for Thornton, he gained the open field in front of Morgan's works. He extended the 85th so as to cover the whole field and with sailors formed in column on the road. He held the marines in reserve as he advanced steadily on Morgan's lines. He supported these troops with his boats in the river, each with its carronade firing from the foredeck. [578]

When the British on the Eastbank heard sounds of gunfire on the Westbank, their hopes soared. Sir John Cooke, a member of the 43rd Regiment of Light Infantry, relates the effect: *"All at once we heard, on the other side of the river, pop, pop, pop, followed by a volley of musketry, interspersed with a few hasty rounds of artillery, which ceased as suddenly as it had begun, and everyone spontaneously said "Bravo' the batteries are taken, and the Americans are done for."*[579]

Colonel Gubbins commanded the 85th, Major Adair the marines, and Captain Money the seamen. With a grand display of Congreve rockets and the piercing sound of bugles, the British assaulted Morgan's line. The Americans fired what artillery they had which caused the enemy to briefly recoil. Captain Money was killed. Thornton, seeing the danger, led a spirited charge up the weak center of Morgan's line while the 85th attacked to the right of Davis' position. This was done in combination with the naval carronades firing at Morgan's left. The Americans, recognizing that they were about to be flanked, fled the field in great confusion. As for Thornton, his act of bravery came at personal cost. He was severely wounded in this assault.

Commodore Patterson's letter to the Secretary of the Navy dated January 13th best describes his interpretation of events: *"At this time the enemy's force had approached General Morgan's lines . . . when in a few minutes I had the extreme mortification and chagrin to observe general Morgan's right wing, composed of Kentucky Militia . . . abandon their breastwork and flying in a most shameful and dastardly manner, almost without a shot . . . after firing a few rounds, was followed by the whole of General Morgan's Command."*[580]

For a moment, Patterson entertained some hope of success, only to have it immediately dashed: *"By the great efforts of those officers at short stand was effected on the field when a discharge of rockets from the enemy, caused them to again retreat in such a manner that no efforts could stop them."*[581]

Morgan attempted to rally Davis' men to no avail. *"Halt, Halt! Men and resume your position."* He yelled. A wounded Adjutant Stephens shouted *"Shame, Shame! Boys, stand by your general."* But to no avail. All of his attempts to rally his men failed.

With the British overtaking the breastworks to the right, the Louisiana militia fired several volleys then broke and ran in terror. Panic had been achieved by the British when they charged aggressively across the open field through the blinding smoke of the American gunfire.

Patterson's Battery, which had been so decisive in sending volleys across the river, now found itself vulnerable. He turned his cannons to confront the advancing British and was about to order his guns to fire *". . . into the damn cowards"*. He was willing to kill his own men to stop the British. When challenged by a subordinate, he countermanded his order, spiked his guns, and had the powder thrown into the river.

Patterson then abandoned his battery cursing both the British and the Kentuckians as he embarked to the safety of the ship *"Louisiana"* which had been standing by about 300 yards to the rear of his battery.[582]

The British gained the American position, their tents, supplies and eighteen cannons. One of which had inscribed on its barrel: *"Captured at Yorktown"* . . . a prize of considerable value to the British.[583]

Although repulsed on the Eastbank, the British soldiers had not given up hope of victory. The action on the Westbank promised to turn the day to their advantage: *"We waited and waited, still exposed to a cannonade from the front, and in our turn expected to hear all the captured guns open fire and enfilade the American entrenchments from the right to the left, exactly in the same way that the American sloop had raked the English bivouac on the first night of landing, but no such agreeable sounds greeted our ears, the Americans having spiked their guns on the right bank of the river before they were taken possession of.* '[584]

Having achieved the pinnacle of victory in Chalmette, Andrew Jackson and his engineer Arsene de Latour witnessed with frightful realization a potential defeat on the Westbank. Just what Jackson feared most and what the British had expected to occur in Chalmette happened on the Westbank. Undisciplined American troops fled in the face of an organized attack by a determined and coordinated army.

The real fear that this could occur had caused Jackson's deep anxiety for some time. If the British gained control over the Westbank, they could attack the city of New Orleans from Algiers Point with cannons and rockets. Would the city surrender? That is why he felt all could be lost as the British advance on the Westbank proceeded unchecked.[585]

Jackson responded to the crisis. He ordered General Humbert, a former French officer, over to the Westbank with reinforcements. Unfortunately, jealousy on the part of some of the militia officers towards this distinguished foreign military hero prevented Morgan and his assistants from listening to this noble war veteran. Perhaps, had they done so they might have escaped the disgrace of Morgan's defeat. The American militia's refusal to serve under Humbert, and their failure to execute his orders, produced a delay. These petty feelings not only injured the pride of Humbert and proved unworthy of the American officer but contributed to the failure to defend the Westbank. [586]

The ethnic tensions British officers hoped for at the beginning of the campaign up to this time had failed to appear. On the Westbank they surfaced!

Having successfully taken Patterson's Battery, Colonel Thornton anxiously looked across the river to see what had transpired there. Unfortunately, by the time he had achieved his goal the tide had turned on the Chalmette battlefield. When Thornton had the opportunity to look across the river, shock awaited his gaze. Horror gripped his soul.

He witnessed the near total destruction of an honored British army. The ground was strewed with the dead and broken bodies of his comrades accompanied by the chaotic retreat of the remaining British forces from the field of battle. His plan to turn the guns against Jackson's own position was dashed. He could do nothing to help Pakenham now but seize the Westbank and turn this flanking maneuver to his commander's advantage. It now fell to Thornton to lead what had become the main attack!

"But still Thornton had accomplished everything that was desirable, or that the most sanguine expectations could have been contemplated. And although Sir Edward was no more, his ultimate plans had been realized by the able conduct of Colonel Thornton, who had seized the happy instant of making his successful charge."[587]

Undaunted by what had befallen his comrades on the east bank, the impervious Thornton, continued his drive forward. Crossing canals, he proceeded to advance up-river pushing the Americans before them with the intention of taking Algiers Point from which position he could have successfully launched his intended artillery and Congreve rocket attack on the French Quarter itself.

The British continued their advance for an additional two miles upriver before being ordered to halt. These brave Brits had rowed across the current of the Mississippi River all night. They had advanced and fought the Americans all morning. His men were exhausted, hungry, tired, and thirsty. They needed rest before any further engagement.

The Louisiana militia persisted in its retreat until it reached the last line of defense. The final American defensive position was erected at Bois Gervais line. Finally, Morgan gained reinforcements and secured control over his frantic men. Here they awaited another onslaught, which they knew would soon occur.

The wounded Thornton urgently needed medical attention. His men evacuated him across the river to the Jumonville Plantation hospital to dress his wounds and seek reinforcements.

His junior officer, Gubbins, took over command and recognizing the strengthening American lines, stopped to rest his men and consider the new situation. He was prepared to drive the Americans further up river. His persistent goal was to gain a position from which he could bombard the city.

Gubbins settled in and awaited what he presumed would be the successful attempt of Colonel Thornton to gain the reinforcements in men, artillery, and material needed to force the American lines and open the door to New Orleans. No one could deny the surprising success of the Westbank operation.

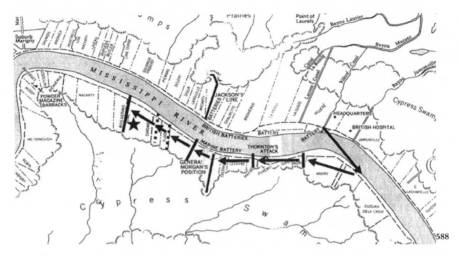

Map Showing Thornton's Weswtbank Advance

The result of the attack on the Westbank cost the British 78 men killed and wounded, including the injuries inflicted on the intractable Colonel Thornton. The Americans lost one man killed and five wounded. [589]

Fear gripped the local civilian population as this battle raged. Emily Clement, in her letter to Jacob Wood described action on the Westbank: *". . . in the heat of the action, some of the enemy crossed the River, drove our men who were placed there with some large cannons from the field . . . The enemy pursued them up to within 3 miles of our powder magazine . . . we saw our troops flying . . . and thought our destruction inevitable until we heard of their retreat."*[590]

When he arrived at headquarters, Thornton was shocked to learn that nearly all of the British command staff had been killed or seriously wounded: General Pakenham was dead, so were General Gibbs, Colonel Rennie, and Colonel Wilkinson. General Keane had suffered a severe wound and was out of action. Only General Lambert remained in charge in command of the reserves and what remained of a tattered main army.

General Lambert had become nearly totally distraught over what had occurred. He could not rally his panicked troops for another assault and seemed incapable of comprehending the magnitude of the disaster that lay before him. Thoughts of another assault were likely far from his mind.

The wounded Thornton informed Lambert of his success on the Westbank and requested reinforcements in men and artillery to seize the advantage. He felt certain that momentum remained in his favor. The Americans had retreated to their last line of defense located at Beau Gervias. A properly organized and equipped attack could easily take that position as well which would place the entire Westbank under British control.

From that position, the British would be able to launch artillery directly into the Vieux Carre' and create panic in the city, thereby demoralizing Jackson's forces in Chalmette. The impact this would have had on Jackson's troops on the Eastbank is impossible to gauge. That bombardment would have terrorized the civilian population.

Jackson's defenders were mere citizens and not highly disciplined professional soldiers; many may well have abandoned their lines to rush home to defend their families. This would have shattered Jackson's defensive line at Chalmette in the face of a bloodied, but still powerful British force fully capable of mounting another assault, this time against a much weaker line of defense.

Surrender of New Orleans might yet be only a matter of time. Prospects for a British victory remained. *"Ten armed boats, with carronades in their bows, floated on the waters of the Mississippi, and forty more boats were ready to follow them, if necessary, and batter the right flank of the Americans to the very portals of New Orleans, who did not possess a flotilla to engage them."*[591]

Lambert was not convinced. He had witnessed so much carnage and had no experienced officers with whom to confer. Any decision was his alone to make.

Events in Chalmette would blunt the British advance. Thornton advised General Lambert, now in charge after Pakenham's death, that he could succeed in taking the Westbank and could still turn the tide of battle. Lambert hesitated. He sent Lieutenant-Colonel Alexander Dickson, Pakenham's artillery commander, across the river to appraise the situation for himself. When Dickson returned he informed Lambert that maintaining that offensive would require the commitment of over 2,000 additional troops and artillery. But Lambert had had enough. He denied Thornton's request.

Pakenham did not know at the time he planned the Westbank operation that the moment he placed boats in the Mississippi, he gained command of the river. The only vessel Jackson had was the *Louisiana* which had been stripped of guns and converted into a floating powder magazine. Lambert failed to appreciate this critical advantage.

The decision to halt operations had a devastating impact on the British army. Many were shocked that Lambert would not take advantage of the Westbank victory. British officer Cook expressed his dismay: *"Here was a glorious position! Here was another opening to the streets of New Orleans, and dame fortune soared aloft in the favour of the English General. This was not the time to count the dead. This was not the time to cover the drum with crape, to sound the funeral knell, or trumpets to blast the dead march in Saul. This was the moment, and the balance between victory and defeat: instead of which a military extinguisher was placed over the bright flame of enterprise, which was as suddenly put out as a greased rush or a farthing candle."*[592]

Lambert decided to enter into truce discussions with Jackson to recover his dead and wounded. Under a flag of truce, he sent a message to Jackson requesting talks. This action took the Americans by surprise as one witness described the event:

About noon on the 8th, several Americans who had advanced some distance from the front lines, announced the approach of a party from the British camp. It consisted of an officer in full uniform, a trumpeter, and a soldier bearing a white flag. The three advanced on the levee to a position within three hundred yards of Jackson's lines, when the trumpeter blew a loud blast, and the standard bearer waved the white flag. The whole army gathered on the summit of the parapet, and looked on in anxious suspense and curiosity."[593]

Jackson sent out Major Butler to receive this detachment. They presented Butler with a note. The note was simply signed "Lambert". Jackson, having never heard that name, returned the message with a request for clarification. Who was "Lambert"?

The messenger returned with the same note signed *"John Lambert Commander-in-Chief of the British Forces."* It was only then that Jackson learned of the depth of destruction visited upon the British command structure.

After meeting, the American and British agreed that a line should be marked off about three hundred yards below the American position. Here elements of both armies would be assembled for the purpose of caring for the wounded and collecting the dead.

The bodies of the British who had fallen into or close to the ramparts were immediately brought to the awaiting comrades at the truce line. Next, the dead were placed upon Colonel Mullins' discarded boarding ladders and carried into the British lines. The British then examined the cruelly shattered bodies and attempted to identify their friends. *"The collection of the dead and the digging of graves consumed the day."*[594]

That evening, by the light of torches, the whole British army, ceremoniously laid their dead to rest in wet and shallow graves. As an interesting side note, sources state that: *"So numerous were they, and buried so imperfectly, that the place was not approachable during the succeeding summer.*[595]

While this dismal task continued, Jackson, recognizing his advantage on the East Bank sought to secure this victory by negotiating a "status quo" only there. He offered no such peace on the Westbank. His intention was to reinforce his troops there and attempt to drive the British back.

Fearing for the safety of his exposed Westbank troops, Lambert informed Jackson that he would withdraw from the Westbank. He then immediately sent Colonel Dickerson back across the river with orders for Gubbins to begin the retreat.[596]

The British army took this news hard: *"We retired two hours after dark to the original ground the troops had marched from in the morning; and when we found that Colonel Thornton's troops had been withdrawn from the opposite side of the river, and relanded, and that the boats were again got into the canal, then, and not till then, all further hopes of victory were blasted. At such a piece of information it is impossible to convey an adequate idea of our astonishment at such an advantage being given up"*[597]

G.R. Gleig, shared Cooke's opinion concerning the error of surrendering the Westbank. As a participant in the campaign, his view deserves credit: *"Again, the recall of the victorious detachment from the left to the right bank of the Mississippi, and the consequent abandonment of that complete command of the river which this partial success had obtained, was a military error of the gravest kind."*[598]

Greig then widened the scope of this criticism far beyond events on the Westbank. First, he believed the entire expedition had been compromised at some point because the Americans knew they were coming and were prepared. Whereas, the British soldiers themselves had no knowledge of their destination or mission. He reserved particular vitriol for the navy because of its failure to secure enough barges to effectively deploy the men and supply them with ammunition and food while in the battlefield.

Whatever the cause, line officers and soldiers of Great Britain felt betrayed by numerous decisions senior officers made, but particular anger centered on the Westbank debacle. That one effort, which could have retrieved their honor and sacrifices, had been abandoned.

Jackson shared the disbelief expressed by many British soldiers. His letter dated January 9, 1815, the day after the battle, expresses astonishment over his good luck. *"The enemy now occupied a position from which he might annoy us without hazard; and by means of which he might have been enabled to defeat, in great measure, the effect of our success on this side of the river."*[599]

Jackson continued: *"His Excellency Major-General Lambert begged time to consider of these propositions until ten o'clock of today and in the meantime re-crossed his troops. I need not tell you with how much eagerness I immediately regained possession of the position he had thus hastily quitted."*[500]

There is no question but that the military rank involved in the battle stood in agreement. The reports issued by American officers as well as statements made by many British officers and soldiers viewed Thornton's successful flanking maneuver on the Westbank as an open door to victory.

Lambert's failure to recognize this sudden change in momentum and take advantage of its opportunity condemned the British attack on New Orleans to failure. He had the men, the vessels, the artillery, and the ground position for success. Some would argue that he lacked only the will to fight.

Lambert would later defend his actions in a letter to the Earl of Bathurst dated January 28, 1815. He composed this after the retreat while on Admiral Cochrane's flag ship *Tonnant*, Lambert wrote: *"After maturely deliberating on the situation of this army, after the command had unfortunately devolved upon me, on the 8th instant, and duly considering what probability now remained of carrying on with success . . . it appeared to me that it ought not to be persisted in."*[501]

No purpose in second guessing, the decision had been made. Now was the time to implement the truce. At midday, the aforementioned line was drawn a few hundred yards from the American lines. The Americans handed over the bodies of about 300 dead British soldiers, *". . . many of them naked, having been stripped of their uniforms, to be hawked about the streets of New Orleans in triumph."*[502]

While the surviving British soldiers were burying their dead, the Americans began to collect the discarded weapons that lay scattered over the battlefield. These trophies were to be kept as mementos or sold for a profit. About 300 severely wounded British soldiers were taken to New Orleans for medical care where they were treated with the utmost respect.

Disheartening to the British, many of the Americans who left their lines to help were so overwhelmed with the magnitude of their victory that they began to make jests about the unbalanced outcome. This caused anger among some of the British officers and men, but the honor of a truce had to be maintained at all costs. Smothering their fury, these men set about the grizzly task before them while grumbling beneath their breath.

In the words of one unidentified British officer on the scene: *"An American officer stood by, smoking a cigar, and apparently counting the slain, with a look of savage exultation, and repeating, over and over, to each individual that approached him, that their loss amounted to eight men killed and fourteen wounded. I confess that when I beheld this scene, I hung down my head, half and sorrow and half in anger."*[603]

The bodies of those officers who had fallen near the American lines were delivered to the British: Colonel Rennie, Major Wittaker, Captain Henry, and Majors Wilkinson and King were carefully received *". . . with sorrowful and tearful silence . . . they were amongst the foremost in all perilous enterprises."* Their remains were respectfully interred in the garden of the Villere Plantation. [604]

On January 9th, the British had settled in at their base camp. Although about one and a quarter miles from Jackson's line, the Americans continued to harass their British foes with musketry and artillery. Although they sustained only a few additional casualties, the continual bombardment tormented them. Both sides also decided to annoy one another by having military bands play martial music.

Shortages of food plagued these British combatants. The sailors had been pressed into service evacuating the wounded by barge to the fleet. In return, they brought what supplies they could. But, being exhausted, maintaining lines of supply proved to be arduous. Besides, what victuals they to eat had been drawn from common ship stores, salted meat and hard tack.

On one occasion a shell exploded over the tent of some British officers while sleeping: *". . . which cut off the feet of Lieutenant D'Arcy, the one just below the knee, the other at the ankle-joint, and he crawled out of the hut in this horrible situation. One of his feet was driven so far into the soft mould that it was obliged to be dug out the following day."*[605]

Their suffering continued. The British evacuation proved to be an ordeal. The sailors had to row wounded from the battlefield to the fleet, then return again with supplies only to repeat the operation day and night. After a month of persistent exertion in cold wet weather facing contrary winds, they had reached their limits of endurance.

As for the soldiers in Chalmette, their physical condition deteriorated as well. All of the food available for forage had been exhausted. They now depended upon sea biscuits and salt meat: *"The consequence was that the consumption was beyond produce; on some days we did not taste food, and when we did, it was served in such small quantities as only to tantalize our voracious appetites."*[606]

For ten days they endured these debilitating conditions. Then matters got worse: *"One morning before daylight we were disturbed (having been kept awake half the night by the usual salutations of shot and shell) by water pouring into our huts, as soon as the objects could be discerned, what a dreary prospect presented itself to view! The Mississippi had overflown its banks, and nothing but a sheet of water was to be seen, except for a few straggling huts and one house, the lines of the Americans and the forest trees. It was nearly dark before the water subsided. The whole day the troops were enveloped in muddy blankets, shivering with cold, as hungry as hunters, and looked like polar bears standing on their hind legs.*[607]

General Lambert issued orders for a full retreat to begin on the night of January 18th. What guns that could be removed were taken back to the ships. The remaining old ship guns were abandoned as trophies for the Americans.

Leaving the field of battle proved to be more difficult than arriving. Before they could even disembark, cannon balls rained in from across the river. There seemed to be no end to their torment.

The retreat had to be carefully planned. They had arrived in three battalions brought in by barges. They could not afford to divide their forces for the withdrawal. They had to move secretly and simultaneously.

Lambert employed deception. He ordered his pickets to take the uniforms off some of the dead and stuff them with reeds. When the time came to evacuate, these were dummies erected, complete with weapons, to leave the impression that pickets had been posted.

The Americans were fooled. The British had departed before Jackson and his forces realized what had occurred. The Americans maintained constant vigilance on the British camp but saw only that their huts were standing, flags were fluttering, and pickets posted. Nevertheless, something just didn't seem quite right. It was too quiet.

At last Jackson asked French General Humbert, for his opinion. The French officer took a careful view through the telescope and immediately exclaimed: *"They are Gone!"* What caught his attention? He focused on to a crow flying close by one of the sentinels. That would only happen if the sentinels were fake . . . dummies. Humbert proved to be right.[608]

Jackson ordered a party to investigate. Before these men could advance too far they encountered a British medical officer approaching under a flag of truce. He handed Jackson a letter from Lambert requesting that he attend to the eighty wounded men who circumstances had forced him to abandon. Jackson's men welcomed this news with hurrahs.

At about the same time, January 17th, Henry Chotard conveyed orders from Jackson to Morgan urging him to: *". . . march with 600 men down the river, observing the movement of the enemy who seem to be retreating. You will procure boats wherever you will find them and have them carried to caution to the point on your side of the river that you will select for the embarking your troops . . . you will land on the other side of the river below the British camp and will take such positions as will enable you to harass the enemy by attacking him on his rear.*[609]

Jackson sought to cut off the British retreat, but there is little indication that this order to Morgan was ever implemented. Perhaps he never received it, or neglected to follow it. Whatever the case, the British withdrew without molestation.

The British had begun their quiet march at 9:00 P.M. using the cover of night. They retreated further to the east of Bayou Bienvenue. The clever deception allowed them to leave unmolested. Engineers had preceded them cutting reeds and palmetto trying to place some firm ground under foot in the marsh for the infantry to pass over.

Cooke colorfully describes their ordeal: *"For a short way we proceeded on the hard road, following the preceding column, and then entered the swamp, and the first step sank up to the knees in mud, and we continued to drag one leg after the other, sometimes falling on our faces, other sinking in up to their hips, and anyone unluckily stepping off this road was almost certain of going over head and ears. At one spot the men came to a stop; an officer, more valiant than wise, pushed everyone aside and boldly stepped forward to lead the way; but courage availed him little, for in an instant he was up to his neck, and had it not been for the timely exertion of those present, in two seconds he would have disappeared."*[610]

They continued this procession throughout the night carrying their muskets crosswise so when they fell they would not sink into the muck. *"During the whole of the night we scrambled and tumbled about in this bog, and when morning broke, a scene presented itself which beggars all description. The straggling files of the soldiery extended along the quagmire for miles, enclosed by high reeds, every countenance was plastered with mire; in fact, the whole army were covered with a cake of mud from the top of the head to the sole of the feet . . ."* They did not reach the Fisherman's Village where their ordeal began twenty-seven days before until ten o'clock in the morning. [611]

To defend their position, Lambert ordered two barges armed with carronades up Bayou Bienvenue. He feared that the Americans might attack his retreating and vulnerable men. His caution was well founded because the Americans did indeed attempt to attack his lines, but were repulsed with several volleys of grape-shot.

The British were forced to remain in the marsh until the sailors from the fleet were able to retrieve them through the relay of barges. Cold, wet, hunger, and dirt were bad enough. What terrified them most now were the presence of some very large alligators. Gleig's express his fears: *"Nearly all night I stood a few paces from the entrance of the hut, not daring to enter, under the apprehension that an alligator might push his broad snout through the reeds and gobble me up!*[612]

It wasn't until the evening of January 25th that Cooke and his compatriots managed to escape the "morass" and were rowed with fifty other men by barge to the fleet. Finally, their horrible ordeal had ended . . . a full month after it had begun.

A few days later the fleet weighed anchor and with a following wind worked their way towards Mobile Bay. Within twenty-four hours they dropped anchor opposite Dauphin Island where they disembarked. This time they set their tents on firm clean sandy soil. They washed themselves, their clothes, and their equipment. They found proper forage, ate well, and recovered their spirits. Still, at this time, they had no knowledge that a treaty had been signed on December 24th.

Considering the events as they unfolded on the Westbank January 8th, questions persist to this day. Had Lambert immediately reinforced his Westbank forces as Thornton had urged, could he have driven the exhausted and fearful Americans back once again? In which case, he would have effectively flanked Jackson and been in a position to terrorize the city of New Orleans. Many of his officers and men believed this to be so. Certainly, the American command staff thought so.

Or, would the Americans have finally held their ground and successfully defended their city? The answer to that question will remain forever unknown.

Prior to the opening of hostilities, some members of the Louisiana legislature wanted to surrender rather than lose the city. They feared its destruction. An artillery attack on the French Quarter from Algiers might have turned the tide. General Lambert had the troops, but he lacked the initiative. In effect, after so much sacrifice, he snatched defeat from the jaws of victory. Yet another example of Pakenham's last words: *"Lost for want of courage!"*

Perhaps Sir John Henry Cooke expressed the feelings of many British soldiers and officers best: *"Had all the generals brought their troops into action like Colonel Thornton and Lieutenant-Colonel Renny, a most brilliant conquest would have crowned the enterprise, would have added new luster to the British arms, and closed this bloody war by a glorious achievement, as worthy of record as it is now unworthy."*[613]

But that was not to be.

The final tally of casualties for the entire campaign was high and disproportionate. On the American side casualties numbered: 55 killed, 185 wounded, and 99 missing for a total of 333. As for Great Britain, their losses were tremendous. A total of 4,000 were killed, wounded and missing. Actual distribution of deaths and injuries are not available. [614]

The main battle of a two and a half month campaign to take the city of New Orleans had ended. Victory was a simple matter. Or so thought the British when they opened the enterprise. But a combination of events, some so simple as to boggle the mind, conspired to cause one of the greatest defeats endured by one of the grandest armies Great Britain ever placed in the field. It proved to be a total disaster!

Back in New Orleans the suspense must have been overwhelming throughout the battle. One can only imagine the sounds emanating from the Chalmette Battlefield in the early morning hours of January 8, 1815 . . . just seven miles from the corner of Canal Street and the Mississippi River!

Citizens were awakened by Captain Shotts' first artillery salvo directed against the British troops just becoming visible through the rising mist. The roar of cannons and the crack of muskets tore the air as the battle raged on the outskirts of town. Those looking east from rooftops likely saw the rising columns of smoke marking the site of the intense conflict and witnessed the traces of Congreve rockets arcing through the sky.

"The morn of the day of the decisive battle came and with it the roar of the cannon from the Chalmette field and the crackle and volleys of the Kentucky and Tennessee rifle. As the morning hours wore away . . . rumors of defeat became frequent."[615]

Gradually, the intensity of combat slowed. The musket cracks eased . . . then ceased. Yet the cannons still roared. By afternoon they, too, had fallen silent. What is amiss? What has happened?

All fears of defeat subsided and changed to cries of joy as horsemen from Chalmette riding through the streets of New Orleans heralded the news that a tremendous victory had been achieved. The Americans had won! The peels of "Victoire", the name of the St. Louis Cathedral's main bell, rang throughout the streets.

The news arrived in the late morning. The city is saved. General Andrew Jackson and his almost ridiculous army had turned back a major invasion by Great Britain, the world's foremost military power.

The only military force remaining to defend the city under the command of Captain DeBuys ". . . *hastily assembled, and with a drum and fife paraded the streets amid the salutes and hurras of the people waving of the snowy handkerchiefs of the ladies, and the boundless exultation and noisy joy of the juveniles."*[616]

Then word went out for all surgeons, nurses, and apothecaries to immediately assemble with whatever carts were available to rush to the front. There was great need for medical attention: *"All who possessed any knowledge of the curative art, who could amputate or set a limb, or take up an artery, hurried to the camp. Next there came up from the camp to dispatch all the carts and other vehicles to the lines."*[617]

"It was late in the day before the purpose of this order was clearly perceived, as a long and melancholy procession of the carts, followed by a crowd of men, was seen slowly and silently winding it way along the levee from the field of battle."[618]

Some sources recount how over forty cartloads and ten boat-loads of wounded British soldiers and officers had been sent to the city for care, along with a large detachment of prisoners.

"Those far-famed nurses, the quadroon women of New Orleans, freely gave their kind attentions to the wounded British, and watched at their bedsides night and day." Some of the officers were taken into the homes of Creole families. Some would never return to England.[619]

General Coffee wrote his wife about his experiences in the battle and his long love for her. He states that he is uncertain of his date of return, hopefully being home sometime in March. On reflection he states: *"we are, and have been at perfect ease for eight days past. The enemy have entirely left our shores and no doubt will leave this coast as soon as they possibly can. It is generally believed they will go to Bermuda where they can deposit their sick and wounded and get supplies etc . . . all doubts are removed here, everything is cheerfulness. The name of Tennessee is revered, and General Jackson idolized."*[620]

While the battle raged in New Orleans that bloody morning of January 8th, the negotiators in Ghent, Belgium had concluded their talks two weeks before. On December 24th, they had initialed the Treaty of Ghent which brought hostilities to an end (subject to ratification). On Christmas Day they gathered at St Bravo's Cathedral for Mass and were preparing for a formal dinner celebrating the treaty agreement hosted by the town council of Ghent to be held in the Throne Room the evening of that same bloody January 8th.

So many lives were lost; so many men were terribly injured during the intervening days between the initial signing of the Treaty of Ghent and its final ratification. That is why some consider the January 8th battle of little historical significance. Yet one must consider. Despite the seemingly meaningless sacrifice, the fact remains that had the British prevailed on that day and taken New Orleans, those same losses may have altered the history of the United States.

Chapter 10

ASSAULT ON FORT ST. PHILLIP . . .

The Americans continued to hammer the British camp with artillery and musketry after January 8th. Commodore Patterson established a battery forward of Morgan's position from which place he could accurately strike the British base at the Villere Plantation.

This harassment continued until January 11th when sounds of heavy cannon were heard coming from downriver. Admiral Cochrane had sent gunboats upriver to assault Fort St. Philip on the Westbank of the river. This fort is located about forty miles above the mouth of the river.

Thankfully, Jackson had reinforced this fort in December. Its armaments consisted of: "*. . . twenty-nine guns: two thirty-pounders, the others were twenty-fours, one thirteen inch mortar, and several howitzers.*" Several detachments of troops had also been sent down and now took up a defensive position. The total defense consisted of 406 men under command of Major Overton.[621]

One would have expected this naval operation to have been deployed in advance of Pakenham's assault; at a minimum, it should have occurred in coordination with it. This would have divided Jackson's attention, complicated his planning, perhaps aided in the overall British plan of attack and possibly resulted in a victory.

What is most surprising, Cochrane failed to seize the opportunity of having control over the Mississippi River. Jackson possessed only the now disarmed ship *Louisiana* which was being used as a powder magazine. The British barges were the only effective naval force in the river.

Despite this advantage, no attempt to move up the Mississippi took place prior to January 8th. For whatever reason, Cochrane waited to enter the river and strike at the forts well after the Chalmette debacle, not before: *"It manifests a palpable want of combination and military skill in the British generals, that their plan of advance upon the city was not so arranged as to secure possession of the river before their land troops occupied its banks."*[622]

It is difficult to believe that after all that had transpired, Cochrane would have believed a small detachment of brigs and gunboats attacking forts downriver would accomplish what a major British army had failed to achieve.

Perhaps he intended a distraction. The British army was under continued attack while attempting to organize its retreat. The soldiers needed time to keep Jackson's forces from threatening them during their vulnerable withdrawal. Cochrane's attack did turn attention further downriver, which may have been its purpose.

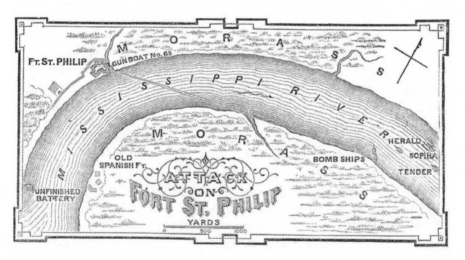

This Map show the positions of Chocrane's Gunboats and American Forts. [623]

His flotilla consisted of two bomb ships, the sloop of war *Sophia*, a brig, and a tender.

Cochrane's flotilla did not arrive within range of Fort St. Philip until the afternoon of January 9th. Overton's guard boat hastened to inform the fort's commander about the arrival of these unwelcomed guests and the Americans *". . . prepared to give them a warm reception."*

At 3:00 P.M., the British bomb vessels approached within a mile and a half of the fort. The Americans fired their 32 pounder. *"They retired out of range then anchored behind a point of land about 3,760 yards from the fort, turned broadsides towards it, and running up their flags, commenced the action."*[624]

Ranging their weapons, the sailors of the British gunboats fired their first shot short. The next shell burst over the fort, the rest rained down around the structure. Unfortunately for the British, the fuses on their mortar shells were set too long and they merely plunged deeply into the soft earth before exploding resulting only in muffled tremors and eruptions of muck.

The British employed four sea-mortars, two of thirteen inch and two of ten inch. The assault continued throughout the night, a shell being fired nearly every two minutes. All had little effect. In darkness, they sent out small vessels to reconnoiter. They approached so close that those in the fort could hear their voices.

The bombardment continued through January 10th and 11th. The Americans returned fire more for morale purposes than any hope of hitting their target, the British being out of range. Late on the 11th, a lucky shot tore the American flag from its pole. An American sailor bravely scaled the structure and, sitting on the cross-tree for nearly an hour, nailed it back in place while under continual attack.[625]

Shells rained down on the fort. The contractor's house was struck killing one man and wounding another. Cannon balls pummeled Fort St. Philip incessantly throughout the 12th, 13th, and 14th of January. Another man was killed and several wounded when a bomb burst over one of the American 32 pounders. Throughout it all, a heavy rain pelted down rendering the interior of the fort a shallow lake. Everyone was cold and wet throughout the attack.

The fort received supplies on January 13th, including ammunition from New Orleans. Finally, one of the American shells struck home on a bomb vessel, causing some confusion among the British sailors but no significant damage.

On January 17th, the shelling became more concentrated and accurate. The fort itself took several hits. But all came to a sudden end on January 18[th.] At dawn Cochrane's little flotilla hoisted sail and sped downriver to the shouts and hurrahs of the American defenders.

The bombardment was intense and had lasted uninterrupted for nine days. Over 1,000 shells had been fired, amounting to nearly seventy tons of iron and 20,000 pounds of gunpowder. American casualties were two dead and three wounded. The sacrifices of these men are seldom mentioned when accounts are given about the Battle of New Orleans.

It should be noted that January 18th also marked the evening when the British had made good their escape from the Villere Plantation and were retreating toward Lake Borgne. The campaign against New Orleans finally ended. The British expedition withdrew on the 18th of January without gaining the promised spoils or glory." [626]

The Battle of New Orleans was over! The importance of the Battle of New Orleans cannot be over-estimated and the residents of New Orleans were overcome with joy. The Americans had won a splendid victory over the most powerful nation in the world. America had reaffirmed the independence won in the American Revolution. America had secured the gains of the Louisiana Purchase. America had gained the respect of European powers. America had joined the international community on a firm footing.

Throughout this bombardment, Jackson remained in Chalmette. He maintained vigilance lest the British mount another assault. They still had over 10,000 troops in the field and the capacity to commit to another offensive.

Jackson did not feel secure in leaving his lines until having been assured that the British had evacuated the Villere Plantation and were well on their way back to the fleet. Thus, he waited until January 20th before arriving in New Orleans, nearly a month after having left his Vieux Carre' headquarters on the evening of December 23rd.

Because of these apprehensions, Jackson ordered most of his men to maintain their positions at Line Jackson in Chalmette and on the Westbank and other locations. Some he allowed to accompany him. This caused considerable grief, because one can imagine that all participants in this wonderful victory wished to participate in the coming celebrations. But Jackson would have none of it. They were ordered to remain in place. This brewed resentment.

"It is needless to attempt to describe the ovation which attended the return of the victorious army to New Orleans. It can be more easily imagined. The whole population was in the streets, at the balconies, at the windows, even on the tops of houses. There was joy in every breast, joy in every face, there were such greetings as the heart alone can give . . ."[627]

When he arrived, the people of New Orleans received him with *". . . boundless demonstrations of joy . . . the first display of popular feeling was too wild to be controlled by any regular method or system."*[628]

At Jackson's request the Apostolic Prefect of the State of Louisiana, Abbe' Dubourg, appointed January 23rd as *". . . a Day of Public*

Thanksgiving to the Almighty for his signal interposition in behalf of the safety and honor of the country."

Festivities began with a discharge of artillery, which apparently shocked some uninformed citizens into believing that hostilities had begun again. The remainder of the population gathered outside of the Place' d' Armes to welcome their hero and celebrate the grand victory that protected their city from enemy occupation.

The St. Louis Cathedral had been cleaned up and decorated, the Place d'Armes (to be re-named Jackson Square on January 28, 1815) was ablaze in beauty with a triumphal arch supported by six evergreen-covered, Corinthian columns in the center where the statue of Jackson presently resides.

"Beneath the arch stood two young girls on pedestals, holding laurel wreaths, whilst near them, as if their guardian angels, was a bright damsel, representing Liberty, and a more sedate one personifying Justice. From the arch to the entrance of the cathedral the loveliest girls of the city had been ranged in two rows, to represent the various states and Territories. They were dressed in pure white, with blue veils and silver stars on their brows. Each bore a small flag, inscribed with the name of the state she represented, and a small basket trimmed with blue ribands and full of flowers. Behind each a shield and lance were stuck in the ground, with the name, motto, and seal of each of the states. The shields were linked together with verdant festoons, which extended from the arch to the door of the cathedral."[629]

At the appointed time, General Andrew Jackson arrived at the front gate of the Place' de Armes with his staff and was welcomed with salvos from the artillery. He then marched through the gate and into the square where the *". . . two little girls, reaching forward with blushing, smiling faces, placed the laurel wreath on his brow. What a benign smile relieved the sternness of that heroic countenance, when the innocent faces of the pretty little ones arose to his view, as with so much pride and delight they performed the high task assigned to them."*[630]

Plauche's Battalion stood at attention in full dress with bayonets glistening in the sun as they awaited the arrival of General Andrew Jackson. As the hero arrived, triumphant cheers rose from the gathering crowd. Cannon fired. Music played.

Following that performance, the general then descended the stairs of the arch only to be met by a beautiful young Creole woman *". . . with face, form, manners, and expression such as the most aspiring artist might have dreamed of as a model for his Venus."* He delivered a glowing speech expressing the gratitude of a devoted city which he had spared from foreign destruction.

Jackson's response is lost. The noise of celebration obscured his humble words, and a shower of flowers covered his body. That having been done, Jackson and his staff were escorted into the cathedral where he was met by Abbe Dubourg and the local priests who delivered yet another speech before entering the church for the *Te Deum* which is traditional on such occasions.

"To him, therefore, our most fervent thanks are due for our late **unexpected** *(emphasis added) rescue considering you, General, as the man of his right hand, whom he has taken pains to call out for the important commission of our defense."*[631]

Following the religious commemorations, the city erupted into levity which continued throughout the night being: *". . . no longer disturbed by dreams of sack, ruin, bloodshed, and devastation."*[632]

Despite the festivities, Jackson remained on guard. The enemy had yet to abandon the shores of Louisiana, and the British still had the means of producing more mischief. Jackson's forces were weak, tired, and had reduced themselves to acceptance of victory even while the British fleet remained anchored in Lake Borgne, merely a few miles away.

Louisiana historian Charles Gayarre summed up Jackson's concerns best: *"Peace, whenever it shall be reestablished on fair and honorable terms, is an event in which both nations ought to rejoice; but whether the Article which are said to have been signed for its restoration will be approved by those whose province is to give to them their final confirmation, is yet uncertain. Until they shall be rectified by the Prince Regent and the President of the United States, peace, though much desired, may still be distant. When that shall be done, the happy intelligence will be publicly and speedily announced"*[633]

Although Jackson's men were finally receiving the long delayed arms shipments, the British had also been reinforced. Their honor was at stake. Would they merely accept an ignoble defeat and leave, or would they mount another offensive? They possessed both the men and material to re-engage if they chose to. Jackson had to consider every possibility.

This was not the time to relax. Jackson intended to maintain his position of vigilance until officially informed by the War Department that he could stand down, and he would not ease his defensive until such notification, including his insistence on maintaining Martial Law!

The fact that an American had been killed when a detachment under Hinds, Humbert, and Latrobe had advanced to reconnoiter the British retreat and were fired upon provided ample evidence for the need to stay at arms.

With these concerns on his mind, Jackson found himself in the unpopular position of having to inform his soldiers that they must maintain their lines of defense despite the now public accounts of a treaty having been concluded in Ghent the past December. The defenses in Chalmette, Fort St. Philip, Fort St. John, Chef Menteur, the Rigolets, all of the American outposts, had to be maintained until there was certainty that the British had no intention to return.

The British did not leave the proximity of Louisiana until January 27th. They had sailed east and had set up camp at Dauphin Island in Mobile Bay, only a day's sail away. Here the British refreshed themselves, performed military scrimmages among themselves, and awaited further orders. Cook, a British officer, best described the scene: *"In a few days almost the whole of the tents were hidden from view, and the labyrinths of the camp presented a most picturesque appearance."*[634]

They even constructed a thirty by sixty foot theater complete with canvas ceiling made from a main-sail, stage, and orchestra pit. The ships' carpenters constructed it all. Having secured costumes from a captured cargo ship, the men dressed accordingly and put on performances of *"Honeymoon"* and *"Mayor of Garret."* The Brits had settled in as they awaited further orders.[635]

On February 4th, Jackson assembled a collection of dignitaries to meet with the British. He sent his personal aid Edward Livingston, Captain Maunsel White of the Louisiana Blues, and R.D Shepherd an Aid to Commodore Patterson, to the British fleet.

Their mission was to negotiate for the exchange of prisoners and the return of slaves taken away by the British army. They arrived at a most inopportune moment. The British were preparing for the invasion of Fort Bowyer at Mobile Point.

They would stay aboard Admiral Cochrane's flag ship *H.M.S. Tonnant* for several days, during which time a generally warm relationship developed among these combatants. Of particular note was the presentation to the British of a sword found on the Chalmette battlefield claimed by General Keane but belonging to Major-General Sir Edward Pakenham. He had lost it when wounded in the conflict.[636]

Conversations among these American negotiators and their British counterparts continued with discussions on a variety of topics. The British expressed their disappointment over failing to prevail at Chalmette and the disappointment of some of the civilian administrators over not having the opportunity to govern in New Orleans.

While these conversations continued, the British organized and deployed an invasion force that took Fort Bowyer. Assaulted from both land and sea and facing overwhelming odds, Colonel Lawrence surrendered. Plans for taking Mobile next were prepared with the intention of at least bringing some honor back from the British expedition.

An interesting exchange then took place between the representatives of these two governments. Admiral Cochrane requested the honor of his American counterparts for dinner in his quarters aboard the *Tonnant*. After dinner had been consumed and wine was served, Cochrane had a curtain which covered the rear window of his cabin drawn to reveal the American flag over Fort Bowyer being replaced with the British Union Jack.

"Well Colonel Livingston, you perceive that our day has commenced", said British Admiral Codrington. Without hesitating a moment, Livingston responded while raising his glass: *"To Your Health, we do not begrudge you that small consolation."* [637]

Thirty-one British soldiers and eleven American lives were lost in this engagement . . . the very last violent exchange of the War of 1812.

One must consider, since Mobile was now in British hands, could the original plan of attack be re-organized? Despite the losses, the British still had sufficient forces to re-initiate an invasion. One must acknowledge, however, that the lack of field officers would have made this a problem.

Indeed, the British victory celebration was short lived. Just two days after the surrender of Fort Bowyer a gig arrived alongside of the *Tonnant* with a message. Shepherd was conversing with Admiral Malcolm on deck when the admiral opened the dispatch, read the contents, then took off his cap and said: *"Good News! Good News! We are friends! The HMS Brazen has just arrived outside with news of peace. I am delighted"* Then he added, *"I have hated this war from the beginning,"* [638]

Jackson's emissaries returned to report about the end of hostilities on February 19th. Jackson happily announced the peace to his troops but reminded them that it had not as yet been ratified and they *". . . should not be thrown off their guard by a mere report."*

Back in New Orleans, Jackson insisted on maintaining Martial Law until officially informed that he could stand down. His reputation for ruthlessness in demanding obedience to his orders began to grate on his men. Some began to falter. Illness in the inclement conditions took its toll. Over five hundred Americans became infected with dysentery within a month of the battle. [639]

Murmurs of frustration became loud and open among Jackson's troops. Friends of the soldiers forced to stay in camp echoed their anger. Some Frenchmen who had served, but not become naturalized citizens, sought the protection of the French consul and were thus able to abandon their posts.[640]

The French Consul, Chevalier de Tousard, issued certificates proving their French national origins. Jackson signed them and allowed the soldiers to be discharged. However, within days so many of these certificates were issued that Jackson became suspicious, and he questioned the consul.[641]

Not satisfied with the response, on February 28th Jackson ordered all Frenchmen who were not citizens and were unwilling to adhere to Martial Law to be removed from the city and not be nearer than Baton Rouge. This *"excited some indignation"*. At the same time, his old problems with the State Legislature began to surface. They took the opportunity provided by his relations with the French to publicly castigate him in publications.

Jackson then learned that one Louaillier, a member of the legislature and *"a very active and useful citizen during the defense of the city"* had authored one very brutal criticism. Jackson had him arrested in Masparo's Exchange on March 5th and confined in the barracks. He was tried under Martial Law for mutiny. This generated anger among the legislator's friends and associates.[642]

His attorney Morel sought a writ of *Habeas Corpus* from Judge Xavier Martin of the Supreme Court who refused to intercede. Next his attorney turned to United States District Court Judge Dominic A. Hall, an Englishman by birth. When Federal Judge Hall granted the defendant's appeal of his case for his release under *habeas corpus,* Jackson ordered Colonel Arbuckle to arrest Judge Hall for *"Aiding, abetting and exciting mutiny"* . . . a violation of Martial Law.

Jackson's actions generated controversy. Both men enjoyed extensive community support. When Louaillier was tried, the court found for the accused on March 9th. Jackson was furious and refused to release the prisoner in violation of the court's order.

Anticipating the court rendering a similar verdict in his case against Judge Hall, Jackson had the judge removed from the city and ordered: *". . . not to return before ratification of the treaty of peace should be regularly announced, or the British have departed from the Southern coast."*[643]

The glory of January 8th and the revelry of January 20th were rapidly eclipsed by anger and frustration. Jackson's star began to fade. The reason he had earned the appellation "Old Hickory" became obvious to everyone. He was indeed difficult to work as the coming weeks would soon attest.

Two days after taking this action against Judge Hall, on March 13th, cannons boomed in the city announcing the arrival of the formal declaration of peace. The War of 1812 was officially over!

Jackson, a soldier to his boots, had awaited official notification from the federal government about peace. This would not occur until March 14, 1815, a full 80 days after both nations' representatives in Ghent had initialed documents of peace and over a month after official ratification by King George III, President Madison, and the United States Senate on February 16th, 1815.

He addressed the citizens of Louisiana: *"Peace, whenever it shall be reestablished on fair and honorable terms, is an event in which both nations ought to rejoice; but whether the Article which are said to have been signed for its restoration will be approved by those whose province is to give to them their final confirmation, is yet uncertain. Until they shall be rectified by the Prince Regent and the President of the United States, peace, though much desired, may still be distant. When that shall be done, the happy intelligence will be publicly and speedily announced"*[644]

Jackson ended Martial Law, ordered his army to stand down, and released all arrested men from prison. But the controversies did not end. Judge Dominck Hall remained furious over his imprisonment. He imposed a fine of $1,000 on Jackson for Contempt of Court ($15,000 in 2013 dollars). The arguments on both sides were sound. Hall believed Jackson had exceeded his authority by imprisoning a federal judge. Jackson argued that Martial Law had no limits.

Jackson defused the raw emotions by calmly drafting a check for the $1,000 and handed it to the marshal. He then retired from the courtroom: *". . . greeted by cheers from the crowd in the streets."*

Jackson returned to Maspero's Coffee House on the corner of Rue Charters and Rue St. Louis where his friends had gathered and to collect $1,000 to be deposited in the general's account. Jackson refused to take the money and, instead, had it given to the widows and orphans of those men who had sacrificed their lives in the long campaign.

As an interesting aside, it should be noted that even when Jackson had retired from public life and was quite ill, some remembered this blemish on his career. They solicited Congress to have the fine refunded thus removing any mark of dishonor that might attend his reputation.[645]

Shortly after these legal transactions, General Andrew Jackson turned over command of his Louisiana forces to General Gaines and left New Orleans for his home in Nashville.

"And thus Jackson parted from his comrades in arms, leaving in the hearts of them all, feelings, which still animate the souls of the few remaining veterans

of that epoch, who linger among their descendants, as beacons to guide and excite the patriotism of the present generation. "[646]

In Ghent, Belgium, representatives of both nations had initialed the treaty of peace ending the war on December 24, 1814. That same treaty would be ratified February 18, 1815. During the interim, a very bloody campaign unfolded on a collection of sugar plantations below the city of New Orleans. The failure of the British expedition secured that peace.

Few would argue that the dogged determination of one man played an essential role in the American victory. General Andrew Jackson inspired men to accomplish what many believed to be impossible. That same stubborn single minded sense of purpose would also cause him problems.

The fact that many New Orleanians had expressed deep concerns or even hostility to Jackson's persistence in maintaining Martial Law for such an extended time was of no concern to him. Jackson did so despite so many reports of a treaty. A British Admiral, a British General, and most newspapers had announced peace. This added to his problem, and further fueled local anger. Was Jackson wrong?

Jackson raises the question at the core of the Battle of New Orleans controversy. His first notification of peace had come from General Lambert of the Royal Army. Could he be believed? Or, was this a ruse to make him drop his defenses? Could he afford to be wrong? Lambert still possessed a considerable force, far in excess of anything Jackson could place in the field.

The later communications, though believable, were not official. As a general in direct command of a region recently at war, should he respond to press reports, rumor, and documents in the enemy's possession? Or, is he obligated and duty bound to await official notification from his superiors?

A lesser man may have caved to pressure, not Andrew Jackson. He finished what he started without compromise.

The Treaty of Ghent which ended the War of 1812 was not ratified until February 18, 1815. This supports Jackson's position. The war was NOT officially over at the time he ordered his men to maintain their defensive positions! To further complicate his position, he did not receive official notification about the treaty until March, 1815; over eighty days after the treaty had been agreed to.

One can appreciate the attitude of the men under his command who so urgently desired to rejoin their friends and families, especially in light of the fact that a considerable number succumbed to dysentery and a variety of other diseases while maintaining their posts. But one must also understand the peculiar pressures Jackson faced.

By March of 1815, the Battle of New Orleans and the War of 1812 were officially over.

Throughout the campaign, a series of incidents on both sides might have altered the outcome of the conflict. Thornton not being allowed to attack New Orleans on December 23rd, Gibb's recall on December 28th, and Mullins dereliction of duty by failing to secure the fascines and ladders on January 8th all contributed to Britain's defeat.

Despite all these failings, the British expedition might still have succeeded had Thornton's Westbank flanking maneuver achieved its goal in a timely manner. Or, if he had been granted the much needed reinforcements he requested once he had taken command of the Westbank. Despite all other mistakes and delays, the failure to calculate the current of the Mississippi River when Thornton disembarked on the morning of January 8th condemned Pakenham's carefully calculated plan to failure.

It is almost impossible to imagine that the 1814-15 British expedition against the Gulf coast of the United States, one of the largest military expeditions ever assembled up to that time, might have succeeded and the future of the United States of America might have been decidedly different . . .

. . . But for a Piece of Wood!

Chapter 11

EPILOGUE

The British campaign for New Orleans had come to an end. On February 18, 1815, the United States Senate and President James Madison ratified the Treaty of Ghent which officially concluded the War of 1812. Peaceful relations developed between the United States and Great Britain from this day forward, an alliance which would continue into the 21ˢᵗ century. The Battle of New Orleans would be the last time these two nations opposed one another in combat.

As for the feelings of British citizens about this defeat, they were distracted by the escape of Napoleon from the Island of Elba. News arrived in London about both events simultaneously on February 23, 1815. William Cobbett, a liberal essayist and author, wrote this about their New Orleans disaster: *". . . and this was all the people of the duped nation ever heard of the matter. Bonaparte had landed from Elba and the battle of Waterloo soon succeeded. Both the government and the people were glad to forget all about this unmerciful beating in America."*

He attributed the victory to*: "Providence, nothing less than providence could have baffled and beaten such a powerful foe!"*

Cobbet went further in honoring General Andrew Jackson: *"This Battle of New Orleans broke the heart of European despotism. The man who won it did, in that one act, more for the good and the honor of the human race than ever was done by any other man."* [647]

American losses during the conflicts around New Orleans were considerably more than popular belief holds. A total of 370 men became casualties of this conflict including losses sustained in the Battle of Lake Borgne.

Battle	Killed	Wounded	Missing
Lake Borgne	5	30	None
December 23rd	24	115	74
December 28th	9	8	None
January 1st	11	23	None
January 8th	13	39	19
Total	62	215	93

648

Once hostilities ended, investigations began. Incidents that had occurred on both sides during the military campaign for New Orleans came under review. Men had to be held accountable for actions taken or not taken.

Nations need to maintain military discipline. To achieve that end, military actions go under careful review by superior officers at their conclusion. That occurred after the Battle of New Orleans, just as it does today.

Andrew Jackson focused his attention on two individuals: Major Jacques Villere and General Morgan. Villere received Jackson's ire for disobeying orders and leaving Bayou Bienvenue open. Morgan showed cowardice in the line of duty.

Major Jacques Villere disobeyed direct orders by not blocking access through Bayou Bienvenue. This allowed the British to make a landing below New Orleans. Why did Major Jacques Villere defy his commanding officer's direct order to close all bayous?

Jackson directed his first fury at Major Jacques Villere. He was angry on December 23rd when he first learned of the British arrival through Bayou Bienvenue which Villere left unblocked. On December 27th he mentioned this in his letter to Secretary of War Monroe. *"Unfortunately, however, a picquet which the general had established at the mouth of the bayou Bienvenue, and with, notwithstanding my orders, had been left unobstructed, was completely surprised and the enemy penetrated through a canal leading to his farm."*

The judges conducting the court martial in the case of Major Villere on March 15, 1815 found him *"not guilty"* of *". . . the charges and specifications exhibited against him, and do acquit him of all and every one of them."* Robert Butler, Adjutant General for the court further declared that Villere *". . . appears to have performed his duty, from the moment he was left in command under the orders of Major-General Villere, with zeal and fidelity; and that the circumstance of his surprise and capture by the enemy, though much to be regretted, might have occurred to the most vigilant officer, and must be attributed to the loss of the whole of his picquet or advanced guard, and the extraordinary rapidity with which the enemy moved from that point."*

That ended Jackson's case against Jacques Villere. Apparently the court found no guilt for failure to close Bayou Bienvenue in violation of a direct order.[649]

Jackson convened a second court of inquiry to examine events on the Westbank with particular focus on the actions taken and not taken by General Morgan and other militia members with particular emphasis on the Kentucky Militia's actions. All was nearly lost by the failure of the American forces to hold the line on the Westbank. How did this happen?

When told of the brave defense against unequal odds, Jackson bristled. He knew better. He had requested the casualty list for those killed, wounded, and missing in the Westbank defense from December 23rd to January 8th. If indeed the fighting had been as robust as Morgan reported, casualties would naturally result. Few casualties were reported which reinforced Jackson's position that little resistance had been offered by the defenders.[650]

Jackson publicly held the Kentucky Militia accountable for the near disaster on the Westbank. Relying on reports by General Morgan and Commodore Patterson, Jackson wrote to the Secretary of War in his official report that: *". . . the Kentucky reinforcement, in whom so much reliance had been placed, ingloriously fled, drawing after them by their example the remainder of the forces and thus yielding to the enemy that most formidable position."*[651]

The official report denouncing the Kentucky Militia for cowardice in the face of the enemy angered all Kentuckians, in particular, those brave men and officers who contributed so much throughout the War of 1812 and the Battle of New Orleans. Something had to be done!

General Adair, commander of all Kentucky forces, took offense at this report and officially defended his men. On February 9, 1815 William Carroll ordered that General Morgan attend the Court of Inquiry under way at the request of General Adair of the Kentucky regiments. Adair believed that Jackson was mistaken in blaming the Kentucky militia for the retreat on the Westbank and that he was reacting to reports from General Morgan and Commodore Patterson who sought merely to cover their own errors of judgment by blaming the Kentuckians.

The Court of Inquiry sustained his position on February 19, 1815. In this instance the Court of Inquiry conducted by Major General William Carroll, President of the Court, found that the: *". . . conduct of Colonel Davis, Dijon, and Cavallier, in the addition and retreat on the 8th of January, on the Westbank of the Mississippi, is not reprehensible, nor do they know of any misconduct, as officers, in either since that time."*

The court further decided that the cause of the retreat should be: *". . . attributed to the shameful flight of the command of Major Arnaud, sent to oppose the landing of the enemy; the retreat of the Kentucky militia, which considering their position, the deficiency of their arms, and other causes, may be excusable . . ."*[652]

In other words, the respective military tribunals snubbed Jackson's attempt to assess blame for the near disastrous outcome for the Battle of New Orleans on Major Jacques Villere and the Kentucky militia. Obviously, since a glorious victory had been achieved, there was little stomach for assessing blame for what might have happened.

Arsene de Latour sought to hear Morgan's side of the story for clarification before publishing his book on the campaign. On April 10, 1815 Latour wrote Morgan about the *". . . publication he was preparing upon the last campaigns relating to the transactions that took place on the fight bank on the 8th of January last."*[653]

Latour goes on to write: *". . . I am of the opinion that you are to hear of the shame of our disgrace on that part of our defense, I thought myself duty bound as a man of honor, to impart to you what I wrote on the subject previous to my putting it to the press. What I have stated, is, I believe unreservedly true, However, you are in a situation to furnish me with such reservations(?) which may tend to rectify what should not be published . . ."*[654]

Latour ends on a kind note commenting that: *". . . I have no animosity against you, on the contrary as a private citizen, I have the regard for you that I think you deserve"*

Evidently, Latour desired to write an accurate account of the War of 1812 and sought input from all participants. Even though he shared Jackson's assessment of Morgan's performance, it did not prevent him from trying to contact the disgraced general to provide him with an opportunity to defend his actions. There is no record of a response.

It would not end there. The rancor between these once friendly comrades in arms, General Adair and General Jackson, would fester for years. Bitter correspondence ended between these once good friends on a sourer note two years later when Jackson responded to Adair with words *"beyond all restraint."* It had become too personal. It nearly ended in tragedy as the two men agreed to meet on the field of honor at the border between their respective states to settle the question at gun point. They did meet, but their seconds prevailed upon them to end their discord peacefully, which they did and thus avoided a most tragic end to an unfortunate affair. The settlement may have preserved the life of a future President of the United States.

Not so for the British. Someone had to be held accountable for the defeat. For them, there were many failures, mistakes, miscalculations, and incidents of negligence all of which contributed to the disaster. One can question the many critical decisions made by Admiral Cochrane; General Pakenham's determination to go forward on January 8th knowing that his plans were faltering; the failure of British naval officers to bring up enough artillery and ammunition to achieve victory; the manner in which the troops were overburdened as they advanced that fateful day and the tactics employed during the assault of January 8th. General Lambert's surrender of the Westbank had to be considered as well.

Despite the multitude of failings, only one man became the object of particular attention and distain. For the British, all fault lay with Lieutenant-Colonel Thomas Mullins, captain of the 44th Regiment of Foot. Despite being given direct orders to advance ahead of General Gibbs' assault with the ladders and fascines needed to scale Jackson's breastworks during the decisive battle of January 8th, Mullins failed to follow this order. When the attack failed, the British Army laid the responsibility on this one man. The bitterness of the surviving officers can best be described in the words of S.R. Gleig: *". . . the behavior of Colonel Mullins was however, disgraceful in the highest degree."* Gleig also held Mullins responsible for the death of General Pakenham, because had he performed his task, Pakenham would not have had to place his life in jeopardy trying to muster the 44th to do its duty. The British army needed to know what happened and why.[655]

On July 11, 181,5 the British Army held a General Court Martial at the Royal Barracks in Dublin, Ireland. Lieutenant-General Meyrick presided over a tribunal composed of fourteen other officers ranging in rank from Colonel to Major.

Colonel Mullins was arraigned on three counts, as a reading of the official record recounts:

1. "For having on the 8th of January, 1815, shamefully neglected and disobeyed the orders he has received from the late Major-General Gibbs, commanding the 2nd Brigade, to collect fascines and ladders, and to be formed with them at the head of

the column of attack at the time directed, and in disobedience of said orders, suffering the Regiment under his command to pass the redoubt where the fascines and ladders were lodged, and remaining at the head of the column for half an hour upwards, without taking any steps to put the 44th Regiment in possession of the fascines and ladders, in conformity with said orders, knowing the period of attack to be momentarily approaching, in consequence of such disobedience and neglect the 44th Regiment on being sent to the redoubt, and returning hurriedly with the fascines etc was thrown into confusion, and moved off to the attack in an irregular and disconnected manner leading to the fire and disorder which ensued in the attacking column, and the disasters attending it.

2. For scandalous and infamous behavior before the enemy, near New Orleans, on the 8th of January, 1815, in not leading and conducting the 44th Regiment under his command up to the enemy's works; in not placing the ladders and fascines in the ditch as he was ordered to do; and in not setting that example of gallantry to the soldiers, so indispensable requisite, a part of an officers duty to insure the success of such an attack, in consequence of such misbehavior, the 44th Regiment did not perform the service allotted to them, never having made an attempt to place the fascines in the ditch, and thereby leading to the cause of the failure of the attack.

3. For scandalous conduct having said to an officer of his Regiment, on 7th January, 1815, when informed the 44th was destined to carry the fascines etc. It is a forlorn hope, and the Regiment must be sacrificed or words to that effect, such an expression being calculated to dispirit those under his command to render them discontented and the service allotted to the, demonstrative of the feeling with which he undertook the enterprise, and infamous and disgraceful to the character of a commanding officer of a British Regiment.[656]"

These were very serious charges and if found guilty the penalty would be severe. The prosecution presented its case, and Mullins mustered thirteen witnesses who testified in his favor. Colonel Mullins conducted his own defense, questioned witnesses, and addressed the court.

Many of the questions concerned the presence of Mullins near the front. Several officers and men responded that they did not see him, while a number of others represented that they saw Mullins near the "ditch", which was the term applied to Jackson's breastwork along the Rodriguez Canal.

The prosecutions problem stemmed from the fact that none of the superior officers whose testimony would have carried the greatest weight were present at the Court Martial. All had been killed in action.

In his closing argument, Mullins aggressively took to his defense: *"On the evidence of those thirteen witnesses of all ranks, who saw me there, in contradiction to the ungenerous surmises of the few, who did not see me at all, I now call upon this high minded court, the members of which, with my entire concurrence, now sit as judges on my conduct, and arbiters of my character, with the feeling that becomes my situation, but in the firmness that benefits my innocence, I call upon you in your justice, by your decision, to expunge this blot upon the British Army, this stigma upon the Irish name, this infamous slander on an injured man."*[657]

Mullins argued that to place the blame for the disaster of January 8th on one matter, the placement of ladders and fascines by the 44th Regiment, understates the magnitude of the disaster and places responsibility solely on one event when the facts prove otherwise. Many decisions made and not made contributed to the defeat.

Furthermore, the defeat could not be the responsibility of just one man, as some accusers would want the court to believe. He introduced into the record an extract of General Lambert's report which detailed the difficulties. He made particular mention of Patterson's battery on the Westbank: *"It is a strong corroboration of this opinion, that the American General, in his dispatch, agrees with the British General in ascribing the greatest importance to the taking or losing of this battery; and the young staff officers, in their endeavors, in their opinions, to load me exclusively with this disaster, have not only said positively that the circumstances connected with the fascines and ladders was the sole cause, but have added positively, that the battery had no connection whatsoever with the repulse."* [658]

With this final comment Mullins ended his defense and left his fate in the hands of the court. The members of the court retired to consider the charges, and then returned to issue their judgment:

On the first count . . . *"Shamefully neglected and disobeyed the orders he had received from the late Major-General Gibbs"*, they found Mullins guilty.

On the second count . . . *"Scandalous and infamous misbehavior before the enemy in not leading 44th did not perform the service allotted to them."* The court found Mullins guilty for not placing the ladders and fascines in the ditch as ordered, but they also found that the prisoner *". . . did not evince any want of personal courage, and that he is NOT guilty of scandalous and infamous misbehavior before the enemy."*

On the third and final count . . . that charge relating to his conversations upon being given his orders that "*it is a forlorn hope, the Regiment must be sacrificed*" the court found that although the evidence indicates that the prisoner did indeed express such apprehensions, but these comments were made to a fellow officer in private, and the court therefore acquitted him of this charge.[659]

Following these findings, the court then passed sentence. Lieutenant-Colonel Thomas Mullins of the 44th Regiment "*shall be cashiered.*" He was dishonorably dismissed from the army. Thus ended the career of Colonel Thomas Mullins.

At the conclusion of Mullins' trial, the British Army officially closed the book on the New Orleans campaign and the War of 1812. For them, the story had come to a close.

However, the site of the Battle of New Orleans remained alive in the minds of those Americans who fought and lived through the carnage. But time and circumstance gradually began to erase public memories of this historic event.

In 1839, twenty-four years after the battle, a group of men assembled under the name Young Men's Jackson Committee to raise money to commemorate that great day. They desired to build a monument. Unfortunately, this effort was still-born.

The next year another committee of citizens invited former President Andrew Jackson to come to New Orleans. This group of active citizens made careful preparations for the arrival of the great hero who arrived aboard the steamer *Vicksburg* on January 8, 1840 . . . the twenty-fifth anniversary of that decisive battle in Chalmette.[660]

Thousands of New Orleans' residents lined the curb of Canal Street as Jackson paraded to the Place d'Armes. Unfortunately, on the same day a large crowd assembled at the Chalmette Battlefield for the laying of a cornerstone to build a monument. Jackson never arrived and there was no cornerstone to be laid. The disappointed crowd which had arrived: "*. . . by steamboats, towboats, railroad cars, coaches, cabs, cabriolets, hacks, horses, wagons sand carts, go carts, hand carts, drays, dugouts, in short every description of land carriage and water craft . . . in short all orders were there . . . there was no Jackson and no cornerstone.*" No one knows how the misinformation was circulated.[661]

Jackson did visit the battlefield, but it was two days later on January 10th. The general then left New Orleans on January 13th. Sadly, there actually was a cornerstone ordered for delivery with the date "Eighth of January, 1815" engraved upon it The granite block arrived late, the men on the riverboat off-loaded the stone where it was: "*. . . placed,* *fixed, or laid in some spot, position or situation, we don't know which, or what, by three or four gentlemen, all there were on board.*[662]

The stone was never found. Jackson did lay one cornerstone during his visit. That was in the Place d'Armes. It was the last time he came to New Orleans. Jackson died in 1845.

Seven years after Jackson's death, in 1851, a new committee called the *Jackson Monument Association* came into being. The new committee was composed of some of the city's most illustrious men, included among them the aging General Jean Baptiste Plauche' who served with Jackson and the noted historian Charles Gayarre'. They agreed to raise the necessary funds to construct a monument in Chalmette.

Unfortunately, after six months of work, the committee had raised only $4,140.00. They appealed to the state for official recognition and gained that distinction along with an appropriation of $10,000.00 for the erection of a statue honoring Jackson in the Place d'Armes and $5,000 to acquire a site for a monument in the Chalmette Battlefield. On February 14, 1855 M. Bachelot sold the property to the committee. It took three years to consummate the sale.

Next came determining the monument's design. On October 19, 1854, the committee decided on the location for the monument at 767 feet from the river along what had been General Jackson's breastworks. In April of 1855, the association examined numerous designs. They even considered one to be constructed of bronze at a height of seventy-five feet. This was rejected in favor of a taller structure.

Four proposals arrived and the one selected resembled an Egyptian obelisk of 150 feet in height, mounted on a pedestal of steps, with four Egyptian styled doors, one on each face. Only one of these doors was to be functional, opening to a circular staircase allowing visitors to ascend to the top and view the surrounding area through several narrow vertical windows. The Association chose this design so that it might: "*. . . form a conspicuous point of attraction and elevation which could be discerned at a distance of many miles . . .*"

Newton Richards, a stone mason and architect from New England, won the design contest. On May 30, 1855, by unanimous vote, the Association awarded the contract to Richards & Stroud for the actual construction of the marble edifice at a cost of $57,000 with payments to be made based upon achieving specified vertical benchmarks.

The *Jackson Monument Association* thus had two projects to complete: an equestrian statue of General Andrew Jackson contracted to artist Clark Mills and a 150 foot obelisk in Chalmette.

Almost immediately the costs of these projects exceeded expectations. Priority went to the statue which was dedicated in

February 1856 when the Place d'Armes was renamed Jackson Square. With cost overruns, this left the Association with only $12,153.00 to complete the Chalmette Monument. That allowed for enough material to complete a mere sixty feet.

Although the Louisiana legislature allocated an additional $15,000, the funds were soon nearly exhausted. In 1856, construction stopped. The contractors started again on April 1, 1857 to build the shaft to a height of fifty-six feet. Payment for that work was made on May 2, 1859. The builders then stopped working again with the obelisk at fifty-six feet ten inches on its base which brought the monument to a total height of sixty-nine feet four inches.

Because work had to be stopped, the workers *"temporarily topped it off with a pyramidal-shaped wooden roof."*

By the late 1800s the monument site had become an overgrown field. A visitor in 1890 stated that those coming approached at their own hazard: *"The approach from the river is through a narrow lane, so grown up in weeds and underbrush that even the narrow foot path is almost impassable for ladies by reason for this growth, reaching eight or ten feet in height."*

The situation became so disgraceful that outrage arose. A group of dedicated and influential ladies formed a new organization: *The Louisiana Society of United States Daughters 1776 and 1812.* They responded to a letter in a local paper that: *". . . called attention to the neglected condition of the Chalmette battleground and the unfinished monument."*

The Society incorporated in 1894 and the Louisiana state legislature placed the monument into their trust. The state then awarded them $2,000 to renew work on the project. By 1896 the new association had organized and retained the architects Favrot & Livaudais to prepare plans for the monument's completion.

Still lacking the necessary funds, in 1902, at the request of the Society, the state asked the federal government to take over the monument and complete it within five years then return it to the Daughters. Congress took no action.

In 1906, Alfred Theard, a civil engineer and member of the *Louisiana Engineering Society,* completed a study of the unfinished obelisk. He determined that it would take about $25,000 to finish. Congress appropriated the money and Theard was appointed by the War Department as project engineer.

According to his assessment, the monument could be completed with the existing foundation, but only to a height of one hundred feet, not one hundred and fifty feet. This destroyed the overall aesthetic dimensions of the obelisk, but nothing else could be done.

Captain Milton P. Doullut won the contract to complete the structure. Another problem arose. The marble used on the original site came from a closed quarry in New York. Doullut was forced to scrounge for the matching marble from dismantled former structures. Because of the delay in completion and the need to search for suitable marble, a close examination of the edifice reveals exactly where the old construction ended and the new began. The monument displays a clear line of demarcation.

After much toil, the *Chalmette Monument* was completed in 1908. On March 16, 1909 *The United States Daughters of 1776 and 1812* held a dedication ceremony with the keys being returned to their President, Mrs. Victor Meyer. An additional $40,000 in federal funds had been committed to finish the job.

Interesting to note that in November of 1929, the *Daughters* informed the War Department that they lacked the means of maintaining the site and asked the federal government for assistance. On December 12th, 1929, Congressman James O'Connor introduced a bill into Congress to establish the Chalmette Battlefield as a historic park.

Nearly ten years later, on August 10, 1939, the Chalmette site was designated a National Historical Park and placed under the jurisdiction of the Park Service where it remains to this day.[663]

Since that date celebrations have been held annually at the Chalmette Battlefield marking the historic struggle that occurred there. Recently, these include historic re-enactors who provide visitors with a true sense of what life was like for the combatants on both sides of this conflict. Today the week of January 8th is commemorated with night tours of the American and British encampments, re-enactments of historic battles, lectures, a mass at St. Louis Cathedral, a similar mass conducted at Our Lady of Prompt Succor Church in Chalmette, and memorials on both the battlefield and Jackson Square.

So ends the story that occurred nearly 200 years ago.

As for the monument, it stands tall as a majestic reminder over the field that marks the grandest victory in American History and the most humiliating defeat in the annals of Great Britain.

The surrounding land in no way resembles what it did so many years ago. Industries, highways, ports, residential developments, and businesses now mark the area where once sugar plantations thrived. Only one open field commemorates the actual site of the battlefield where so many suffered and died in the cause of their national honor.

664

Bibliography

Albright, Harry. "New Orleans, Battle of the Bayous" New York: Hippoicrene Books, 1990

Arthur, Stanley Clisby. "The Story of the Battle of New Orleans" New Orleans: Louisiana Historical Society, 1915

Avalon Project. "Treaty of Ghent 1814", Yale Law School

Christian, Marcus. "Negro Soldiers in the Battle of New Orleans" New Orleans: The Battle of New Orleans 150th Anniversary Committee of Louisiana, 1965

Cerami, Charles. "Jefferson's Great Gamble" Naperville, IL: Scourcebooks Inc., 2003

Clement, William Edwards. "Plantation Life on the Mississippi" New Orleans: Pelican Publishing Company, 1952

Cooke, Sir John Henry. "A Narrative of Events in the South of France, and or the Attacks on New Orleans, in 1814 and 1815" London: T & W Boone, 1835

Cope, Sir William. "The History of the Rifle Brigade" London: Chatto & Windus; Piccadilly, 1877

Dasey, Powel. "Louisiana at the Battle of New Orleans" Louisiana: The Battle of New Orleans 150th Anniversary Committee of Louisiana, 1965

Davis, Edwin. "Louisiana: A Narrative History" Baton Rouge, Clayton's Book Store, 1965

Davis, William. "The Pirates Lafitte: The Treacherous World of the Corsairs of the Gulf" Boston: Houghton Mifflin Harcourt, 2006

Darling, Anthony. "Red Coat and Brown Bess" London: Museum Restoration Service, 1970

Davis, Edwin. "Louisiana: A Narrative History" Baton Rouge: Claitor's Bookstore, 1965 de Verges, Marie Cruza. "American Forces at Chalmette" Louisiana:The Battle of New Orleans 150th Anniversary Committee of Louisiana 1965

Dixon, Richard. "The Battle on the West Bank" Louisiana:The Battle of New Orleans 150th Anniversary Committee of Louisiana, 1965

Dorsey, Florence. "Master of the Mississippi: Henry Shreve and the Conquest of the Mississippi" Boston: Houghton Mifflin Co., 1941

Fortier, Alcee. "A History of Louisiana" Baton Rouge: Claitor's Publishing Division, Volumes 1-4, 1985

Gayarre', Charles. "History of Louisiana Vol IV" New Orleans: Pelican Publishing Company, 1974

Gleig, G.R. "The Campaigns of the British Army at Washington and New Orleans 1814-1815" (Boston: IndyPublish, 2006

Hickey, Donald, "The War of 1812: A short History" Chicago: University of Illinois Press, 1995

Huber, Leonard. "New Orleans as it Was in 1815" Louisiana:The Battle of New Orleans 150th Anniversary Committee of Louisiana, 1965

Huber, Leonard. "The Battle of New Orleans and its Monument" New Orleans: Laborde Printing, 1983

James, William. "Full and Correct Account of the Military Occurrences of the Late War Between Great Britain and the United States of America" London: Black, Kingsbury, and Allen, 1818)

Kendall, John Smith; "History of New Orleans" New Orleans: 1922 1922

Latour, Arsene la Carriere. "Historical Memoir of the War in West Florida and Louisiana in 1846" New Orleans, Historic New Orleans Collection, 1999

Lossing, Benson. "The Pictorial Field-Book for the War of 181"; New York: Harper & Brothers Publishers, 1869

Louisiana Gazette. (Newspaper) Williams Research Center microfilm

McAfee, Robert Breckinidge. "History of the Late War in the Western Country" Lexington, Ky: Worsley & Smith 1816 reprint 1966:University Microfilms.

Neumann, George C. "The Brown Bess" (The American Rifleman, April 2001.)

Hezekiah Niles, Niles National Register, (Baltimore) 1811-1849, THNOC

Owsley, Frank Lawrence Jr. "Struggle for the Gulf Borderlands: The Creek War and the Battle of New Orleans 1812-1815" Tuscaloosa: The University of Alabama Press, 2000

Parton, James. "Makers of American History: General Jackson" New York: The University Society 1905

Patterson, Benton Rain. "The Generals: Andrew Jackson, Sir Edward Pakenham, and the Road to the Battle of New Orleans" New York & London: New York University Press, 1929)

Patton, Charles, Chalmette. "The Battle for New Orleans and How the British Nearly Stole the Louisiana Territory" Bowling Green, Kentucky: Hickory Tales Publishing, 2001

Pickles, Tim. "New Orleans 1815; Andrew Jackson Crushes the British" Great Britain: Osprey Publishing, 1993

Reilly, Robin. "The British at the Gates, The New Orleans Campaign in the War of 1812" New York, G.P. Putnam's Sons, 1974

Remini, Robert. "The Battle of New Orleans, Andrew Jackson's and America's First Military Victory" New York: Penguin Books, 1999

Remini, Robert V. "Andrew Jackson and his Indian Wars" New York: Penquin Group, 2001)

Scott, Valerie McNair. "Major-General Sir Edward M. Pakenham" Louisiana:The Battle of New Orleans 150th Anniversary Committee of Louisiana, 1965

Smith, Zackary F.; "The Battle of New Orleans" Georgia:Wayne & Judy Dasher 2008 Reprint from original (1904: Louisville, KY, Filson Club)

The Currier (Newspaper) Williams Research Center Microfilm)

Thomson, John Lewis, "1816: Historical Sketches of the Late War Between the United States and Great Britain" (Philadelphia: Thomas Desilver, 1816)

Walker, Alexander. "Life of Andrew Jackson to which is added an Authentic Narrative of the Memorable Achievements of the American Army at New Orleans in the Winter of 1814,1815" Philadelphia: G.G. Evans, 1860

Williams Research Center, Charters Street New Orleans (most complete repository for primary information on the Battle of New Orleans)

Williams Research Center, The Historic New Orleans Collection (THNOC): "Louisiana and War of 1812 Related documents from the British National Archives"; There are 28 reels of Microfilm divided into two phases. **Phase one**: Admiralty Office Records 1814 (reels `1-7); Foreign Office (reels 10-14); Colonial Office Records (reels 8 & 9); War Office Records (reels 15-18). **Phase Two:**

Represent the last ten reels of the project: Colonial Office (reel
    19); Foreign Office (reels 20-27), and War Office (reel 28).
Wilson, Samuel, "Plantation Houses on the Battlefield of New Orleans"
    Louisiana:The Battle of New Orleans 150th Anniversary Committee
    of Louisiana, 1965

Maps of the Theater of Operations
During
The Battle of New Orleans

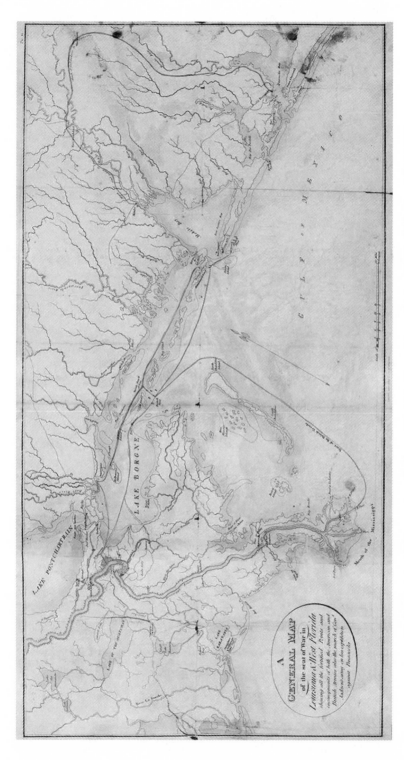

A
GENERAL MAP
of the seat of War in
Louisiana & West Florida
showing all the Nautical Route and
encampments of both the American and
British Armies who the march of Gen.
Andrew Jackson in his expedition
against Pensacola

This map provides an overall view of British Operations in the Gulf of Mexico 1814-1815

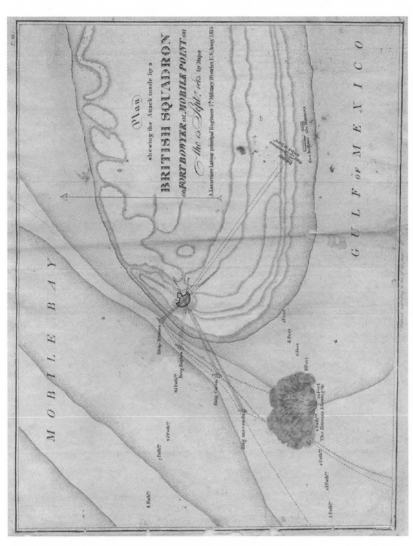

British Attack on Fort Bowyer located at Mobile Point at the beginning of British operations in the Gulf of Mexico.

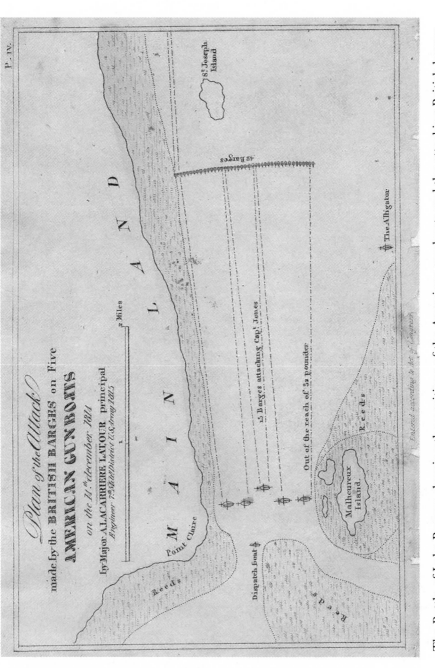

The Battle of Lake Borgne showing the positions of the American gunboats and the attacking British barges.

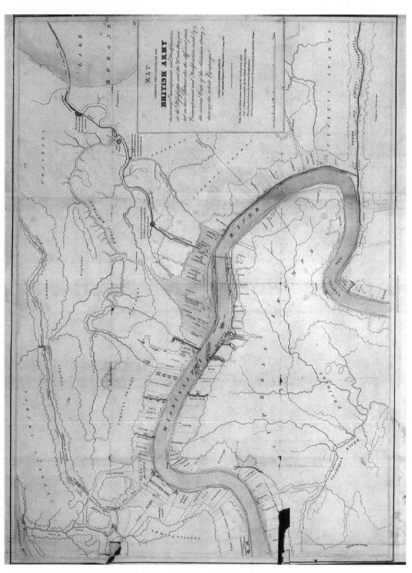

The map above shows the position of the American troops and the British army in relation to the location of the plantations that would form the battlefield.

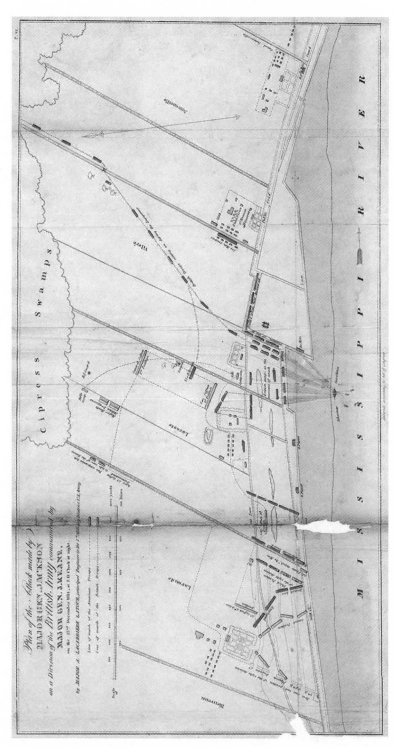

This map depicts the engagement between Jackson's forces and the British on the night of the Battle of December 23rd.

Letter, dated January 3, 1815, from General Andrew Jackson
to Headquarters of the 7th Military District. For health
reasons he requests to be relieved of command.

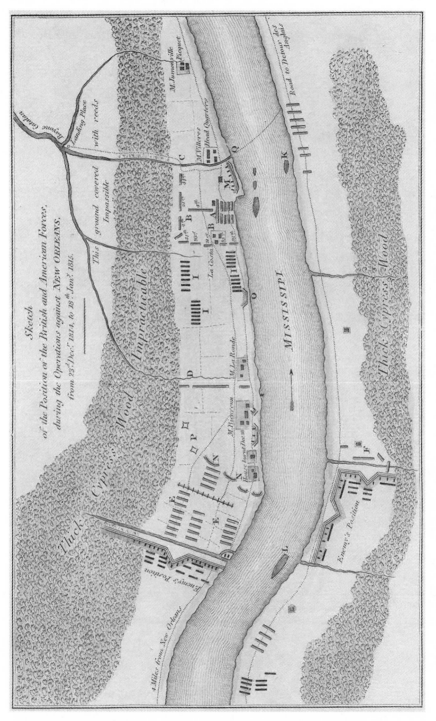

This map shows the relative position of the British and American troops just prior to the January 8th battle.

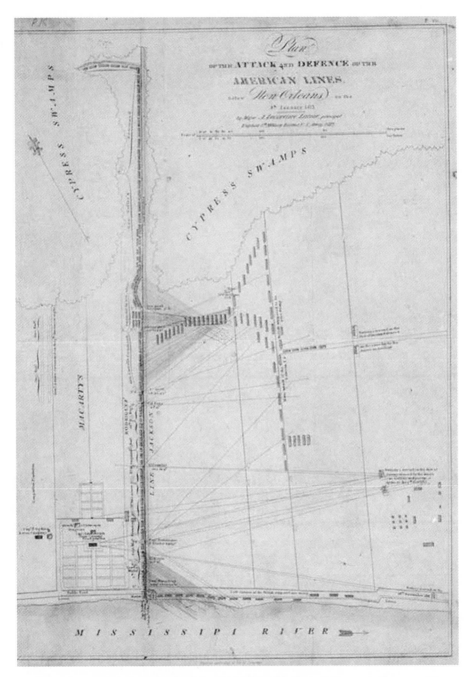

This map shows the attack of the British on Jackson's lines on January 8th.

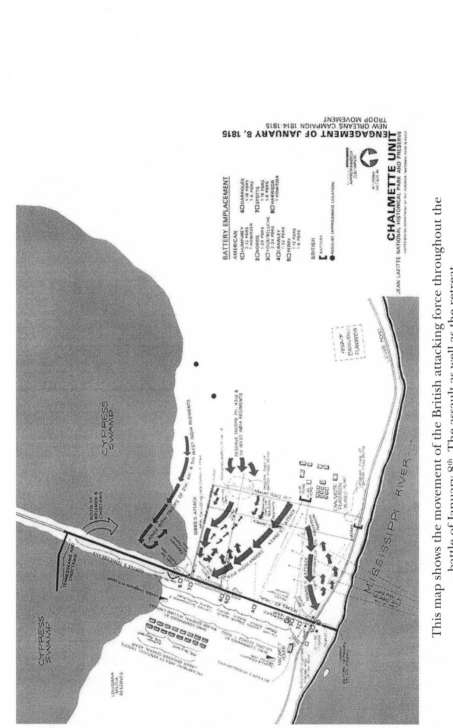

This map shows the movement of the British attacking force throughout the battle of January 8th. The assault as well as the retreat.

Pl. VIII.

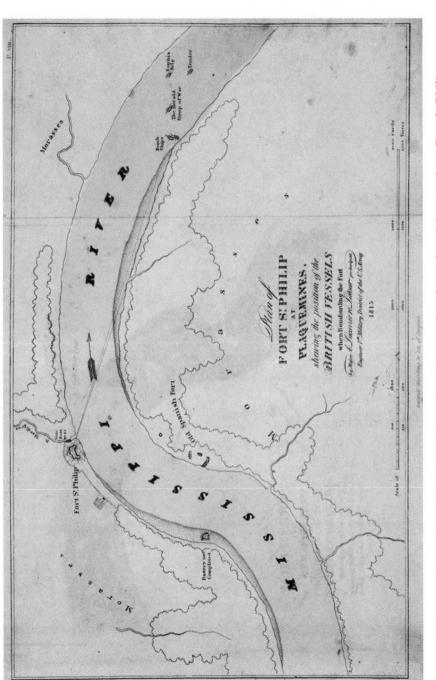

Plan of
FORT St. PHILIP
AT
PLAQUEMINES,
shewing the position of the
BRITISH VESSELS
when Bombarding the Fort
by Capt. A. Lacarrier Latour, engineer
Engineer 7th Military District of the U.S. Army
1815

This map shows the position of Cochrane's gunboats when he ordered the attack on Fort St. Philip.

This image shows what the city of New Orleans looked like in 1814.

Appendix

DAMAGES TO DENIS DE LA RONDE PLANTATION

An Itemized List

The damages done to the de la Ronde Plantation were extensive. De la Ronde's itemized inventory of damage and the prices he requested for reimbursement from the United States Government provide some insights into the value of property in 1815.

The British occupied this home and used it as a Headquarters for the duration of the Battle of New Orleans. They left the home intact. The damages occurred when the American forces enter the home and savaged the place.

The Inventory

- 66 Arpents of cane burned for fuel by General Coffee........ $$7,200
- 40,000 lbs sugar in 14 hogsheads destroyed or stolen.......... $11,200
- fence pickets, corn, potatoes, beans, hay carts,
    800 bottles of wine.. $925.00
- A demijohn of honey and 15 earthen ware pots............................?
- Glassware, furnishings, bedding, personal clothing.......................?
- 25 robes for my wife and daughters..................................... $125.00
- Paper hangings for 8 rooms... $244.00

- 2 clocks broken to pieces, 2 shades with plated stands
  & Candle sticks, 2 handsome stands plated in bronze
  for 3 flambeaux, 1 book case, 2 marble tables with
  Mahogany frames, 1 pair card tables, 1 toilette table,
  2 dining tables, 4 dozen chairs, 12 beautiful
  engravings, and a quantity of medicine ....?
- cattle and poultry, powder, shot, fowling pieces,
  carpentry tools, cabinate making tools,
  agricultural utensils, carriages, harnesses, saddle....................?
- 400 book volumes ....?
- 8 slaves $7,200
- Damages to sugar mill, dwelling, corn mill, outhouses........ $794.20

Appendix #1

ANONYMOUS.

To Commodore Daniel T Patterson, New Orleans.
Pensacola, 5th December, 1814.

Sir,

I feel it a duty to apprize you of a very large force of the enemy off this port, and it is generally understood New Orleans is the object of attack. It amounts at present to about eighty vessels, and more than double that number are momentarily looked for, to form a junction, when an immediate commencement of their operations will take place. I am not able to learn, how, when, or where the attack will be made; but I heard that they have vessels of all descriptions, and a large body of troops. Admiral Cochrane commands, and his ship, the *Tonnant,* lies at this moment just outside the bar; they certainly appear to have swept the West Indies of troops, and probably no means will be left untried to obtain their object.-The admiral arrived only yesterday noon.

I am yours, &c.
N***.

Appendix #2

PROCLAMATION

By lieutenant-colonel Edward Nicholls, commanding
his Britannic Majesty Forces in the Floridas.

Natives of Louisiana! On you the first call is made to assist in liberating from a faithless, imbecile government, your paternal soil: Spaniards, Frenchmen, Italians, and British, whether settled or residing for a time, in Louisiana, on you, also, I call to aid me in this just cause: the American usurpation in this country must be abolished, and the lawful owners of the soil put in possession. I am at the head of a large body of Indians, well armed, disciplined, and commanded by British officers-a good train of artillery with every requisite, seconded by the powerful aid of a numerous British and Spanish squadron of ships and vessels of war. Be not alarmed, inhabitants of the country, at our approach; the same good faith and disinterestedness which has distinguished the conduct of Britons in Europe, accompanies them here; you will have no fear of litigious taxes imposed on you for the purpose of carrying on an unnatural and unjust war; your property, your laws, the peace and tranquility of your country, will be guaranteed to you by men who will suffer no infringement of theirs; rest assured that these brave red men only burn with an ardent desire of satisfaction, for the wrongs they have suffered from the Americans, to join you in liberating these southern provinces from their yoke, and drive them into those limits formerly prescribed by my sovereign. The Indians have pledged themselves, in the most solemn manner not to injure, in the slightest degree, the persons or properties of any but enemies; to their Spanish or English fathers, a flag over any door, whether Spanish, French, or British, will be a certain protection, nor dare any Indian put his foot on the threshold thereof, under penalty of death from his own countrymen; not even an enemy will an Indian put to death, except resisting in arms, and as for injuring helpless women and children, the red men, by their good conduct and treatment to them, will (if it be possible) make the Americans blush for their more inhuman conduct lately on the Escambia, and within a neutral territory.

Inhabitants of Kentucky, you have too long home with grievous impositions-the whole brunt of the war has fallen on your brave sons; be imposed on no longer, but either range yourselves under the standard of your forefathers, or observe a strict neutrality; if you comply with either of these offers, whatever provisions you send down, will be paid for in dollars, and the safety of the persons bringing it, as well as the free navigation of the Mississippi, guaranteed to you.

Men of Kentucky, let me call to your view (and I trust to your abhorrence) the conduct of those factions, which hurried you into this civil, unjust, and unnatural war, at a time when Great Britain was straining every nerve in defense of her own and the liberties of the world-when the bravest of her sons were fighting and bleeding in so sacred a cause-when she was spending millions of her treasure in endeavoring to pull down one of the most formidable and dangerous tyrants that ever disgraced the form of man-when groaning Europe was almost in her last gasp-when Britons alone showed an undaunted front-basely did those assassins endeavour to stab her from the rear; she has turned on them, renovated from the bloody but successful struggle-Europe is happy and free, and she now hastens justly to avenge the unprovoked insult. Show them that you are not collectively unjust; leave that contemptible few to shift for themselves; let those slaves of the tyrant send an embassy to Elba, and implore his aid; but let every honest, upright American, spurn them with united contempt. After the experience of twenty-one years, can you any longer support those brawlers for liberty, who call it freedom, when themselves are free; be no longer their dupes-accept of my offers-everything I have promised in this paper I guarantee to you, on the sacred honour of a British officer.

> Given under my hand at my Head-Quarters,
> Pensacola, this 29th day of August, 1814.
> EDWARD NICHOLLS.

Appendix #3

[These letters prove that British troops anticipated looting and plundering New Orleans]

From Admiral Cockburn to Captain Evans.
Head-Quarters, Cumberland Island, 11th February, 1815.

No general, however, as you now know, has come here; you have had them all your way, and though I have learnt by a few hasty lines the unfortunate result of our first endeavours against New Orleans, yet excepting as far as relates to the poor generals and to the gross numbers you lost, I know no particulars, not even which of my many friends amongst you are dead or alive, or which have broken bones or whole sldns. I trust, however, it will prove that you are amongst the latter, and I hope you will when at leisure favour me with a detailed account of all that has passed in your neighbourhood.

We have been more fortunate here in our small way. We have taken St. Mary's, a tolerably rich place, and with little loss have managed to do much damage to the enemy, and we are now in tolerable security, upon a large fertile island in Georgia, though an ugly account of peace being signed (the particulars of which I have sent to Sir Admiral Cochrane) seems to promise a speedy dismissal to us from this coast.

From Mr Swainson to lieutenant Douglas, of H.M.
brig Sophie, off New Orleans.
9th February, 1815.

We had some fine times at St. Mary's; the bombs were at the town, and had plenty of plunder. How are you for tables, and chests of drawers, etc?

From Capt. Gallon to Capt. O'Neil, Esq. on board H.M.
ship Tenant, off New Orleans.
Cumberland Island, 9th February, 1815.

We have had fine fun since I saw you. What with the Rappahannock and various other places, we have contrived to pick up a few trifling things, such as mahogany tables, chests of drawers, &c.

Appendix #4

Edward Nicholls to Mr. Laffite or the commandant at Bara aria.
Head-quarters, Pensacola, August 31, 1814.

Sir,

I have arrived in the Floridas for the purpose of annoying the only enemy Great Britain has in the world, as France and England are now friends. I call on you, with your brave followers, to enter into the service of Great Britain, in which you shall have the rank of a captain; lands will be given to you all, in proportion to your respective ranks, on a peace taking place, and I invite you on the following terms. Your property shall be guaranteed to you, and your persons protected: in return for which I ask you to cease all hostilities against Spain, or the allies of Great Britain.-Your ships and vessels to be placed under the orders of the commanding officer on this station, until the commander-in-chief's pleasure is known; but I guarantee their fair value at all events. I herewith enclose you a copy of my proclamation to the inhabitants of Louisiana, which will, I trust, point out to you the honourable intentions of my government. You may be a useful assistant to me, in forwarding them; therefore, if you determine, lose no time. The bearer of this, Captain M'Williams, will satisfy you on another point you may be anxious to learn, as will captain Lockyer of the Sophia, who brings him to you. We have a powerful re-enforcement on its way here, and I hope to cut out some other work for the Americans than oppressing the inhabitants of Louisiana. Be expeditious in your resolves, and rely on the verity of

Your very humble servant,
EDWARD NICHOLLS.

Appendix #5

Letter from Mr. Laffite to his Excellency WC. C Claiborne.

SIR,

In the firm persuasion that the choice made of you to fill the office of first magistrate of this state, was dictated by the esteem of your fellow-citizens, and was conferred on merit, I confidently address you on an affair on which may depend the safety of this country.

I offer to you to restore to this state several citizens, who perhaps in your eyes have lost that sacred title. I offer you them, however, such as you could wish to find them, ready to exert their utmost efforts in defense of the country. This point of Louisiana, which I occupy, is of great importance in the present crisis. I tender my services to defend it; and the only reward I ask is that a stop be put to the proscription against me and my adherents, by an act of oblivion for all that has been done hitherto. I am the stray sheep, wishing to return to the sheepfold. If you were thoroughly acquainted with the nature of my offences, I should appear to you much less guilty, and still worthy to discharge the duties of a good citizen. I have never sailed under any flag but that of the republic of Carthagena, and my vessels are perfectly regular in that respect.

If I could have brought my lawful prizes into the ports of this state, I should not have employed the illicit means that have caused me to be proscribed. I decline saying more on the subject, until I have the honour of your Excellency's answer, which I am persuaded can be dictated only by wisdom. Should your answer not be favourable to my ardent desires, I declare to you that I will instantly leave the country, to avoid the imputation of having co-operated towards an invasion on this point, which cannot fail to take place, and to rest secure in the acquittal of my own conscience.

> I have the honour to be
> Your Excellency's &c.
> J. LAFF

Appendix #6

PROCLAMATION.

Head-quarters, 7th military district, Mobile, September 21, 1814.
To the free Coloured inhabitants of Louisiana.

Through a mistaken policy you have heretofore been deprived of a participation in the glorious struggle for national rights in which our country is engaged. This no longer shall exist.

As sons of freedom, you are now called upon to defend our most inestimable blessing. As Americans, your country looks with confidence to her adopted children, for a valorous support, as a faithful return for the advantages enjoyed under her mild and equitable government. As fathers, husbands, and brothers, you are summoned to rally round the standard of the eagle, to defend all which is dear in existence.

Your country, although calling for your exertions, does not wish you to engage in her cause, without amply remunerating you for the services rendered. Your intelligent minds are not to be led away by false representations.-Your love of honour would cause you to despise the man who should attempt to deceive you. In the sincerity of a soldier, and the language of truth I address you.

To every noble-hearted, generous freeman of colour, volunteering to serve during the present contest with Great Britain, and no longer, there will be paid the same bounty in money and lands, now received by the white soldiers of the United States, viz. one hundred and twenty-four dollars in money, and one hundred and sixty acres of land. The non-commissioned officers and privates will also be entitled to the same monthly pay and daily rations, and clothes furnished to any American soldier.

On enrolling yourselves in companies, the major-general commanding will select officers for your government, from your white fellow citizens. Your non-commissioned officers will be appointed from among yourselves.

Due regard will be paid to the feelings of freemen and soldiers. You will not, by being associated with white men in the same corps, be exposed to improper comparisons or unjust sarcasm. As a distinct, independent battalion or regiment, pursuing the path of glory, you will, undivided, receive the applause and gratitude of your countrymen.

To assure you of the sincerity of my intentions and my anxiety to engage your invaluable services to our country, I have communicated my wishes to the governor of Louisiana, who is fully informed as to the manner of enrolment, and will give you every necessary information on the subject of this address.

ANDREW JACKSON,
Major-general commanding.

Appendix #7

Letter from Admiral Cockrane to General Jackson.
H.B.M. ship Tonnant, off Mobile Bay, 13th February, 1815.

Sir,

I have exceeding satisfaction in sending to you a copy of a bulletin that I have this moment received from Jamaica, proclaiming that a treaty of peace was signed be-tween our respective plenipotentiaries at Ghent, on the 24th December, 1814, upon which I beg leave to offer you my sincere congratulations.

> I have the honour to be, sit, &c.
> (Signed) ALEX. COCHRANE.

Appendix #8

Copy of a letter from the Secretary of War to General Jackson.

Department of War,
March 13, 1815.
Major General Andrew Jackson,

Sir,

You will have received my communication, informing you that a treaty had been signed, on the 24 December, at Ghent, by the commissioners on the part of the United States & Great Britain; and that the exchange of the ratification took place here on the 17 ultimo. It is expected that you have already taken the necessary measures for carrying into effect, within your military district, the stipulations of the first article of the treaty, as were respecting the surrender of the ports and places held by the British forces, as the slaves, and other private property, stipulated to be delivered up.

The movements of the British forces against Mobile, and their previous conduct at Pensacola, give some cause to apprehend that there may have been some arrangement between the British & Spanish governments, respecting the occupation of West Florida. Should the British forces have obtained possession of any part of that country, formerly claimed as part of West Florida, west of the Perdido River, and refuse to deliver it up, under the stipulations of the first article of the treaty, you will make use of the forces under your command to expel them from it. All that part of West Florida being considered as a part of the United States, it must be defended as such.

I have the honor to be
JAMES MONROE.

Appendix #9

TREATY OF PEACE.
JAMES MADISON, PRESIDENT OF THE UNITED STATES,

To all and singular to whom these presents shall come, greeting.

Whereas a treaty of peace and amity between the United States of America and his Britannic majesty was signed at Ghent, on the twenty-fourth day of December, one thousand eight hundred and fourteen, by plenipotentiaries respectively appointed for that purpose; and the said treaty having been, by and with the advice and consent of the senate of the United States; duly accepted, ratified and confirmed, on the seven-tenth day of February, one thousand eight hundred and fifteen; and ratified copies thereof having been exchanged agreeably to the tenor of the said treaty, which is in the words following, to wit:

TREATY OF PEACE AND AMITY BETWEEN HIS BRITANNIC
MAJESTY AND THE UNITED STATES OF AMERICA.

His Britannic majesty and the United States of America, desirous of terminating the war which has unhappily subsisted between the two countries, and of restoring, upon principles of perfect reciprocity, peace, friendship, and good understanding between them, have, for that purpose, appointed their respective plenipotentiaries, that is to say: his Britannic majesty, on his part, has appointed the right honourable James lord Gambier, late admiral of the white, now admiral of the red squadron of his majesty's fleet, Henry Goulbourn, esq. member of the imperial parliament, and under secretary of state, and William Adams, Esq. doctor of civil laws:-and the president of the United States, by and with the advice and consent of the senate thereof, has appointed John Quincy Adams, James A. Bayard, Henry Clay, Jonathan Russel, and Albert Gallatin, citizens of the United States, who, after a reciprocal communication of their respective full powers, have agreed upon the following articles:

ART. I.-There shall be a firm and universal peace between his Britannic majesty and the United States, and between their respective countries, territories, cities, towns and people, of every degree, without exception of places or persons. All hostilities, both by sea and land, shall cease as soon as this treaty has been ratified by both parties, as hereinafter mentioned. All territories, places, and possessions whatsoever, taken from either party by the other, during the war, or which may be taken after the signing of this treaty, excepting only the islands hereinafter mentioned, shall be restored without delay, and without causing any destruction, or carrying away any of the artillery or other public property originally captured in the said forts or places, and which shall remain therein, upon the exchange of the ratifications of this treaty, or any slaves or other private property, and all archives, records, deeds, and papers, either of a public nature, or belonging to private persons, which, in the course of the war, may have fallen into the hands of the officers of either party, shall be, as far as may be practicable, **forthwith restored and delivered to the proper authorities and persons to whom they respectively belong**. Such of the islands in the bay of Passamaquoddy as are claimed by both parties, shall remain in the possession of the party in whose occupation they may be at the time of the exchange of the ratifications of this treaty, until the decision respecting the title to the said islands shall have been made, in conformity with the fourth article of this treaty. No disposition made by this treaty, as to such possession of the islands and territories claimed by both parties, shall, in any manner whatever, be construed to affect the right of either.

ART. II.-Immediately after the ratification of this treaty by both parties, as herein after mentioned, orders shall be sent to the armies, squadrons, officers, subjects and citizens of the two powers to cease from all hostilities: and to prevent all causes of complaint which might arise on account of the prizes which may be taken at sea after the ratifications of this treaty, it is reciprocally agreed, that all vessels and effects which may be taken after the space of twelve days from the said ratifications, upon all parts of the coast of North America, from the latitude of twenty-three degrees north, to the latitude of fifty degrees north, as far eastward in the Atlantic ocean, as the thirty-sixth degree of west longitude from the meridian of Greenwich, shall be restored on each side: That the time shall be thirty days in all other parts of the Atlantic ocean, north of the equinoxial line or equator, and the same time for the British and Irish channels, for the gulf of Mexico, and all parts of the West Indies: forty days for the North Seas, for the

Baltic, and for all parts of the Mediterranean. Sixty days for the Atlantic ocean south of the equator as far as the latitude of the Cape of Good Hope: ninety days for every part of the world south of the equator: and one hundred and twenty days for all other parts of the world, without exception.

ART. III.-All prisoners of war taken on either side, as well by land as by sea, shall be restored as soon as practicable after the ratification of this treaty, as hereinafter mentioned, on their paying the debts which they may have contracted during their captivity. The two contracting parties respectively engage to discharge, in specie, the advances which may have been made by the other, for the sustenance and maintenance of such prisoners.

ART. IV-Whereas it was stipulated by the second article in the treaty of peace of one thousand seven hundred and eighty three, between his Britannic majesty and the United States of America, that the boundary of the United States should comprehend all islands within twenty leagues of any part of the shores of the United States, and lying between lines to be drawn due east from the points where the aforesaid boundaries between Nova-Scotia, on the one part, and East Florida on the other, shall respectively touch the Bay of Fundy, and the Atlantic ocean, excepting such islands as now are, or heretofore have been within the limits of Nova-Scotia: and whereas the several islands in the Bay of Passamaquoddy, which is part of the Bay of Fundy, and the Island of Grand Menan, in the said Bay of Fundy, are claimed by the United States as being comprehended within their aforesaid boundaries, which said islands are claimed as belonging to his Britannic majesty as having been at the time of, and previous to, the aforesaid treaty of one thousand seven hundred and eighty three, within the limits of the province of Nova Scotia: in order, therefore, finally to decide upon these claims, it is agreed that they shall be referred to two commissioners, to be appointed in the following manner, viz. One commissioner shall be appointed by his Britannic majesty, and one by the president of the United States, by and with the advice and consent of the senate thereof, and the said two commissioners so appointed shall be sworn impartially to examine and decide upon the said claims according to such evidence as shall be laid before them on the part of his Britannic majesty and of the United States respectively. The said commissioners shall meet at St. Andrews, in the province of New Brunswick, and shall have power to adjourn to such other place or places as they shall think fit. The said commissioners shall, by a declaration or report under their hands and seals, decide to which of the two contracting parties the several islands aforesaid do respectively belong, in conformity with the true intent of the said treaty of peace of one thousand seven hundred and eighty-three. And if the said commissioners shall agree in their decision, both parties shall consider such decision as final and conclusive. It is further agreed, that in the event of the two commissioners differing upon all or any of the matters so referred to them, or in the event of both or either of the said commissioners refusing or declining, or willfully omitting, to act as such, they shall make jointly or separately, a report or reports, as well to the government of his Britannic majesty, as to that of the United States, stating in detail the points on which they differ, and the grounds upon which their respective opinions have been formed, or the grounds upon which they, or either of them, have so refused, declined, or omitted to act. And his Britannic majesty, and the government of the United States, hereby agree to refer the report or reports of the said commissioners, to some friendly sovereign state, to be then named for that purpose, and who shall be requested to decide on the differences which may be stated in the said report or reports, or upon the report of one commissioner, together with the grounds upon which the other commissioner shall be refused, declined, or omitted to act, as the case may be. And if the commissioner so refusing, declining, or omitting to act, shall also willfully omit to a state the grounds upon which he has so done, in such manner that the said statement may be referred to such friendly sovereign or state, together with the report of such other commissioner, then such sovereign or state, shall decide exparte upon the said report alone. And his Britannic majesty and the government of the United States engage to consider the decision of some friendly sovereign or state to be final and conclusive, on all matters so referred.

ART. V-Whereas neither that point of the high lands lying due north from the source of the river St. Croix, and designated in the former treaty of peace between the two powers as the northwest angle of Nova Scotia, now the northwesternmost head of Connecticut river, has yet been ascertained; and whereas that part of the boundary line between the dominion of the two powers which extends from the source of the river St. Croix directly north to the above mentioned northwest angle of Nova Scotia, thence along the said high lands which divide those rivers that empty themselves into the river St. Lawrence from those which fall into the Atlantic ocean, to the north-westernmost head of Connecticut river, thence down along the middle of that river to the forty-fifth degree of north latitude: thence by a line due west on said latitude until it strikes the river Iroquois or Cataraguy, has not yet been surveyed: it is agreed, that for these several purposes, two commissioners shall be appointed, sworn, and authorized, to act exactly in the manner directed with respect to those mentioned in the next preceding article, unless otherwise specified in the present article. The said commissioners shall meet at St. Andrews, in the province of New Brunswick, and shall have power to adjourn to such other place or places as they shall think fit. The said commissioners shall have power to ascertain and determine the points above mentioned, in conformity with the provisions of the said treaty of peace of one thousand seven hundred and eighty-three, and shall cause the boundary aforesaid, from the source of the river St. Croix, to the river Iroquois or Cataraguy, to be surveyed and marked according to the said provisions. The said commissioners shall make a map of the said boundary, and annex it to a declaration under their hands and seals, certifying it to be the true map of the said boundary, and particularizing the latitude and longitude of the northwest angle of Nova Scotia, of the northwesternmost head of Connecticut river, and of such other points of the said boundary as they may deem proper. And both parties agree to consider such map and declaration as finally and conclusively fixing the said boundary. And in the event of the said two commissioners differing, or both, or either of them, refusing or declining, or willfully omitting to act, such reports, declarations, or statements, shall be made by them, or either of them, and such reference to a friendly sovereign or state, shall be made, in all respects as in the latter part of the fourth article is contained, and in as full a manner as if the same was herein repeated.

ART. VI.-Whereas by the former treaty of peace, that portion of the boundary of the United States from the point where the forty-fifth degree of north latitude strikes the river Iroquois or Cataraguy to the lake Superior, was declared to be "along the middle of said river into lake Ontario, through the middle of said lake until it strikes the communication by water between that lake and lake Erie, thence along the middle of said communication into lake Erie, through the middle of said lake until it arrives at the water communication into the lake Huron, thence through the middle of said lake to the water communication between that lake and lake Superior." And whereas doubts have arisen what the middle of said river, lakes, and water communications, and whether certain islands lying in the same were within the dominions of his Britannic majesty or of the United States: in order, therefore, finally to decide these doubts, they shall be referred to two commissioners, to be appointed, sworn, and authorized to act exactly in the manner directed with respect to those mentioned in the next preceding article, unless otherwise specified in this present article. The said commissioners shall meet, in the first instance at Albany, in the state of New York, and shall have power to adjourn to such other place or places as they shall think fit. The said commissioners shall, by a report or declaration, under their hands and seals, designate the boundary through the said river, lakes, or water communications, and decide to which of the two contracting parties the several islands lying within the said river, lakes, and water communications, do respectively belong, in conformity with the true intent of the said treaty of one thousand seven hundred and eighty-three. And both parties agree to consider such designation and decision as final and conclusive. And in the event of the said two commissioners differing, or both, or either of them, refusing, declining, or willfully omitting to act, such reports, declarations, or statements, shall be made by them, or either of them; and such reference to a friendly sovereign or state shall be made in all respects as in the latter part of the fourth article is contained, and in as full a manner as if the same was herein repeated.

ART. VII-It is further agreed that the said two last mentioned commissioners, after they shall have executed the duties assigned to them in the preceding article, shall be, and they are hereby authorized, upon their oaths, impartially to fix and determine, according to the true intent of the said treaty of peace of one thousand seven hundred and eighty-three, that part of the boundary between the dominions of the two powers, which extends from the water communication between lake Huron and lake Superior, to the most northwestern point of the lake of the Woods, to decide to which of the two parties the several islands lying in the lakes, water communications and rivers, forming the said boundary, do respectively belong, in conformity with the true intent of the said treaty of peace of one thousand seven hundred and eighty-three; and to cause such parts of the said boundary, as require it, to be surveyed and marked. The said commissioners shall, by a report or declaration under their hands and seals, designate the boundary line aforesaid, state their decisions on the points thus referred to them, and particularize the latitude and longitude of the most northwestern point of the lake of the Woods, and of such other parts of the said boundary, as they may deem proper. And both parties agree to consider such designation and decision as final and conclusive. And in the event of the said two commissioners differing, or both, or either of them, refusing, declining, or willfully omitting to act, such reports, declarations, or statements, shall be made by them, or either of them, and such reference to a friendly sovereign or state, shall be made in all respects, as in the latter part of the fourth article is contained, and in as full a manner as if the same was herein repeated.

ART. VIII-The several boards of two commissioners mentioned in the four preceding articles, shall respectively have power to appoint a secretary, and to employ such surveyors or other persons as they shall judge necessary. Duplicates of all their respective reports, declarations, statements, and decisions, and of their accounts and of the journal of their proceedings, shall be delivered by them to the agents of his Britannic majesty, and to the agents of the United States, who may be respectively appointed and authorized to manage the business on behalf of their respective governments. The said commissioners shall be respectively paid in such manner as shall be agreed between the two contracting parties, such agreement being to be settled at the time of the exchange of the ratifications of this treaty; and all other expenses attending said commissioners shall be defrayed equally by the two parties. And in case of death, sickness, resignation, or necessary absence, the place of every such commissioner respectively shall be supplied in the same manner as such commissioner was first appointed, and the new commissioner shall take the same oath or affirmation, and do the same duties. It is further agreed between the two contracting parties, that in case any of the islands mentioned in any of the preceding articles, which were in the possession of one of the parties prior to the commencement of the present war between the countries, should, by the decision of any of the boards of commissioners aforesaid, or of the sovereign or state so referred to, as in the four next preceding articles contained, fall within the dominions of the other party, all grants of land made previous to the commencement of the war, by the party having had such possession, shall be as valid as if such island or islands, had by such decision or decisions, been adjudged to be within the dominions of the party having such possession.

ART. IX.-The United States of America engage to put an end, immediately after the ratification of the present treaty, to hostilities with all the tribes or nations of Indians, with whom they may be at war at the time of such ratification and forthwith to restore to such tribes or nations, respectively, all the possessions, rights, and privileges, which they may have enjoyed or been entitled to in one thousand eight hundred and eleven, previous to such hostilities: Provided always, that such tribes or nations shall agree to desist from all hostilities against the United States of America, their citizens and subjects, upon the ratification of the present treaty being notified to such tribes or nations, and shall so desist accordingly. And his Britannic majesty engages, on his part, to put an end immediately after the ratification of the present treaty, to hostilities with all the tribes or nations of Indians with whom he may be at war at the time of such ratification, and forthwith to restore to such tribes or nations respectively, all the possessions, rights, and privileges, which they may have enjoyed, or been entitled to in one thousand eight hundred and eleven, previous to such hostilities: Provided always, that such tribes or nations shall agree to desist from all hostilities against his Britannic majesty, and his subjects, upon the ratification of the present treaty being notified to such tribes or nations, and shall so desist accordingly.

ART. X.-Whereas the traffic in slaves is irreconcilable with the principles of humanity and justice, and whereas both his Britannic majesty and the United States are desirous of continuing their efforts to promote its entire abolition, it is hereby agreed that both the contracting parties shall use their best endeavours to accomplish so desirable an object.

ART. XI.-This treaty, when the same shall have been ratified on both sides, without alteration by either of the contracting parties and the ratifications mutually exchanged, shall be binding on both parties, and the ratifications shall be exchanged at Washington, in the space of four months from this day, or sooner if practicable.

In faith whereof, we the respective plenipotentiaries, have signed this treaty, and have thereunto affixed our seals.

Done, in triplicate, at Ghent, the twenty-fourth day of December, one thousand eight hundred and fourteen.

(L.S.) GAMBIER, (L.S.) HENRY GOULBOURN, (L.S.) MLLIAM ADAMS, (L.S.) JOHN QUINCY ADAMS, (L.S.) J. A. BAYARD, (L.S.) H. CLAY, (L.S.) JONATHAN RUSSELL, (L.S.) ALBERT GALLATIN.

Now, therefore, to the end that the said treaty of peace and amity may be observed with good faith, on the part of the United States, 1, JAMES MADISON, president as aforesaid, have caused the premises to be made public: and I do hereby enjoin all persons bearing office, civil or military, within the United States, and all others, citizens or inhabitants thereof, or being within the same, faithfully to observe and fulfill the said treaty and every clause and article thereof.

In testimony whereof I have caused the seal of the United States to be affixed to these presents, and signed the same with my hand.

Done at the city of Washington, this eighteenth day of February, in the year of our Lord one thousand eight hundred and fifteen, and of the sovereignty and independence of the United States the thirty-ninth.

By the President,
JAMES MADISON.
JAMES MONROE.

Appendix #10

Letter from General Lambert to General Jackson.
Head-Quarters, Isle Dauphine, March 18, 1815.

SIR-

I received with great pleasure, by the hands of major Woodruff, on the evening of the 16th, about nine o'clock, yours of the 13th instant. I communicated the contents immediately to rear admiral Malcolm, and orders were issued for the cessation of hostilities, and to all detached posts and ships to be withdrawn in our respective commands. I daily expect an official communication (similar to what you have received) from Mr. Baker. In the meantime every preparation is making for the embarkation of this force, and ships are now sent away, when we are able to put sufficient provisions on board to take them to Bermuda. Victuallers from Jamaica must be here in a very few days, when everything will be put on board as quickly as possible; and should I by that time not have received any intelligence, the admiral and myself will have no hesitation in putting to sea directly. I have requested major Woodruff, who went up to Mobile yesterday, to acquaint the commanding officer that I would let him know the moment we were prepared to give up the fort, which would be when the transports could get out of the bay. The fort would be restored in every respect as when it fell into our possession, with the exception only of a brass mortar, cast in George the Second's reign, which had been sent away the day after.

In the fulfilling the first article of the treaty, I cannot consider the meaning of "not causing any destruction, or carrying away any artillery, or other public property, originally captured in the said forts or places, and to which shall remain therein upon the exchange of the ratification of this treaty, or any slave, or other property," having reference to any antecedent period to the 18th of February, the day of the exchange of ratifications; because it is only from that time that the article could be fulfilled in a long war. If those negroes (the matter now in question) belonged to the territory or city we were annually in occupation of, I should conceive we had no right to take them away; but by their coming away, they are virtually the same as deserters or property taken away at any time of the war. I am obliged to say so much in justification of the right; but I have from the first done all I could to prevent, and subsequently, together with admiral Malcolm, have given every facility, and used every persuasion that they should return to their masters, and many have done so; but I could not reconcile it to myself to abandon any, who, from false reasoning perhaps, joined us during the period of hostilities and have thus acted in violation of the laws of their country, and besides become obnoxious to their masters.

Had it been an object to take the negroes away, they could have been embarked in the first instance; but they have been permitted to remain in the hopes that they might return.

I am much obliged to you for your offer of supplies, and comforts for the sick and wounded. I send a commissary, to make a few purchases, and have directed him to call on Mr. Livingston with this letter.

Appendix #11

Letter from General Jackson to the Secretary of War
Head-quarters, 7th military districts

New Orleans, March 16, 1815.

Sir,

I have the honour to acknowledge the receipt of your letter of the 16th ult. advising me of the ratification of the treaty of peace between Great Britain and the United States.

In conformity with your directions, I have forwarded to the officer commanding his Britannic majesty's forces, in this quarter, information of that event. The Tennessee and Kentucky militia will be immediately marched to their respective states, and discharged without receiving any pay beforehand. The Louisiana and Mississippi militia will be discharged and paid here. It is hoped that funds will be provided for the payment of the former in suitable time. Difficulties are experienced from the want of means to procure forage, and transportation on the return march, colonel Knight having not yet arrived. On this ac-count I have offered my bills on the governor of Tennessee, payable in treasury notes at Nashville.

I have received no intelligence of colonel Knight, except by your letter of the 7th ult.

The greater portion of the regulars in this quarter having enlisted to serve during the war, expect to be immediately discharged. As you have not mentioned them in your instructions, I shall be glad to hear from you on the subject as soon as possible.

It is my intention, so soon as I get the troops mustered out of service here, to remove my head-quarters to Nashville, where I shall expect to receive the orders of the government.

Major-general Gaines is placed in the immediate command of this section of the district, and I am happy to commit it to one in whom die government has such high and deserved confidence.

I have the honour to be, &c.
A.JACKSON

Appendix #12

COURT OF INQUIRY

Extracts of the Proceedings of a Court of inquiry relative to the Retreat on the Right Bank of the Mississippi, on the 8th of January, 1815.

THE court, on mature deliberation, are of opinion that the conduct of colonel Daris, Dijan and Cavallier, in the action and retreat on the 8th of January, on the western bank of the Mississippi, is not reprehensible, nor do they know of any misconduct, as officers, in either since that time.

The causes of the retreat are attributed to the shameful flight of the command of major Arnaud, sent to oppose the landing of the enemy;-the retreat of the Kentucky militia, which, considering their position, the deficiency of their arms, and other causes, may be excusable;-and the panic and confusion introduced in every part of the line, thereby occasioning the retreat and confusion of the Orleans and Louisiana drafted militia.

Whilst the court find much to applaud in the zeal and gallantry of the officer immediately commanding, they believe that a farther reason for the retreat may be found in the manner in which the force was posted on the line, which they consider exceptionable. The commands of colonels Dijan, Cavallier and Declauett, composing five hundred men, supported by three pieces of artillery, having in front a strong breastwork, occupying only a space of two hundred yards, whilst the Kentucky militia, only one hundred and seventy men strong, without artillery, occupied more than three hundred yards, covered by a small ditch only.

W'M. CARROLL, Maj. Gen. President of the Court.

Appendix #13

DECISION OF THE COURT MARTIAL
IN THE CASE OF MAJOR VILLERE.

Head-Quarters, Adjutant-General's Office, New Orleans, March 15, 1815.

After a full examination of all the testimony for and against the prosecution, the court find the said major Villere "not guilty" of the charges and specifications exhibited against him, and do acquit him of all and every one of them.-And the court consider it due to the accused, further to declare, that major Villere appears to have performed his duty, from the moment he was left in command under the orders of major-general Villere, with zeal and fidelity; and that the circumstance of his surprise and capture by the enemy, though much to be regretted, might have occurred to the most vigilant officer, and must be attributed to the loss of the whole of his picquet or advanced guard, and the extraordinary rapidity with which the enemy moved from that point.

The major-general commanding approved the foregoing sentence of the general court martial, and ordered major Villere to resume his sword without delay.

By order, ROBERT BUTLER, Adj. Gen. NOTE.-Major Villere did not introduce any testimony in his behalf.

Appendix # 14

New Orleans 9ᵗᵉ Jany 1815

My dear Sir

Yesterday the british experienced the most bloody
butchery ever recorded in american history in an attack which
they made against the strong lines of Genl Jackson, where they
were entirely Slaughtered from the heavy fire of 18 or 20
pieces of artillery playing upon them with round balls & grape
Shot. The prudence & forbearance of General Jackson
reminds me of that of Genl Washington. The british
attacked the line with an undaunted bravery; many were
Killed on the Parapet, after having crossed the ditch over
the bodies of their men, they had filled it with. The field
of battle is covered with dead and wounded — What may
appear to you almost incredible and still is litterally true
the Loss of the British of which follows the statement,
is reckoned 1500, and yet the americans, covered with their
lines, lost only nine Killed and about 20 wounded.
Intercourse have been kept between the two Camps this morning
They say their loss is 830 killed, but I suppose they include
many of the wounded that have not returned to their corps.
There is now in town, besides those which were sent to Natchez
104 in number; in the Geole 163 prisoners. In the Barracks 296
wounded, five Sixths of which can not recover having five
Seven and more wounds. In the hospital at the Camp a vast
number are Still, which are hourly Sent to town in barges
& carts — upwards of 200 prisoners are Still at Jackson's Camp.

Endnotes

Introduction

I am deeply indebted to those historians who preceded me in writing about this exciting episode in American History. Were it not for their efforts, this work would not be possible. I learned so much from their labors. I commend them and have sought to provide proper credit for their work. My goal has been to gather and condense all the information available about this historic event thereby providing readers with a grand overview of the campaign to conquer New Orleans and the Gulf of Mexico.

[1] The Impressment of American Sailors had become so serious that many ports issued documents certifying the citizenship of sailors leaving their ports in hopes to protect them from impressments by the British. How successful theses efforts were is open to conjecture. Also, it should be noted that Great Britain suspended the offensive Orders in Council days before the Americans declared war. In an age of modern communication, the war might never have occurred.

[2] Zachary F. Smith. *The Battle of New Orleans*; (Louisville Kentucky, John P. Morgan Printers to the Filson Club 1904. reprint 2008 Wayne & Judy Dasher Nashville Tennessee) p. 95-97

[3] Ibid.

[4] Ibid.

[5] Ibid.

[6] Arsene de LaTour p. *Historical Memoir of the War in West Florida and Louisiana* (New Orleans: Historic New Orleans Collection) 185 (See

Appendix #3); Niles Register November 5, 1814 #9 Vol VII p.134 (Colonel Nicholls' Proclamation)

[7] Appendix #9 . . . Article #1 *Treaty of Ghent*, December 1814.

[8] *Louisiana Historical Quarterly* (1961: Volume 44 Issue 1 p. 94 "General Lambert had not made up his mind Whether or not to leave the island [Dauphin Island] before ratification of the peace."

[9] Treaty of Ghent . . . Article the First

[10] Ibid.

[11] Some sources cite February 16th

[12] Charles Cerami, *Jefferson's Great Gamble* (Sourcebooks Inc., Naperville Il) p. 239.

[13] Latour, p. 180 (letter from Monroe to the Governor of Tennessee September 25, 1814)

[14] Letter: Wellington to Longford (May 22, 1815) Louisiana Historical Quarterly 1926: Volume 9 Issue 1 p. 14

[15] Charles Gayarre *"History of Louisiana"* Vol .1 (New Orleans: Pelican Publising Compay, 1974) p. 387

Chapter 1

[16] Hickey, Donald: The War of 1812, *A Short History*; (Chicago, IL; University of Illinois Press, 1995) p.16

[17] ibid. p. 52

[18] ibid. p.53

[19] Valerie McNair Scott, *Major-General Sir Edward Pakenham* (1965, The battle of New Orleans 150th Anniversary Committee of Louisiana. P.3

[20] Ibid. p. 4

[21] Ibid. p. 8

[22] Ibid. p. 13

[23] Ibid.

[24] Ibid. p. 14

[25] Ibid. p.16

[26] Pakenham p. 34.

[27] Ibid p.36

[28] Ibid p. 35

[29] Ibid p.37

[30] Life of Sir George Napier, Pakenham p. 36

[31] Pakenham p.37

[32] Ibid. p. 37

[33] Benton Raid Patterson, *The Generals*, (2005: New York University Press) p.3-6 Much of this personal sketch comes from the pages of this work and ·a variety of other biographies. The content here is general knowledge.

[34] Patterson, *The Generals*, p. 103

Chapter 2

[35] Benson Lossing, *Pictorial Field Book for the War of 1812*, (New York: Harper & Brothers, 1869) p. 740-41 9 (It should be mentioned here that the territories annexed to Louisiana at this time became would be call the "Florida Parishes")

[36] Ibid.

[37] Public Domain, University of Alabama Archives

[38] Ibid.

[39] Charles Patton; Chalmette; *The Battle for New Orleans and How the British Nearly Stole the Louisiana Territory* (Bowling Green KY; Hickory Tales Publishing, 2001) location 282 (Kindle Version)

[40] Ibid; (location 293)

[41] Williams Research Center, British Admiralty Records Reel 2 (AR19)

[42] William Garrott Brown *Andrew Jackson* (NY. NY, Houghton, Mifflin & Co. 1900) p. 47

[43] Lossing, 1869: p. 746

[44] Public Domain, Encyclopedia of Alabama

[45] Jackson's response to some of the actions of his volunteers who sought to return home are legendary. He demonstrated his iron will to the point of executing several men under his command.

[46] Ibid. p. 115

[47] Ibid. p. 161

[48] www.sui.edu; Mississippi State University

[49] Williams Research Center, MF 2.2-Louisiana and War of 1812 Related documents from the British National Archives; Reel 01: Admiralty Office Records 1814

[50] Williams Research Center, MF 2.2-Louisiana and War of 1812 Related documents from the British National Archives; Reel 02: Admiralty Office Records 1814; Proclamation of Admiral Alexander Cochrane in Bermuda April 25, 1814.

[51] Ibid.

[52] Ibid.

[53] Gayarre Vol. IV p. 377

[54] Williams Research Center, British Admiralty Records Reel 2 (AR13)

[55] Williams Research Center, British Admiralty Records Reel 2 (AR13)

[56] British Admiralty Records Reel 2. Williams Research Center (letter from Captain Pigot of HMS Orpheus)

[57] Ibid

[58] British Admiralty Records Reel 2; Williams Research Center (letter from five Creek Indian Chiefs to British

[59] Ibid.

[60] Ibid. (It is difficult to decipher the names of the tribes

[61] Ibid

[62] Ibid

[63] Ibid. The fact that Cochrane refers to Americans as "rebellious subjects" betrays a common feeling among many British.

[64] Admiralty Records; Letter from Admiral Cochrane to Indian Chiefs.

[65] Ibid.

[66] Admiralty Records Reel 2; Letter from Cochrane to Lords Commissioners of Admiralty July 23, 1814 (AR16)

[67] Ibid.

[68] Admiralty Records Reel 2; Letter from Cochrane to Lords Commissioners of Admiralty concering plan of attack in southern theater. (undated) (AR15)

[69] Ibid.

[70] THNOC 1980.32

[71] Patton, (location 608)

[72] Admiralty Records Reel 1 (2?); Letter from Captain Percy to Admiral Cochrane September 16, 1814

[73] Ibid.

[74] Ibid.

[75] THNOC MSS 557.9.78 Letter from Gideon Granger expressing concern for safety of New Orleans.

[76] Ibid.

[77] Ibid. p. 163

[78] Ibid. p. 164-65

[79] Lossing, p. 1022

[80] Admiralty Records, Reel 2 (AR7) Letter from Captain Percy to Governor General of Havana dated November 3, 1814.

[81] Admiralty Records (Reel 2) Letter from Captain James Gordon of HMS Seahorse to Governor of Pensacola Nov. 2, 1814

[82] Admiralty Records Reel 2 (AR12) Letter from General Jackson to Spanish Governor in Pensacola . . . dated November 6, 1814

[83] Lossing, p. 1023

[84] Admiralty Records Reel 2 (AR8) Letter from Captain Gordon HMS *Seahorse* to Captain General Havana November 7, 1814.

[85] Ibid.

[86] Admiralty Records Reel 2 ((AR10) Letter from Captain James Gordon of *HMS Seahorse* to Admiral Cochrane November 18, 1814.

[87] Ibid

[88] Ibid

[89] Ibid

90 Admiralty records Reel 2 (AR 1) Letter from Admiral Cochrane to Lord Commissioners of Admiralty December 7, 1814

91 Ibid.

92 Gayarre Vol. IV p. 377

93 The Story of the Battle of New Orleans (1915: Louisiana Historical Society) p. 17

94 Historic New Orleans Collection (MSS 557. 4. 17) Letter from Col. Frederick Stovin to mother dated December 5, 1814.

95 The Story of the Battle of New Orleans (1915: Louisiana Historical Society. p. 18

96 Ibid.

97 Ibid.

Chapter 3

98 Define term Creole: generally it means a person of French or Spanish descent born in the colonies and not the homeland.

99 John Smith Kendall, History of New Orleans, (New Orleans 1922) p. 91

100 Davis, William, *The Pirates Lafitte: The Treacherous World of Corsairs in the Gulf*, (New York: Houghton, Mifflin, Harcourt, 2006) p. 45.

101 Alcee Fortier, *A History of Louisiana* (Baton Rouge, Claitors Publishing Division, 1985) Vol. 3 p. 10

102 Robert Breckinridge McAfee, *War in the Western Country*, (Lexington, KY: Worsley & Smith, 1816) reprint 1966 University Microfilms p. 501-2

103 *Louisiana Historical Quarterly*: (1961: Volume 44 Issue 1 p. 37)

104 La Tour p. 185 (Appendix #3)

105 Congressional Record February 9, 1811.

106 Kendall, *History of New Orleans*, p. 95

107 Gayarre' Vol. IV p. 875

108 Contemporaries often cited New England's desire to secede. But noted historian Samuel Elliot Morrison argues that those who contend "secession" are inaccurate. The delegates to the Hartford Convention merely attempted to express their opposition to the war in the strongest possible terms. Since few records of this meeting exist, there is no way to properly document their true intentions.

109 Kendall, *History of New Orleans*, p. 96

110 Ibid. p.95

111 Alexander Walker, *Life of Jackson, to which is added an Authentic Narrative of the Memorable Achievements of the American Army at New Orleans in the Winter of 1814-15*, (Philadelphia: G>G> Evans, 1860) p. 30-31

112 Davis, *The Pirates Lafitte*, p. 50

113 Sketch by Ron Chapman

114   *Life of Jackson.* p, 34
115   Ibid.
116   Ibid.
117   Davis, *The Pirates Lafitte*, p.53
118   THNOC 0.42
119   Ibid, p.73
120   "Life of Jackson". p. 134
121   "Life of Jackson" p. 35-36; Davis, *The Pirates Lafitte*, p.71
122   Davis, *The Pirates Lafitte*, p.73
123   "Walker, *Life of Jackson.* p. 38
124   Ibid. p. 39
125   Niles Register #9 Vol. VII; Page 134 (Williams Research center) Letter of Captain Percy of HMS Hermes
126   Ibid.
127   , Lyle Saxon, *Laffite the Pirate*, (D. Appleton-Century Company, New York, 1930) p.131.
128   Walker, *Life of Jackson* p.130
129   Ibid; p131-132
130   Ibid; p.137
131   Ibid; p. 135, Benson Lossing, *Pictorial Field Book of the War of 1812*, p. 1018
132   Saxon, *Lafitte the Pirate*, p.136
133   Davis, *The Pirates Lafitte*, p.170
134   Arthur, Stanley Clishy "Old New Orleans: A History of the Vieux Carre' " (2007, Heritage Books, Maryland) p. 44
135   Ibid, p. 146
136   Kendall, *History of New Orleans*, p 97
137   Walker, *Life of Jackson* p, 38
138   Davis, *The Pirates Lafitte*, p.185
139   Saxon, *Lafitte the Pirate*, p. 148
140   *Louisiana Gazette*, (October 11, 1814) Williams Research Center microfilm
141   The Niles Register November 5, 1814 #9 Vol II (Williams Research Center)
142   Ibid.
143   Saxon, Lafitte the Pirate. p. 149-150
144   Ibid. p. 146
145   Ibid. p. 153
146   Davis, *The Pirates Lafitte*, p. 186
147   Saxon, *Lafitte the Pirate*. p.154
148   Ibid. p.157
149   *Louisiana Gazette (September 24, 1814) Williams Research Center Microfilm File.*
150   Ibid.
151   Ibid. (October 20th)

[152]   Ibid. p. 158
[153]
[154]   Ibid. p. 159
[155]   *Louisiana Historical Quarterly*; (1961:Volume 44 Issue 1 p. 44) Interesting interpretation of the origins of the name "Old Hickory"
[156]   Ibid
[157]   Ibid.
[158]   Ibid. p. 174
[159]   Documents supplied by Alberta & Jim Lewis, Sabastopol Plantation, St. Bernard Parish.
[160]   Kendall, *New Orleans*, p. 95
[161]   Louisiana Historical Society Annual Banquet Lecture, 2010
[162]   Alberta Lewis Collection (St. Bernard Parish: Sabastopol Plantation, 2005)
[163]   Ibid.
[164]   Freemasonary & the American Revolution. (internet)
[165]   Letters on the Masonic Institution by John Quincy Adams
[166]   Saxon, *Lafitte the Pirate*, p. 183
[167]   Both of these buildings sustained considerable damage during Hurricane Katrina in 2005. The Andrew Jackson lodge has been rebuilt, the Dominique Youx lodge is currently under construction.
[168]   Pictures taken by Ron Chapman
[169]   James Parton: *Makers of American History: General Jackson* (1905: New York, The University Press) p. 145
[170]   Kendall, *History of New Orleans*, p. 98
[171]   *Louisiana Gazette, September 28, 1814*
[172]   Ibid. (October 4, 1814)
[173]   Ibid.
[174]   Kendall, *History of New Orleans*, p. 98
[175]   *Louisiana Gazette* October 25, 11814 (Sadly, the Gazette accounts of events leading up to the campaign against New Orleans ends here and does not pick up again until February 15, 1815. What happened to the newspapers during the intervening and most important months of the conflict is not known. In fact, there appears to be no local newspapers in existence that cover this most important period of the area's history.
[176]   Ibid. p. 145

Chapter 4

[177]   Picture by Ron Chapman
[178]   Picture by Ron Chapman
[179]   www.cherrys.com
[180]   George Neumann, *The Brown Bess* (*The American Rifleman*, April 2001) p. 10

[181]   Picture taken by Ron Chapman

[182]   Picture taken by Ron Chapman

[183]   www.ctie.moash.edu.au (redrawn by author)

[184]   Image taken from U.S. Park Service leaflet redrawn by author

[185]   Dorsey, Florence; <u>Master of the Mississippi: Henry Shreve and the Conquest of the Mississippi,</u> (1941: Houghton, Mifflin co, Boston) p.76-80 There is some debate about the event but since the local newspapers do not exist, it is difficult to prove or disprove. Sufficient records do exist for a second boat. Thus the riverboat did play a roll in the defense of New Orleans.

[186]   <u>Ibid</u>. p. 84-92

[187]   THNOC 74.25.33.24

[188]   <u>Ibid</u>. pp 87

[189]   <u>Ibid</u>. 89p. ; *Louisiana Quarterly* 1920 Vol.3 Issue1 P.40

[190]   <u>Ibid</u>. p. 90

[191]   <u>Ibid</u>.

[192]   <u>Ibid</u>. p. 94

[193]   <u>Ibid</u>. p. 97

[194]   Samuel Clement; *Plantation Life on the Mississippi* (New Orleans, Pelican Publishing, 1952) p.106 The account does have one wondering if only one boat operated but the accounts have become confused.

[195]   <u>Ibid</u>., p. 106

[196]   <u>Ibid</u>., p.113

Chapter 5

[197]   Consider these engagements: Fort Bowyer on Mobile Point, Invasion of Pensacola, Battle of Lake Borgne, December 23rd Night attack, December 27th Reconnaissance in Force, January 1st artillery duel, January 8th Main Attack, and January 19th Bombardment of Fort St. Philip.

[198]   Louisiana State Museum Map Database

[199]   Colonial Office Records (Williams Research Center, Historic New Orleans Collection) MF 2.9 Reel 09 p.19

The following is a list of ships and commanders at Negril Bay, Jamaica:

Ship name	No. of Guns	Commander
Tonnant	80	Admiral Cochrane
Royal Oak	74	Rear-Ad Malcolm
Norge	74	Capt. Dashford
Ship name	No. of Guns	Commander
Bedford	74	Capt. Walker
Rramilies	74	Capt. Sir T. Hardy
Asia	74	Capt. Skene
Dictator	64	Capt Crofton
Diomede	56	Capt Kippen
Gorgon	44	Capt R.B. Bowden
Armide	38	Capt. Sir T. Toubridge
Belle Poule	38	Capt. Baker
Traave	38	Capt. Money
Wesex	38	Capt. Sullivan
Alceste	38	Capt. Lawrence
Hydra	38	Capt. Digby
Fox	36	Capt. Wilcox
Cydnus	36	Capt. Langford
Thames	32	Capt. Hon C.L. Irby
Dover	32	Capt. Rodgers
Buchephalus	32	Capt. D'Aith
Calliope	16	Capt. Codd
Anaconda	16	Capt. Westphalt
Borer	14	Capt. Rawlins
Manly	14	Capt. Locke
Meteor (Bomb Ship)	6	Capt. Roberts.
Volcano (Bomb Ship)	6	Capt. Price
Etna (Bomb Ship)	16	Capt. Gardner
Pigmy (Schooner)	6	Lieutenant Crossman
Jane (cutter)		Lieutenant Johnson

Various Transports: Norfolk, Golden Fleece, Thames, Diana, Active, Woodman, Cyrus, Elizabeth, Kate, Daniel Woodriffe, and George and others not names.

Later HMS Nymph (Capt. Pigett); Dasher (Capt Henderson) sailed for Negril with Schooners Lark and Cossas.

200 *Louisiana Historical Quarterly*: (1961: Volume 44 issue 1 p.34) Dickson's Diary

201 Ibid. p.35

202 Williams Research Center, MF 2.9 Reel 09 p. 22

203 Ibid. p.3

204 THNOC 1979.238.1

205 Paul Laviolette, *Sink or be Sunk: The Naval Battle in the Mississippi Sound that Preceded the Battle of New Orleans* (Annabelle Publishing, 2002) p. 88

206 (http://www.usskidd.com/battles-lakeborgne.html)

207 "Sink r be Sunk", p. 41 (AP is Scottish for "son of")

208 Ibid. p.84

209 *Gayarre' Vol. 4.p.398).*

210 Ibid. p.43-47

211 Ibid, p.27-29

212 Ibid. p 36

213 la Tour, *The War;* p. 51

214 THNOC 1979.238.2 : Lossing p.026

215 Laviolette, *Sink or Be Sunk* p. 111

216 Ibid. p113.

217 Ibid. p. 125

218 Ibid.

219 Ibid. p.13-37

220 Ibid.

221 Ibid. p. 141

222 Lossing, p.102; James, William, *Military Occurrences of the Late War Between Great Britain and the United States of America* (London; Black, Kingsbury, and Allen, 1818) p. 353

223 Laviolette, *Sink or Be Sunk*, p. 141-150

224 THNOC 1969.4

225 Account of the vessels by John Henry Eaton, biographer of Andrew Jackson.

	Boats	Men	Guns
British	43	1200	43
Americans	5	182	23

226 Gene Smith, *A British Eyewitness at the Battle of New Orleans: the Memorial of Royal Navy Admiral Robert Aitchinson, 1808-1827* (2004: Historic New Orleans Collection, New Orleans) p. 58

227 Ibid. p. 150; *(Gayarre' Vol.4 p.401; Lossing p. 1026)*

228 Gayarre' Vol.4 p. 401; Lossing p. 1026

229 James, *Military Occurrences*, p. 354

230 Smith, *A British Eyewitness*, p. 61

Chapter 6

[231] Islenos are immigrants from the Canary Islands who were brought in to Louisiana by Governor Bernardo Galvez to help defend the Spanish Colony from the British during the American Revolution. They stayed in the state and many settled in St. Bernard Parish, likewise named after Bernardo Galvez.

[232] -(*Negro Soldiers*, Marcus Christian p.11)

[233] Marcus Christian, Negro *Soldiers in the Battle of New Orleans*, (The Battle of New Orleans 150th Anniversary Committee of Louisiana, 1965) p.15

[234] La Tour p. 217 (Appendix #XXI); Kendall, *History of New Orleans*, p. 100

[235] Kendall, *History of New Orleans*, p. 100

[236] *Gayarre Vol IV p. 874*

[237] Walker, Alexander, *"Life of Andrew Jackson* p.12-13

[238] Ibid. p.13; (reports have him suffering from intestinal problems throughout most of his life. He could only eat very mild unseasoned foods like hominy grits, rice, etc. During campaigns he would spend hours relieving himself propped between saplings in great discomfort)

[239] Ibid. p 13

[240] Ibid. p. 14

[241] Ibid. p 15; Stanley Cllisby Arthur, *The Story of the Battle of New Orleans*, 1915) (New Orleans: Louisiana Historical Society p. 46

[242] Walker, p 17-18 (there is some confusion about Jackson's Headquarters address because the numbering system has changed over the years.

[243] Arthur, *The Story of the Battle of New Orleans*, p. 51

[244] Ibid. 54

[245] Lossing, p. 1020

[246] Parton, *General Jackson* p. 146

[247] Ibid. p. 147

[248] *Gayarre Vol. IV p.384*

[249] Arthur, *The Story of the Battle of New Orleans*, p.67

[250] Ibid. p. 70

[251] Ibid p.67

[252] Parton, *General Jackson*, p. 150

[253] Ibid.

[254] Ibid.

[255] Parton, *General Jackson*, p. 151

[256] Ibid. p. 153

[257] Arthur, *The Story of the Battle of New Orleans*, p.74

[258] Smith, *Battle of New Orleans*, p. 20-21

[259] Ibid.

[260] Ibid. p 75

[261]   Ibid. p. 75

[262]   *Louisiana Historical Quarterly;* (1961: volume 44 issue1 45

[263]   THNOC 1971.4

[264]   -Gayarre *Vol 4. p. 402*

[265]   Gayarre' *p.416*

[266]   Gayarre' *p.417;* Smith, *Battle of New Orleans, p. 22*

[267]   Smith, *Battle of New Orleans,* p. 123

[268]   *Jackson's December 27th report to the War Department*

[269]   la Tour, *The War, p. 64*

[270]   Ibid. p.65

[271]   Ibid. p. 65

[272]   Walker p. 207

[273]   Walker p. 209 (Private letter in Duke of Wellington's collection)

[274]   Gleig, G.R. *The Campaigns of the British Army at Washington and New Orleans* (2006, IndyPublish.com, Boston) p.131

[275]   Arthur, *The Story of the Battle of New Orleans,* p.78

[276]   Ibid. p. 131

[277]   Walker p. 119

[278]   Cleig p. 131

[279]   Ibid. p. 133

[280]   La Tour, p. 66

[281]   Gayarre, *p.421*

[282]   Arthur, *The Story of the Battle of New Orleans,* p. 83

[283]   Gayarre' p.418); Smith, *Battle of New Orleans,* p.23

[284]   Walker p. 133

[285]   La Tour p. 67

[286]   Ibid. p.67

[287]   *Louisiana Historical Quarterly:* (1961: volume 44 issue1 p. 46

[288]   Ibid.

[289]   Walker, P,134

[290]   Image Courtesy of U.S. Park Service

[291]   Wilson, Plantation on the Battlefield. p.59

[292]   Samuel Wilson Jr, *Plantation Houses on the Battlefield of New Orleans,* (1965, The Battle of New Orleans 150th Anniversary Committee 1965) The Plantation pictures for this section and a portion of the narrative are drawn from this work. There is no need to continually site this book.

[293]   Wilson, *Plantation on the Battlefield.* p.29; Losing 1037

[294]   Wilson, *Plantation on the Battlefield.* p.33

[295]   Wilson, *Plantation houses p.44*

[296]   Lossing p. 1039

[297]   *Plantations p.60*

[298]   *Plantation p.66*

[299] Lossing

[300] Lossing p. 1031

[301] *Plantation p.85*

[302] Lossing p. 1029

[303] No picture of Jumonville Plantation available

[304] Clement, William, *Plantation Life on the Mississippi* (USA, Pelican Publishing Company, 1952) p. p. 82

Chapter 7

[305] James, <u>Military Occurences</u>, p. 355

[306] <u>Ibid</u>. 357; The decision to move up Bayou Bienvenue rather then moving into Lake Pontchartrain was the result of misinformation provided by the American purser Mr. Shields who informed the British that the American Fort Coquille at the Rigolets had 40 pieces of artillery and 500 defenders, not the actual 8 guns and 50 men.

[307] Gleig, p.134, Walker p. 136

[308] Walker, p. 126

[309] <u>Ibid</u>.

[310] <u>Ibid</u>. p. 359

[311] *Louisiana Historical Quarterly* (1961: Volume44 issue1 p. 39)

[312] Gleig p.134

[313] <u>Ibid</u>. p. 136

[314] Walker p. 127

[315] <u>Ibid</u>. p. 128 (some sources have him slaying the dog with his hunting knife.)

[316] Parton, <u>General Jackson</u> p. 159

[317] <u>Ibid</u>. p. 160

[318] Walker p. 138

[319] Parton, *General Jackson*, p. 161

[320] THNOC 11949.8 : Lossing p. 1032

[321] Gleig, p.136

[322] Arthur, *The Story of the Battle of New Orleans*, p. 97-98

[323] Kendall, *History of New Orleans*, p. 102

[324] *Gayarre' p.423; Lossing p.1031*

[325] Arthur, *The Story of the Battle of New Orleans*, p.102 (Kendall cites 1,200 men while Arthur provides evidence of 2,035)

Army and Marines	85
7th U.S.	450
44th U.S.	285
Tennessee Brigade	850

Orleans Battalion 365
Orleans Riflemen 60
Hind's Dragoons 55
Free Men of Color..............175
TOTAL...........................2,325

[326] Ibid.; Parton, *General Jackson*, p. 164

[327] Gleig, p. 137

[328] Gleig, p. 137

[329] *Ibid.*

[330] Lossing p. 1032

[331] Ibid.

[332] Lossing p. 103

[333] Lossing p. 1030

[334] Lossing. 1024

[335] *Louisiana Historical Quarterly*: (1960: volume 44 issue 1 p 40)

[336] Cleig p. 138

[337] Latour p. 80

[338] Latour p. 82

[339] Latour p. 82

[340] Arthur, *The Story of the Battle of New Orleans*, p. 107

[341] Lossing p. 1033

[342] Latour, p. 66-83 (Latour's and Cleig's books offer a more complete portrait of the actions of December 23rd for the perspectives of both the British and the Americans.); Lossing p. 1033; Arthur, *The Story of the Battle of New Orleans*, p.124 (he reports British sources recounting that the engagement did not fully end until 3:00am in the morning.)

[343] *Louisiana Historical Quarterly*: Dickson's Diary (961 volume 44 issue 1 p. 41)

[344] Smith, *Battle of New Orleans*, p. 27

[345] Latour p. 83

[346] Gleig p.142

[347] Gleig p.143

[348] Ibid.

[349] Louisiana Historical Quarterly: Dickson's Diary (1961: volume 44 issue 1 p. 42)

[350] *Latour, The War, p. 82*

[351] *Gayarre; vol.4 p.439*

[352] James, *Military Occurrences*, p. 362.

[353] *Latour p. 327 Appendix #7 (Return of casualties in action near New Orleans 23rd & 24th December 1814)*

[354] Kendall, *History of New Orleans*, p. 104

[355] Arthur, *The Story of the Battle of New Orleans*, p.126

356 Kendall, *History of New Orleans*, p. 103

357 *Louisiana Historical Quarterly:* Dickson's Diary (1961: volume 44 issue 1 p. 43)

358 THNOC mss557.5.33

359 Latour, p. 85

360 Arthur, *The Story of the Battle of New Orleans*, p.138

361 Ibid.

362 Gleig p. 147

363 Ibid p.148

364 Arthur, The Story of the Battle of New Orleans, p.136

365 Ibid. p.148

366 Ibib p. 148

367 James, *Military Occurrences*, p. 363

368 Arthur, *The Story of the Battle of New Orleans*, p.143-143

369 *Gayarre' vol.4, p. 444; Gleig p. 149*

370 Picture taken by Ron Chapman at the Daughters of the War of 1812 museum in Washington D.C. The author owes the Daughters a debt of gratitude for allowing this valuable relic to be included in this work. The nautical sextant is a late 18th century brass, ivory, and ebony instrument housed in a mahogany case. It was donated to the Daughters by James M. Thompson, great-grandson of Lt. Scott.

371 James, *Military Occurrences*, p. 363

372 There is much debate about the use of the term *"Booty and Beauty"*. The phrase has been quoted in many sources, however, British sources indicate that no such enticement was employed.

373 THNOC 1949.18

374 James, *Military Occurrences*, p. 364

375 James, *Military Occurrences*, p. 366

376 Ibid., p. 364

377 Lossing p. 1037

378 Gleig p.149

379 Ibid. p.150

380 Parton, *General Jackson*, p. 179

381 Ibid., p. 181

382 Ibid p185

383 *Louisiana Historical Quarterly*: (1961: volume 44 issue1 p. 282

384 *Louisiana Historical Quarterly*: (1926: volume 2 issue2 p.241

385 Ibid. 283

386 Ibid. 282

387 Ibid. 270

388 Gleig. p.151

389 Parton, *General Jackson*, p. 186

[390]   Ibid. p.151

[391]   Arthur, *The Story of the Battle of New Orleans*, p.149

[392]   Ibid.

[393]   Lossing p. 1037

[394]   James, *Military Occurrences*, p. 368

[395]   Gayarre vol4. P. 453

[396]   Gleig p. 153

[397]   Parton, *General Jackson*, p. 190

[398]   Latour p. 89 [British: 16 killed, 38 wounded, 2 missing: total 56; Americans 9 killed, 8 wounded, 1 wounded on ship: Total 18]

[399]   Arthur, *The Story of the Battle of New Orleans*, p. 153

[400]   Parton, *General Jackson*, p. 191

[401]   *Louisiana Historical Quarterly*: (1961: volume 44 issue1 p.48

[402]   *Louisiana Historical Quarterly*: (1961: volume 44 issue1 p.53

[403]   Ibid.

[404]   Lossing p. 1038

[405]   *Gayarre' vol.4 p. 454*

[406]   Latour, *The War*, p.90

[407]   Lossing p.1038

[408]   Gleig p.154

[409]   James, *Military Occurrences*, p. 369

[410]   *Louisiana Historical Quarterly*: (1961: volume 44 issue1 p.56

[411]   Greig p.; Parton, *General Jackson*, p.194

[412]   Lossing p. 1039; Parton, *General Jackson*, p.192

[413]   *Louisiana Historical Quarterly*: (1961: volume 44 issue1 p.56

[414]   Sources differ on this issue. Many argue that no cotton bales were ever used, other cite the use of them as a stable base for artillery.

[415]   *Louisiana Historical Quarterly*: (1961: volume 44 issue1 p.58

[416]   James, *Military Occurrences, p.* 369

[417]   Parton, *General Jackson*, p. 195

[418]   Gleig p. 156

[419]   Parton, *General Jackson*, p.196

[420]   Ibid.

[421]   Parton, *General Jackson*, p 194-195

[422]   Ibid. 196-197

[423]   James, *Military Occurrences*, p. 369

[424]   Parton, *General Jackson*, p 197

[425]   Latour, The War, p. 92

[426]   Latour p. 97; Parton, *General Jackson*, p.198

[427]   *Louisiana Historical Quarterly*: (1961: volume 44 issue1 p.60

[428]   *Louisiana Historical Quarterly*: (1961: volume 44 issue1 p.59

[429]   Gleig p. 157

[430] Ibid.

[431] Ibid.

[432] The Historic New Orleans Collection (THNOC) MSS 200 4, Letter from General Jackson at camp four miles below New Orleans to the Headquarters of the 7th Military District. Jauary 3, 1814.

[433] Ibid.

[434] Imagine if the present means of immediate communication available today had existed in 1815. Jacksons request for relief of command would have arrived in time for consideration.

[435] Latour p. 101

[436] Latour p.98

[437] Latour p.100-101 (footnote)

[438] Latour p. 101

[439] , Zachary Smith_*Battle of New Orleans*, (Louisville Kentucky, Filsom Club, 1904) location 861 (digital book)

[440] Latour p. 102

[441] Latour p. 105

[442] A French general reviewing the maps of the battle at a later date would criticize Pakenham for wasting so many good men. The swamp, this man argued, was passable for a man if a horse could get through it. That was Jackson's weak flank. He believed if Pakenham would have pressed Jackson's left through the swamp he would have carried the day.

[443] Parton, *General Jackson*, p 201

[444] *Ibid.*

[445] *Louisiana Historical Quarterly*: (1961: volume 44 issue1 p.62

Chapter 8

[446] Lossing p. 1044

[447] Latour Map; This map lays out the positions of the British forces and their approach through Bayou Bienvenue. It also establishes Jackson's three defensive lines as well as Pakenham's plan of action on the Westbank of the river.

[448] Lossing p. 1041; Latour

[449] Gleig p. 159

[450] *Louisiana Historical Quarterly*: (1961: volume 44 issue1 p.64

[451] *Ibid.*

[452] Ibid. p. 66

[453] Walker p. 323

[454] *Louisiana Historical Quarterly*: (1961: volume 44 issue1 p.65

[455] Walker p. 307

[456] U.S. History Images.com

[457] Latour p. 100; Lossing p. 1041; James, *Military Occurrences*, p. 371-72

[458] Latour p. 101

[459] Ibid.

[460] Walker p. 311& p. 317

[461] Walker p. 315 (Walker provides a very detailed description of Jacksons line); James, *Military Occurrences*, p. 367

[462] Parton, *General Jackson*, p 203

[463] THNOC MSS 200.5 Folder 5 pg 1: Letter from General Jackson to General David Morgan. January 7, 1814

[464] THONC MSS 557 .4. 25 : General orders of Col. Shambaugh to camp on right bank.

[465] Walker p. 307

[466] Lossing p. 1044

[467] *Latour, The War, p. 108 (Again, American estimates are higher than British accounts)*

[468] Parton, *General Jackson*, p 208

[469] Parton, *General Jackson*, p. 209

[470] Walker p. 318

[471] Ibid.; Walker p. 318

[472] Walker p. 319

[473] *Ibid* p. 182

[474] www.usskidd.com

[475] Gleig p. 158

[476] *Lossing p. 1045)*

[477] THNOC mss.557.5.33

[478] Parton, General Jackson, p. 212

[479] Parton, General Jackson, p. 211

[480] Ibid.

[481] Walker, p. 323.

[482] British sources refute any mention of "Booty and Beauty" by British officers, in particular they argue that Pakenham would have continence not such talk.

[483] Latour p.109

[484] Walker p. 325

[485] Louisiana State Museum: (This is a British map of the plan of attack)

[486] THNOC 1979.238.4

[487] Parton, *General Jackson*, p. 212

[488] Lossing p. 1045

[489] James, *Military Occurrences*, p. 376

[490] Ibid. p. 375

[491] Gleig p. 160

[492] Gleig p. 160

[493] James, *Military Occurrences* p. 375
[494] Gleig p. 160
[495] James, *Military Occurrences*, p. 377
[496] THNOC 1989.79.135
[497] Walker p. 326
[498] *Louisiana Historical Quarterly*: (1961: volume 44 issue1 p.74
[499] Parton, *General Jackson*, p.213
[500] THNOC MSS 201 Jordan Noble Collection.
[501] THNOC MSS 557.5. 39: Letter from "Cold Steel" to the editor of the U.S. Journal, H. Colburm, London
[502] Arthur, *The story of the Battle of New Orleans*, p. 185-186
[503] Ibid p.188
[504] *Louisiana Historical Quarterly*: (1961: volume 44 issue1 p.71
[505] Lossing p. 1046; Gleig p. 160
[506] Arthur, *The story of the Battle of New Orleans*, p. 196
[507] Ibid
[508] *Louisiana Historical Quarterly*: (1961: volume 44 issue1 p.72; Parton, *General Jackson*, p. 216
[509] James, *Military Occurrences*, p. 377
[510] Ibid.
[511] Lossing, p.1046
[512] THNOC 1949.2 iii
[513] James, *Military Occurrences*, p. 378-79
[514] Ibid.
[515] Walker p. 341
[516] Christian p. 39
[517] Walker p. 332
[518] Ibid.
[519] Parton, General Jackson, p. 218
[520] THNOC 1959.160.5
[521] Ibid.
[522] James, *Military Occurrences* p. 381
[523] Parton, *General Jackson*, p.220 (British Colonel Thornton would often reflect on the civility of the Americans for returning personal items of the dead to their families)
[524] *Louisiana Historical Quarterly*: (1961: volume 44 issue1 p.72
[525] Parton, *General Jackson*, p. 223
[526] Ibid.
[527] *Louisiana Historical Quarterly*: (1961: volume 44 issue1 p. 78
[528] Ibid.
[529] Lossing, p.1048
[530] *Louisiana Historical Quarterly*: (1961: volume 44 issue1 p.224

[531] *Louisiana Historical Quarterly*: (1961: volume 44 issue1 p.224

[532] Walker, p. 338

[533] Walker p. 339

[534] Arthur, *The Story of the Battle of New Orleans*, p. 239

[535] Clement, *Plantation Life on the Mississippi*, p. 129

[536] Arthur, *The Story of the Battle of New Orleans*, p. 239

[537] Ibid. p. 340

[538] Ibid. p. 345

[539] James, *Military Occurrences*, p. 382 (James's numbers differ: 290 killed, 1,262 wounded, 484 missing for a total of 2036. It must be remembered, however, being wounded in battle was tantamount to be killed in those days. For the Americans he quotes: 13 killed, 39 wounded, 19 missing, Total 71

[540] *Lossing p.1050*

[541] Lossing. P. 1050

[542] Letter from Earl of Longford (December 30, 1896) to James Zacherie, Regents Park Barracks N.W.) *Louisiana Historical Quarterly*, 1926; vol9 issue 1 p.12

[543] *Louisiana Historical Quarterly*: (1961: volume 44 issue1 p.47

[544] Letter: *Louisiana Historical Quarterly*; 1926; Massachusetts Volunteer in the Battle of New Orleans p. 30

[545] THNOC MSS 557.4: Letter from William Fort to father Major Abraham Fort of New York. February 24, 1815.

[546] THNOC MSS.557.4: Letter from D.B. Lyles, Baltimore to James Cox February13, 1815

[547] THNOC MSS 557.4.41: Letter from Sir Fredrick Stovin to Mother new Chesterfield England.

[548] Ibid. p. 2

[549] THNOC MSS 557.4.42: Letter from Duchess of Wellington to unknown recipient. January 30, 1815

[550] Latour p. 112

[551] Ibid.

[552] *Louisiana Historical Quarterly*; Letter from Unknown participant sent to one Thaddus Mayhew, New Bedford, Mass. to be forwarded to "Susan".

[553] Ibid.

[554] Ibid.

[555] Ibid.70

[556] Courtesy of U.S. Military Academy

Chapter 9

[557] Cope, Sir William Henry, *History of the Rifle Brigade.*(London: Chatto & WIndus, 1880s)

[558] Owsley, Frank Lawrence, "Struggle for the Gulf Borderlands: The Creek War and the Battle of New Orleans 1812-1815" (1981, The University of Alabama Press) p. 156

[559] Letter from Major-General Jackson to the Secretary of war dated January9, 1815; Latour p. 237 (Appendix)

[560] Latour p. 114

[561] Dixon, Richard Remy; *The Battle on the West Bank* (1965: The Battle of New Orleans 150th)

[562] Dixon, Richard Remy: *The Battle on the West Bank* (1965; The Battle of New Orleans 150th Anniversary Committee of Louisiana)

[563] Latour p. 114

[564] Ibid. p. 115

[565] Richard Dixon, *Battle on the Westbank*, p. 29

[566] Ibid. p. 4

[567] Ibid. p. 115

[568] Latour p. 116

[569] Ibid.

[570] Ibid. p. 117

[571] Smith, *Battle of New Orleans*, p. 70-71

[572] Dixon, *Battle on Westbank*, p. 10

[573] THNOC MSS 200 Folder 5 Page 1: Letter from Jackson to Morgan January7, 1815.

[574] There is some controversy here. Morgan's men contend they were awake but overwhelmed. Colonel Thronton reports that the Americans were taken by surprise while asleep.

[575] Dixon "Battle on the Westbank" p. 13

[576] Walker "Life of Jackson" p. 351

[577] Ibid

[578] Ibid p. 352

[579] Cooke, Sir John Henry, "A Narrative of Events in the South of France, and of the Attack on New Orleans, in 1814 and 1815" (1832; T &W Boon, London) p. 257. John Cooke participated in the battle and his reminiscences are a valuable resource from the British perspective.

[580] Patterson, Letter from Commodore Patterson to the Secretary of the Navy (January 13, 815)

[581] Ibid.

[582] Ibid. p. 354

583 Gleig, *Campaigns* p. 162 (The Battle of Yorktown and General Cornwallis's surrender marked the end of the American Revolution.)

584 Cooke, *Narrative* p. 259

585 Dixon *Battle on the Westbank*

586 Walker, *Life of Andrew Jackson* p. 355

587 Cooke, *Narratives* p.259.

588 THNOC mss 557.5.33

589 Cooke, *Narratives* p.258 (78 British casualties: 85th lost 43, the Marines 16, and the armed sailors 19)

590 Clement, *Plantation Life on the Mississippi*, p. 129-130 (letter from Mrs. Henry Clement to Jacob Wood dated January 11, 1815)

591 Ibid. 260.

592 Cooke, *Narratives* p. 261

593 Walker, *Life of Jackson* p. 356

594 Arthur, *The Story of the Battle of New Orleans*, p.221

595 Ibid. p. 223

596 Dixon *Battle on Westbank* p. 24

597 Cooke, *Narrative* p. 264.

598 Gleig, *The Campaigns of the British Army"*p. 187

599 Cooke, *Narrative* p. 266

600 Jackson, "Letter to Secretary of War James Monroe" (January 9, 1815)

601 Latour, *Historical Memoir*, p. 324 (letter from General Lamber t to Earl of Bathurst)

602 Cooke, *Narrative* p. 263

603 Walker, *Life of Jackson* p. 258

604 Ibid.

605 Cooke, *Narrative* p. 268

606 Ibid. 269

607 Ibid. p. 271

608 Walker, *Life of Andrew Jackson* p. 382

609 THNOC MSS 557 folder 107 p.1: Letter from Chotard to Morgan January17,1815.

610 Cooke, *Narrative* p. 272-273

611 Ibid p. 272

612 Ibid. p. 274

613 Cooke, Narratives p. 259-60.

614 Gayarre, *Histor y of LouisianaVol* IV p.539

615 Arthur, *The Story of the Battle of New Orleans*, p. 218

616 Ibid. p. 219

617 Ibid.

618   Ibid.

619   Ibid.

620   THNOC MSS 547 folder 367 p1 : letter from General John Coffee to wife dated January 30, 1815

Chapter 10

621   Walker, *Life of Andrew Jackson* p. 371

622   Ibid. 373

623   THNOC 1979.238.5 Lossing p. 1051

624   Ibid. p372.

625   Ibid. p.373

626   *Lossing p. 1051*

627   *-(Gayarre' Vol. IV p.507)*

628   Walker, *Life of Jackson* p. 355

629   Ibid p.386

630   Ibid. p.387

631   *Gayarre' Vol. IV p509*

632   Walker, *Narrative* p. 387.

633   *Gayarre; vol.4 p. 579*

634   Cooke, *Narrative*, p. 277

635   Ibid. p.306

636   Walker, *Narrative* p. 392

637   Ibid." p. 395

638   Ibid.

639   Jackson had executed several militia members during the Creek Indian War for attempting to return home when they believed their enlistment was over in contravention of Jackson's orders.

640   Walker, *Life of Jackson*, p. 390

641   Arthur, *The Story of the Battle of New Orleans*, p. 254

642   Ibid. p. 255

643   *Ibid.* p. 255

644   Gayarre; vol.4 p. 579

645   Ibid. p. 409

646   Ibid. p. 406

Chapter 11

647   Smith, *Battle of New Orleans*, p. 99

648   Smith, *Battle of New Orleans*, p. 77

649   Appendix #13 March 15, 1815.

[650] THNOC MSS 557.4.37 Folder 106 P. 1 : letter from Colonel Robert Butler to General David Morgan.

[651] Smith, *Battle of New Orleans* p. 66

[652] Report of the Court in Inquiry Headquarters 7th Military District, New Orleans, LA February 19, 1815

[653] THNOC MSS 19: Letter from Latout to Morgan April 10, 1815.

[654] Ibid.

[655] *Louisiana Historical Quarterly*; (1926: Vol. 9 issue 1 p. 118)

[656] *Louisiana Historical Quarterly*; (1926: vol. 9 issue 1 p. 41-43)

[657] *Louisiana Historical Quarterly*; (1926; vol. 9 issue 1 p. 113)

[658] Ibid. p.115

[659] *Louisiana Historical Quarterly*: (1926: vol. 9 issue 1 p. 15-116)

[660] Huber, *The Battle of New Orleans and its Monument*, p. 12

[661] Ibid.

[662] Ibid.

[663] Ibid. (The story of the monument was taken entirely from Huber's work. Citing every paragraph would have been unnecessarily tedious.)

[664] Picture by Ron Chapman